REPRESENTATION IN CRISIS

SUNY Series in
Political Party Development
Susan J. Tolchin, Editor

REPRESENTATION IN CRISIS

The Constitution, Interest Groups, and Political Parties

David K. Ryden

STATE UNIVERSITY OF NEW YORK PRESS

Production by Ruth Fisher
Marketing by Fran Keneston

Published by
State University of New York Press, Albany

For information, address the State University of New York Press,
State University Plaza, Albany, NY 12246

Library of Congress Cataloging-in-Publication Data

Ryden, David K.
    Representation in crisis : the constitution, interest groups, and
political parties / David K. Ryden.
        p.   cm. — (SUNY series in political party development)
    Includes bibliographical references and index.
    ISBN 0-7914-3057-X (alk. paper). — ISBN 0-7914-3058-8 (pbk. :
alk. paper)
    1. Proportional representation—United States.   2. Representative
government and representation—United States.   3. Political parties—
United States.   4. Pressure groups—United States.   5. United
States—Constitutional law.   I. Title.   II. Series.
JF1075.U6R93   1996
328.73'07347—dc20   95-39220
                                                                      CIP

10 9 8 7 6 5 4 3 2 1

To My Parents, Phil and Marie Ryden

CONTENTS

Chapter Eight

Chapter Nine

Chapter Ten

Appendix A

Appendix B

Appendix C

ACKNOWLEDGMENTS

That I was able to see this project through to completion is a testament to the intellectual and moral support, encouragement and assistance I received from countless sources. First, I owe a chief debt of gratitude to two people who were instrumental in shepherding me through the perils of the dissertation process, from which this book grew; to Dr. John Kenneth White for advice and counsel that was always as practical and pragmatic as it was enlightening and insightful, and to my "chief kibitzer," Dr. Ralph Morris Goldman, who deserves the primary credit for enabling me to uncover the intrigue and value of this subject, and whose unflagging sense of humor and energy were unsurpassed and a constant motivation. Thanks are due to Dr. Steve Schneck, the third member of my dissertation committee, for his always thoughtful comments and insights, especially with respect to the foundational chapters where such comments were most needed. A collective thank you is likewise in order for the other members of the Department of Politics at The Catholic University of America in Washington, D.C. for their frequent words of advice and suggestions, even though they were under no compulsion to do so. I owe a special debt to departmental Chair Dr. David Walsh, who was always intent on facilitating completion of the project rather than creating obstacles to it, and to Dr. Dennis Coyle, who was kind enough to allow me the use of his office and computer equipment while on sabbatical. Helen Foggo, Audrey Whittaker, and other staff at Catholic University are deserving of my appreciation for good-naturedly tolerating my often nettlesome presence and for providing assistance even in the most mundane of tasks. My circle of graduate student colleagues, though they shall remain nameless to safeguard their reputations, provided an invaluable sounding board for ideas and, perhaps more importantly, arranged frequent stress-release activities which are absolutely essential for the completion of a task of this magnitude. Perhaps more important were the members of my WCF covenant group, whose prayers, encouragement, and companionship always kept me grounded with a healthy perspective on what truly matters.

When midway through this project I began teaching at Hope College in Holland, Michigan, I was fortunate enough to step into a truly supportive environment which made completion of the book far easier than should be expected. Sincere thanks to my departmental colleagues, Jack Holmes, Robert Elder, James Zoetewey, and Annie Dandavati, for making me feel so welcome and in doing everything possible to ease the burdens and demands of my first year of teaching so that I could devote sufficient attention to this book. Department secretary Sally Smith never refused my plaintive requests for help, no matter how far afield or inappropriate they might be, and invariably carried them out with saintly patience and good cheer. A number of Hope College students, who assisted at various points and in various ways, deserve recognition. They include Amy Grassman, Hristo Dimitrov, Nicole Rottenberg, Kelly Jansen, and Beth Darr. Mary Beamish's professional editorial eye was invaluable in helping me polish the final manuscript. I am also very appreciative of the generosity of Hope College and Provost Jacob Nyenhuis for a 1995 summer research stipend which allowed me to focus on completion of the manuscript.

I am grateful to everyone at SUNY Press who had a hand in the publishing of this book. In particular, editors Clay Morgan and Ruth Fisher and their staffs helped make my first large-scale publishing venture go so smoothly that I am inclined to try again. Thanks also to Susan Tolchin, who generously provided her knowledge and expertise as the editor for the SUNY series of which this is a part, focusing on institutional aspects of political parties. I have undoubtedly overlooked others who contributed in significant ways to this book, for which I sincerely apologize.

Finally, there is no way to adequately express the depth of the love and gratitude I feel toward my parents and the rest of my family. Their support and encouragement, though it usually came from a distance, carried me through this project. They are the ones to whom I owe the most, and they deserve the final word.

INTRODUCTION

In 1974, the U.S. Supreme Court issued *Buckley v. Valeo*,[1] the seminal decision largely responsible for the current state of campaign
financing. In *Buckley*, the Court dissected and reconstructed a 1974
set of amendments to the Federal Election Campaign Act. Those
amendments represented a comprehensive effort by Congress to
remedy shortcomings in the system of financing campaigns which
became all too apparent in the long shadow of the Watergate
debacle. The Act placed strict limits on what individuals and
groups could give to, and spend on behalf of, candidates and campaign committees. It also placed a ceiling on total campaign spending and imposed disclosure requirements. By the time the Supreme
Court rendered its constitutional judgment on Congress' handiwork, the Act had a much different look. Contributions to candidates could be limited; individual expenditures on their behalf
could not. While full disclosure of campaign contributions was
permissible, Congress could not restrict political speech by cap-
ping total spending on an election.

Buckley had dramatic consequences for the financing of campaigns, and for the soundness of the electoral process generally.
While some of those consequences were clearly intended, others
were not. Yet the country has been struggling with those consequences ever since. The most obvious example is the precipitous
spiralling upward of the expense of campaigns. The Court's sur-
gical removal of total spending limits from the legislation made it
possible for Diane Feinstein and Michael Huffington to spend $44
million in 1994 on their Senate race, and for Chuck Robb and
Ollie North to spend $25 million. Similarly, the Court's rejection
of the clause limiting a candidate's expenditure of personal funds
allowed the wealthy Mr. Huffington to fund his entire campaign,
to the tune of $29 million.

The *Buckley* case is perhaps the most powerful illustration of
two points that lie at the heart of this book. One is the critically
important role played by the courts generally, and the Supreme

1

Court in particular, in shaping the functional operation of our political system. The tendency (of which both scholars and lay people are guilty) is to think of the Court as remote and insulated from the practical dimensions of politics. While perhaps sound political theory, the notion of the Court as removed from practical politics is misguided and inaccurate. Indeed, just the opposite is true. Whenever Congress (or the Executive branch) engages in efforts that affect elections, political parties, and representation, the Supreme Court wields the ultimate check. As *Buckley* demonstrates in such stark fashion, the Court is extremely influential in affecting the nitty-gritty of real-world politics. Consequently, the legal reasoning and theory underlying those decisions pertaining to politics, elections, and representation are a ripe subject for more extensive inquiry.

The second point follows from the first. *Buckley* demonstrated the absence of a coherent theory of representation to guide the Court's decisions, and the serious deleterious consequences of that oversight. A central premise of this book is that political parties provide a set of structures that are integral to the attainment of effective representation. Nevertheless, they are consistently overlooked or disparaged by the Court. In *Buckley*, the Court fundamentally altered the campaign financing ground rules, and did so with virtually no consideration of political parties as strategic players in the effort to ensure a fair system of financing elections. For the most part, parties were treated as essentially indistinguishable from other politically active associations and groups. Yet the consequences of the decision have perhaps been more harmful to political parties than to any other political participants, excepting the voters themselves.

Buckley, along with the *Sun Oil* FEC decision condoning business-related PACs, indirectly and unintentionally set the stage for the meteoric rise in the influence of PACs. The striking down of total spending limits and the escalating costs of campaigns that followed, combined with the absence of any stated maximum amount that PACs could spend overall, created an insatiable demand for money, which PACs stepped in to fill. PACs have made the most of the opportunities given them, as candidate-centered campaigns have come to rely more and more on PAC financing. The heightened influence that has redounded to interest groups is a direct challenge to the parties' role in electoral politics, and has contributed significantly to the continuing decline of political parties in the twentieth century. Again, this case indicates the power of the Court to affect party politics in fundamental ways, even when it may not intend to. *Buckley* is a striking reminder of why it is essential for the Court to fully appreciate the complexities of representation, and to ensure that political parties have a central place in its constitutional jurisprudence.

This is a work on representation, more specifically, on political representation in America and the neglected role of the courts in fashioning it. It seeks to isolate flaws or holes in the Court's view of representation, and suggests how it might bolster its theory of representation. Our political system is one of *tensions* and *contradictions.* Any attempt to define or construct a theory of representation must confront the challenge of alleviating, if not resolving, these contradictions. Our political culture is also one of law and constitution. The arrangements responsible for producing representative government spring from a legal blueprint, which is the written Constitution.

The purpose of what follows is to examine and assess the legal arrangements that are responsible for generating representation. It requires a fleshing-out of the tensions and challenges of representation, based on a review of theories of representation and group politics. It likewise necessitates measuring the extent to which the primary interpreter of the Constitution, the U.S. Supreme Court, has successfully identified those challenges and crafted constitutional principles that address and satisfy them. *Ultimately, the fact that a comprehensive, all-encompassing constitutional theory of representation has eluded the Court compels a redefinition of representative systems and structures which will confront those challenges.*

The focus is on the Court's discernment of and response to the contradictions inherent in a pluralist democracy. That dilemma exists between defined and applied pluralism. The pluralist ideal rests on the group theory of politics, the notion that mass politics compels individuals to participate in group activity if they are to realize political influence. In short, the efficacy of individual participation in a large-scale democracy hinges on the effectiveness of the group or groups to which one belongs. But the pluralist reality is one of inequality and disequilibrium between groups, as some dominate while others go unheard. The dilemma, then, is this; if individual equality is conditional upon parity between groups, how is meaningful and equal political participation by citizens possible in light of group inequality? Stated in terms of representation, the dilemma is how to construct a scheme of representation that accommodates the array of group interests in society while simultaneously promoting individual equality.

Neopluralists like Iris Marion Young and Lani Guinier would modify the electoral system to ensure formal representation for a variety of groups and/or interests. Their goal is to give disadvantaged or powerless groups a voice in the political debate through formal legal mechanisms that would monitor and equalize group influence. The alternative approach, though much less in vogue, embraces political parties as the institutional means of integrating individual and group voices and facilitating their access to the public square, thus ensuring effective participation for all. This avenue has gone largely unexamined, due in considerable part to the failure of the Court to recognize constitutionally the functional benefits of party systems.

The current political climate provides an especially opportune time to think about representation, and especially the role of parties. The electoral earthquake of November 1994 provided a striking reminder that elections still have the potential to drastically alter the makeup of our representative institutions. The stunning victories enjoyed by Republicans at virtually all levels transformed the face of government across the country. The governance that occurred in the months that followed reinforced the point in an astonishing fashion. Led by a remarkably disciplined Republican majority party, the House of Representatives methodically attacked the agenda set out in the Republican campaign manifesto, the Contract with America. Marching in virtual lockstep, House Republicans provided a practical model of responsible party government to an extent few if any political scientists would have thought possible.

This unparalleled tide of party government may prove only temporal. It is certainly possible that it will quickly fade in the chambers of a balky Senate, or be stemmed by the veto pen of a Democratic President. It could well be thwarted at the ballot box in the next election by a public ill at ease with the nature and degree of the changes pursued by the new congressional majority. But even if one of these perils should befall the Republican party, the point remains; representation remains in very large part a product of elections, and the most discernible, powerful changes in representation come through political parties.

We begin with an examination of the nature, themes, and concepts of political representation. How is representation to be conceptualized? What are the modes by which representation operates? What are the purposes underlying these various modes? Is the ultimate aim of representation to enable people to elect representatives who are "like" them? Or is it to guarantee that all relevant interests are present in the governing body? Does representation mean that specific policy preferences of groups and interests must be reflected in policy outcomes? Or is it simply to assure that all pertinent voices are participants in policy dialogues? Finally, what are the contributions of the cast of political actors and institutions in achieving representation?

Chapter One leads to the conclusion that representation is all of these things and more. It resides in formal and descriptive modes and is manifested in relationships and governmental outputs. It has multiple aims, realized through a host of activities and actors. It has individual and collective dimensions, both for those who are represented and those doing the representing. Representation defies easy definition or simple categorization. It is a labyrinth of concepts and forms that synthesize an array of activities and participants through institutional and structural means.

Chapters Two and Three examine the extent to which the complex representative ideal has been incorporated into principles of constitutional law. They reveal a Supreme Court whose understanding of representation has been predominantly shaped in the mold of the American liberal tradition. The individualism at the core of our political philosophy is also the central theme of the Court's notions of political representation. Chapter Two surveys contemporary constitutional jurisprudence in voting rights, redistricting and reapportionment law. Beginning with *Baker v. Carr*[2] and *Reynolds v. Sims*[3], the Court traditionally relied upon an individualistic perception of politics. Focusing exclusively on the principle of "one person one vote" and precise mathematical equality of voting power, the Court abandoned concerns over the quality of representation. Provided that the forms and procedures assured all individuals equal access to electoral processes, fair and effective representation was a given.

The Court's initial preoccupation with individualistic, numerical voting equality ignored the role of groups, if any, in realizing representation. Those issues gradually surfaced with the advent of racial minorities' vote dilution claims, as the Court was forced by political necessity to confront minority group claims to representation. The Court established a group "right" to representation, first for racial minorities, and then for other politically identifiable groups. But its creation of that group right was driven more by political considerations than theoretical or philosophical principle. It was dispensing "group representation" rights without a theoretical understanding of the institutional structures that recognize the representative character inherent in all groups. Lacking a basic premise for defining group rights or for determining those groups entitled to them, the Court was reduced to making descriptive assignments based on political rather than legal considerations. As a result, it found itself confronting a potential morass, making political calculations beyond its capabilities or authority.

While the Court was increasingly aware of the need to account for groups in constitutional analysis, it lacked the framework that would enable it to treat all groups fairly, consistently, and logically as tools of representation. The search for the theoretical basis for judicial cognizance of collective activity is the subject of Chapter Four. Despite the dominance of individualism, our country is also a nation of joiners. Our liberal heritage exists in uneasy tension with the communitarian idea of individuals' finding their bearing through collective associations. Group theories contend that associational affiliations constitute the principal determinant of one's political interests and motivations. Individual political activity becomes meaningful only when one's voice is joined with others who share one's interests. In short, effective individual participation hinges on the collectivities that exist to represent one's interests. It is essential, therefore, that representative structures be cognizant of, and accommodate, a wide variety of group interests in politics.

Group theories yield a pluralist descriptive ideal of government, in which policy decision-making is accomplished through competition and interaction between these collective interests. The greater the number of group interests with access to the policymakers, the sounder the policy outcomes. The pluralist reality, however, raises serious doubts about the fairness and effectiveness of pluralist forms of representation. The system is heavily skewed in favor of certain groups to the detriment or outright exclusion of others, due to group disparities in political resources and influence. Interest group liberalism is the manifestation of a system of policy-producing unions between those with the most to gain, operating privately beyond the public eye and outside the sphere of the public interest. The consequence is to make just policy decisions unlikely. Hence the gulf between pluralism in theory and in practice. Group theory demands formal cognizance of group activity to insure individual effectiveness. But the inequities between groups in a pluralist democracy defeat the underlying objective of individual equality.

For a Supreme Court seeking a framework for incorporating group considerations, this is the central challenge; how to reconcile the fundamental objective of individual equality with the need to remedy organizational inequality. It demands institutional arrangements that enrich the individual in politics while addressing the shortcomings of pluralist representative structures. It compels structures that enhance the representative equality of groups without sacrificing fundamental standards of individual equality.

This is the dilemma to which the legal responses are directed. Chapter Five introduces the neopluralist goal of particularized formal group representation through an illustrative trio of group representation proponents who would elevate the representative status of groups to create a level, fair group playing field. For a better idea of how group representation might look in practice, we move to areas of constitutional doctrine where the Court has adopted neopluralist strategies. The most striking example is the markedly neopluralist framework for judicial attempts to balance and equalize group influence through campaign finance regulation.

Closer scrutiny of the neopluralist philosophy in Chapter Six reveals that group representation theories are saddled with significant theoretical and practical weaknesses. On a theoretical level, the focus on the rights of discrete groups tends to divide and segment the elements of society, rather than unify them. The factionalizing propensities of neopluralism are unlikely to alleviate the tensions of pluralism, and may only intensify them.

On a practical level, neopluralist approaches present complicated empirical challenges in implementation. The empirical reality of the political arena is that only individuals furnish a distinct, definable functional unit by which to gauge political activity. The same cannot be said for collective interests. Groups exist in a multitude of forms and organizations. The empirically impossible task lies in identifying, typing, ranking, and weighting these varied collective entities for purposes of formally assigning representative status.

For example, how do we determine which groups are entitled to greater representation? Groups can be distinguished and categorized by structure or organization, by political resources, by their internal procedures, or by the goals underlying their formation. They can be differentiated by how they are defined, by their functions and activities, on the basis of their political agenda, and in their degree of permanency. Each of these provides a possible basis for typing groups so as to dispense representation. But how are these legal distinctions made? For purposes of representation, what are the relevant distinctions between parties and interest groups, between for-profit and nonprofit corporations, between public-interest and business organizations, between organizations formed around a political or economic interest and groups of sociologically designated people (by gender, race, religion, etc.)? Can these distinctions be accounted for in a rational scheme of representation which is not wholly arbitrary? In the end, the categorizing, ordering, and handicapping of groups for purposes of determining representative status present insurmountable difficulties.

In contrast, the alternative model of vigorous party structures offers a comprehensive response to the myriad of representational demands. A functional assessment reveals parties to be inherently superior in their potential for performing representative democratic functions. Unlike self-interested single-issue groups, parties mediate and reconcile a variety of interests. While formal group recognition tends to "balkanize" or compartmentalize society, parties act as assimilating institutions, bringing together different voices and interests and allowing them to coexist. Parties are uniquely representative both of individuals and groups. They aggregate, shape, and channel individual participation. They also serve as vehicles of group influence by giving groups a forum in which to air their concerns.

Parties are also integrative institutions within government, bringing coherence and cohesiveness to the administration of power. They set agendas, define issues and alternatives, and manage the conflict that is at the heart of politics. Finally, they have an unmatched capacity as civic educators, promoting a common identity among the citizenry. They are essential linkages between the private and public aspects of one's life, enlarging the public sphere of the individual to include more than the sum of his private interests. The parties do none of these tasks perfectly, and do some of them rather poorly. But parties by definition and character differ significantly from other collective interests that exist in the political arena. Their unique organizational, functional, and structural attributes enable them to satisfy the multiple demands of representation, and compel a party-informed constitutional jurisprudence.

The central inquiry of the final chapters is the extent to which the Court's jurisprudence reflects an awareness of the crucial institutional and functional benefits of party systems in attaining representation. Chapter Seven examines the Court's treatment of political parties in the law of reapportionment and redistricting. Chapter Eight surveys state laws affecting the parties' control over their primaries and nominating procedures, and the impact on parties of ballot and voter access regulations. Finally, Chapter Nine scrutinizes the Court's decisions limiting the parties' reliance on patronage practices, an area that directly implicates the standing of parties in constitutional law.

Each of these chapters leads to the same conclusion, that the Court lacks an appreciation of parties and their unique capability to meet the demands of representation. At times, they are treated as equal or inferior to other political groups. In other areas, they are excluded from consideration altogether. When the Court does rule in their favor, it almost seems inadvertent. *In short, party structures are the essential component missing from the Court's theory of representation. Ultimately, these decisions evidence a dangerous indifference by the Court toward the institutional safeguards of representative democracy that reside in the makeup of political parties.*

One of the greatest challenges to altering this state of indifference is the current attitudinal climate. The contemporary environment is not party-friendly. Indeed, it is largely anti-party. Modern parties are held in low esteem in virtually all circles, with the possible exception of party activists themselves. The public, despite its continuing reliance on parties and its need for them, has little respect or appreciation for them. Negative impressions of parties are routinely reinforced by media and politicians themselves. Even academics outside the party renewal camp question their role. Any attempt to rehabilitate the Court's party-poor theory of representation faces the additional hurdle of the hostile antiparty atmosphere in which they must operate.

Nevertheless, the judicial oversight of parties is not irreparable. The role of parties as systems of representation is implicated by issues that will continue to find their way to the Court. As this happens, the challenge for the Court is to reconcile the variety of demands emanating from the web of representation theory, in a way that allays the tension between group activity and the flaws of pluralism. In the concluding chapter, I suggest a fresh way of conceptualizing representation to assist the Court in meeting that challenge. Rather than reducing representation to rights that rigidify the contradictions of representation theory, representation is better conceptualized as a set of "conflicts of interests." By maximizing the conflicts of interests to which legislators and the state are subjected and to which they must respond, the complex demands of representation are better satisfied. Representation theory necessitates institutional means of creating this set of conflicts and of translating them into representative action. The institutionalization of conflicts of interest brings us full circle to the organizational prerequisites of representative democracy, namely party organizations. It is through the subsystems of representation in the form of parties and groups that the optimal set of conflicts of interests are generated and are ultimately resolved.

AN EXPLANATORY NOTE: THE SURVEY OF THE ATTITUDINAL ENVIRONMENT

When struggling with a concept as elusive as political representation, there exists the danger of slipping off into abstract discussions of little relevance to the practical operation of the political system. A similar peril exists when one argues for significant changes in political institutions, as this book does with respect to the Supreme Court and its treatment of political parties. This is that the proposed solutions are unrealistic, unworkable, or simply out of the realm of the possible. In an effort to ward off these potential problems, the author conducted a survey of a cross-section of experts, professionals, and practitioners, who are engaged on a daily basis in the legal battles involving the actual shape and workings of the U.S. political system. The survey, its results, and the conclusions drawn from it are set out in their entirety in Appendix A. References to the survey are also sprinkled throughout the text where relevant to the discussion.

The survey is not intended as a statistical tool or form of quantitative evidence, but constitutes a canvassing of expert attitudes with respect to parties, the courts, and representation. It examines the opinions of those whose work is directly related to the issues and dilemmas of this book: law professors and legal practitioners who litigate or advise on matters in the electoral arena, party leaders and activists, as well as lobbyists and interest group representatives. In short, if there are to be genuine improvements in the electoral system, they will occur with the participation of the people who were the subjects of this survey. Consequently, though their attitudes comprise a relatively modest sampling, those opinions are extremely valuable in enriching the discussion with the pragmatic observations of practitioners.

CHAPTER ONE

The Labyrinth of Representation: Structures, Systems, and Institutions

Ours is a government formed of representative democracy. Its central tenet is one of rule with the consent of the governed. This is accomplished in a large-scale democracy through representative devices. People grant their approval to government by democratic structures and arrangements designed to ensure they are "represented" in the actions that government takes. The ultimate task of this endeavor is to consider legal responses to the challenges of representation in a pluralist democracy. The goal of those efforts is a group-constituted political system that better represents individual citizens. To assess the soundness of the alternative legal remedies necessitates a review of principles of political representation. We cannot judge their merits without first clarifying what they seek to accomplish (or whether they are clear in what they seek to accomplish).

The phrase "political representation" is plagued by an ambiguity that impedes meaningful discussions of its shortcomings and possible remedies. The term has numerous connotations and implications that frame the arguments, whether one is considering the "representation" of individual, local, or national interests, or the "representative" responsibilities imposed on a legislator or the legislative body as a whole, or what it means to be effectively "represented." Representation means different things to different people, and different things in different contexts. Yet students of representation fall into the habit of speaking without defining, assuming that what is being discussed is clear to all. The failure to acknowledge the variety of concepts falling within the rubric of representation, or to elucidate what is meant by representation, precludes a common basis of understanding to facilitate debate.[1]

The objectives of this chapter are twofold. The first is to survey the multitude of concepts, understandings, modes, and processes that must be incorporated into any study of political representation. We do not seek some universal definition for representation, but operate from the premise that a host of interpretations surround representation that are perfectly legitimate, depending on the context in which they are invoked. This review should broaden our perspective of the range of possible connotations of representation, and illuminate the multitude of issues and considerations implicated by such discussions.

A subtext within this discussion is to consider the systematic role of various political actors in a representative democracy. In particular, political parties and interest groups are key players in the pluralist account. The discussion will examine the case for parties and groups, respectively, as critical representative components of pluralist democracy.

The second objective is to distill from the review a paradigm of representation. That paradigm should encompass the principles that form a confluence leading to the most efficacious political representation. It ought to incorporate competing notions, which will yield a richer, more balanced understanding of political representation. It is ultimately the tool for framing the remainder of our discussion, and for assessing legal efforts to cultivate the representative capacity of our political processes.

MODES AND CONCEPTS OF REPRESENTATION

This study begins with the general modes of representation.[2] Political representation exists in and flows from four essential sources: (1) *formal* representation generated by the forms and processes of the electoral system; (2) *descriptive* representation from representatives who embody the characteristics, values, and mindset of the represented; (3) representation dwelling in the *relationship* between the representative and the represented; and (4) representative *activity* on behalf of the represented.

Formalistic Representation

The first set of representative ideas emphasizes the formal structures and arrangements responsible for generating a representative government. These are the institutional forms that allow a democracy to properly call itself representative. Formalistic concepts presuppose that, provided the proper forms and processes are in place, representation is a given. If the appropriate democratic operations from which representation flows have been implemented, we need not worry about the actual legislative activity under the system those forms produce. The formalistic conceptualization of representation consists of two parts. One is that point at which the representative is given *authority* to act for the represented, when he is "authorized to act in place of others."[3] Once the requisite grant of authority is given, all that follows necessarily constitutes representation.

Elections are the critical structural arrangements for accomplishing this. For the representative to act he must be granted authority in advance, in the form of elections. Elections bind the represented to the future actions of those whom they elect. Voters, in whom sovereignty ultimately dwells, commit themselves through elections to the acts of those they choose.[4]

The second prong of formal representation theory similarly relies on elections, but from a different vantage point. It views representation as the *accountability* of the representative to those he represents.[5] Representatives are answerable and responsible to those who elected them. Again, the prescribed means by which people hold their representatives to account are periodic elections. The electorate as a sovereign body gives or withholds its consent by approving or rejecting the past actions of the representative. The prospect of elections, combined with the representative's desire to continue in office, furnishes the basis for ensuring that he acts representatively. As John Dewey stated, "one is held responsible in order that he may become responsible, that is, responsive to the needs and claims of others."[6] Elections, then, are the formal guarantee of representation, initiating representation by bestowing authority and equipping the electorate to terminate that representation when dissatisfied.

Reflective Representation

Few would accept the formal mode of representation as sufficient, in itself, to provide effective political representation.[7] While the formal apparatus may be a prerequisite to achieving representation, most agree upon the need to move beyond formalistic explanations. A second set of considerations view representation as satisfied when the representative is *reflective* of those represented. Representation exists to the degree that the people represented are "present" in their representative, when he embodies or mirrors those he represents.

Reflective representation may be achieved in two ways. First, it is realized through the actual reflection of the relevant physical characteristics of those represented. Second, it includes symbolic or expressive acts engaged in by the representative, which the represented perceive as a fundamental reflection of who they are, their values and beliefs. The first idea is grounded in the belief that the representative assembly should be a miniature of society at large. A legislature that personifies the tangible, physical characteristics of the nation is sure to encapsulate the public's thoughts and opinions, and the social forces present in society.[8] Representation is a question of *representativeness*, and depends on whether those who rule bear a resemblance to the governed in those traits that are politically pertinent.[9]

Two assumptions underly this mode of representation. First, representativeness of the vital physical properties is assumed to be accompanied by a similarity of opinions and preferences on political issues. The representative who shares one's personal traits must share one's political views, and can be relied upon to advance those views in the assembly. This, standing alone, will not produce a representative assembly. Rather, it anticipates a second assumption, namely that legislative bodies are deliberative in character. The legislative embodiment of a multiplicity of physical attributes matters only if the legislature operates deliberatively. A properly deliberative assembly need only have all relevant interests voiced to ensure proper action. It need not be concerned with the size or magnitude of different interests represented, only that the array of societal characteristics are reflected physically so that the corollary interests will be present and accounted for.[10] Representation is satisfied by a diverse body of legislators, because (1) legislators who "look" like their constituents will act like them, and (2) this will ensure full deliberation resulting in the right action.

The second type of reflective representation, symbolic representation, is the attempt by the representative to create the perception in her constituents' minds that she shares and stands for that which is essential to them.[11] The representative symbolizes to the people the feelings, expressions, and actions that they wish to see represented. It is an arbitrary concept, a frame of mind, existing in the people's beliefs and "the extent that those subject to his rule accept him, believe in him as a symbol."[12] It is gauged by the level of satisfaction in the minds of the represented.

This amorphous representation does not result from persuasion or rational argument, or even from reacting in response to the people's substantive preferences. It dwells in the emotional, affective, and psychological responses of the represented. The representative's manipulation and use of ceremonial and expressive functions create the proper psychological responses in the represented.[13] In short, representation arises out of that activity which fosters feelings of loyalty, satisfaction, and trust between leaders and the citizenry. It is a perception in the minds of the people that the representative mirrors them. How does one know if this nebulous perception exists? It is whether the representative is believed in and accepted by the people as a symbol.[14]

In the realm of symbolic representation, elections are simply one device, and not an especially important one, for creating the invisible bonds of popular acceptance in the minds of the public. Elections perpetuate the symbolic dimension of representation by enabling the people to "identify themselves, as the ruled, with their representatives, as the rulers."[15] But elections may be much less significant than the representative's appearing at the local parade, holding a town hall meeting, and the like. Like formal accounts of representation, symbolic representation does not account for substantive, policy-oriented representation. It implicates representative activity only to the extent that the representative acts push the right buttons and perform those functions that create the necessary emotive bond.

Representation as Relationship

A third view of representation emphasizes the special relationship between legislator and constituent. Representation is the affinity for the representative that stems from the realization that he is the one through whom the represented affects government. That personal relationship gives the individual entry into the political arena. It furnishes the citizen with a channel for expressing her positions and preferences and for pursuing real input into government. Hence the attempts by the legislator to cultivate a personal relationship with the constituent. The representative (or someone in his office) can be counted on to read and respond to letters, to take constituents' phone calls, and to carry out the other activities attendant to constituency service. The greater the sense of empowerment and political significance imparted to the constituent, the greater the sense of representation. In short, it is through the representative relationship that the individual is made to feel that she counts for something, that she is actually recognized by the system.

Representation as Activity

The forms, reflection, and relationships all fail to capture the core of political representation, which is its substantive dimension. Contemporary concepts of representation are pinned on the substantive activity which is the fulfillment of one's official duties. The legislator "represents" those whose substantive preferences he discerns and pursues.[16] Representation as activity explains those actions one undertakes in office to advance the substantive interests of his constituents. It creates standards to which the representative must conform, providing normative criteria for assessing what the representative is doing in office to further the interests of those he represents.[17]

The meaning of representation as activity is not always clear. An assortment of phrases and tags are invoked to express representation as activity.[18] Depending on the context, each has distinct ramifications for what is expected of the representative in the active fulfillment of his duties.[19] This brief survey does not permit an exhaustive examination of the subtle complexities of representation as activity. A closer look at several of the more prominent questions, however, illustrates the broad implications. One such question is the central controversy in political representation, that which weighs the representative's role as delegate against that of trustee. Is the agent to carry out the mandate of the represented or exercise his judgment as independent actor in order to decide what is best for the subjects?[20] Does representation compel reliance on the representative's independent wisdom and exercise of his detached judgment? Or does it require obedience to the express wishes of those represented, even if contrary to their long-term interests? Or is it on a continuum somewhere between these positions? Or is it an amalgamation of the two? Pitkin sees the representative's obligation as neither to blindly follow his constituents' wishes nor to decide independently, but to act on what is objectively in their interests.[21] As she puts it:

The representative must act in such a way that, although he is independent, and his constituents are capable of action and judgment, no conflict arises between them. He must act in their interest, and this means that he must not normally come into conflict with their wishes.[22]

This does little to resolve the dilemma when there are legitimate differences over what course of action best serves constituents' interests. Who is most competent to decide raises another entire set of considerations, involving the nature of the interests and preferences implicated, the complexities of the issues involved, the respective wisdom and abilities of representative and the represented, and the context in which the decision must be made. The point is not to definitively answer how the representative should act. It is to demonstrate that, provided the representative acts within the two extremes, "there is room for a variety of views on what a good representative should and should not do."[23] Within the framework of the representative's obligations as established by the competing theories, representation permits a wide range of alternative actions.

THE INDIVIDUALIST AND COLLECTIVIST CHARACTER OF REPRESENTATION

Overlaid upon the modes of representation are considerations pertaining to the individualist and collectivist dimensions of representation. The goal of effective political representation has ramifications for the individual, the state, and the countless groups in between. Competing themes of individualism and collectivism exist on both sides of the representation equation; who is being represented, and who is doing the representing. They suggest discordant conclusions regarding (1) the feasibility and advisability of forming structures of representation around individuals versus collectively held interests, and (2) the capacity of individuals compared to collectivities to adequately discharge representative responsibilities. An examination of these contradictory themes reveals the complexity of the task of weaving together a coherent ideal of political representation.

The Representative Relationship: Individual or Corporate?

The modes of representation yield different understandings of the nature and practical operation of representation, and the levels on which it operates. An example is the effort to identify the focus of the representative relationship. To be more precise, does representation dwell primarily in the individual relationship between citizen and the legislator from his district? Or does it consist of the relationship between the citizen and the legislative body that passes laws and administers government resources? The answer hinges on one's understanding of what representation is designed to accomplish.

One such aim is to provide assistance to citizens who have specific needs that require the services of someone in government to resolve. For those entangled in the federal bureaucracy, or in need of help in solving a particular problem, the representative provides that service. Constituency service is a purely individual relationship between constituent and representative.

Another aim is the more nebulous goal of satisfying the citizen's need to feel represented by government. Representational arrangements seek to avoid the alienation resulting from a government seemingly oblivious to one's political existence or interests. Representation on one level should instill confidence in the citizen that he and his interests are acknowledged and accounted for. It provides some reassurance to the citizen that there are means by which to speak and be heard.

This end likewise favors representation as a personal, individual relationship between constituent and representative. One will feel represented when there is a person to whom he can point as his representative, whose office he can call to express his opinions. He will feel represented when he participates in choosing who will serve in Congress and represent his district. He will feel represented by encountering his representative at parades or town meetings, or by enjoying localized benefits acquired for the district. In short, the representative relationship exists on an individual level, between legislator and constituent.

Individualism, then, implicates both the relational and the reflective modes of representation. Symbolic or expressive words or deeds are intended to impart feelings of representation, even without discernible concrete benefits to the constituent.[24] Through racial, ethnic, educational, religious, or occupational bonds, the representative is expected to share the preferences, values, and outlooks of the individuals he is representing. One's sense of being represented is not activated just by observing the representative act in more palpable ways to wield power on one's behalf. It also comes from seeing someone within the power-wielding body who is "like" the constituent and has his defining characteristics.

Representation in this individualistic light has practical ramifications for representative structures. First, the size of the constituency takes on obvious importance, affecting the ability of the
legislator to individually represent those within it. Second, it
heightens the importance of having electoral choices available to
the constituency. It requires that citizens have substantial influence in selecting their personal representative, and that the formal institutions of representation be in place to satisfy them.
Finally, it implicates the level of homogeneity of interests and characteristics of the constituents. The representative can only mirror
group norms or qualities within his geographic district. A highly
homogeneous constituency with fewer distinct traits will be better
able to select a representative who reflects that. This is likely to
increase the degree of satisfaction felt by individual constituents
with their perceived representation. Moreover, the narrower the
constituency can be defined in opinions and interests, the greater
their control over the representative. To the extent constituents
share well-defined interests, the less likely the representative will
be to act contrary to those interests. The represented, better able
to maintain corporate control over their representative, should
individually enjoy a sense of enhanced representation.[25]

Representational Activity as Collective Response

An alternative view of representation focuses on the activity of
the representative body responsible for governing, and generates
a different set of implications. Unlike the individualistic relational
and reflective modes of representation, legislative output requires
corporate representation by the entire legislature.[26] The representative operates not in isolation, but within a network of other
people and political institutions. Representation of constituents
occurs within a framework of influences and constraints from one's
legislative colleagues, one's party, and one's desire for re-election.

Representative activity as the collective acts of the legislative
body presupposes different objectives. It measures representation
by tangible policy outcomes, which are generated in response to
the needs of the represented. Representation is more than the
detection of the preferences of the represented. It also judges the
representatives by their ability to produce results that actually satisfy those preferences. The essence of representative government
is its capacity to respond to constituent needs and wants.

Representation in this light bears little relation to descriptive criteria of what a representative looks like or what he expresses

in symbolic activity. The focus is simply on what is actually accomplished. Representation is the responsiveness of the government as a whole, as reflected in the policies it pursues and the outcomes that result.[27] The essential acts of representing are when the ruling body "defines priorities, collects and distributes resources, and otherwise manages the affairs of the community in a manner responsive to the interests of its citizens."[28] The single representative, then, cannot satisfy the representative needs of the governed. That requires a broader set of institutional structures and relationships. Pitkin describes it as:

> a public, institutional arrangement involving many people and groups, and operating in the complex ways of large-scale social arrangements. *What makes it representation is not any single action by any one participant, but the overall structure and functioning of the system, the patterns emerging from the multiple activities of many people.* It is representation if the people (or a constituency) are present in governmental action.[29]

Limiting representation to the relationship between legislator and constituent falls far short. Reflective representation is one component, but it is an incomplete standard for evaluating representation. The "representativeness" of the legislator provides no real criteria for assessing whether he is acting in constituents' interests.[30] It requires only that he properly reflect the spectrum of characteristics present in his district.[31]

In contrast, an emphasis on legislative activity permits a reasonable means of assessing the representative's responsiveness to his constituents. It establishes behavioral norms and standards against which performance can be measured, thus allowing for the turning-out of the governors if they fail to adhere to those standards.[32] It permits empirical inquiry into the actions of the leaders to determine if the citizenry's interests are being advanced in perceptible ways.[33] Representative activity, therefore, is the benchmark for enforcing legislative accountability.

Representation as corporate activity does not abandon the importance of representative relationships. It does put them in a markedly different light. The focus is shifted from before election day, as a means of choosing representatives, to a post-election device to judge whether the chosen are acting responsively. The focus becomes one of responsiveness, "how governors behave after they have been chosen and after they have been exposed to the preferences of the public."[34]

This suggests a complex, multifaceted vision of representation which is absent from descriptive or symbolic concepts. It encompasses a variety of activities in which people and groups are involved within the political community.[35] It envisions a governing body attempting to weave countless strands of opinion and preference into substantive policies acceptable to those demanding action. Eulau and Prewitt describe it as "the myriad activities, behaviors, and perceptions which link the governors and the governed, and not just in those more specialized activities which have to do with selection and petitioning."[36]

Finally, representation as activity implicates the internal workings of the groups responsible for that activity. To this point, our examination of collective political activity has focused on how individuals seek political influence through groups. Representation lodged in the corporate governing body raises group considerations pertaining to the ways in which the official, institutionalized group arrives at its decisions. A full comprehension of representation requires a scrutiny of the dynamics and forces at work as the legislature, congressional committee, or appellate panel of judges goes about its business.[37]

Who is Represented?: Local vs. National Interests

The individualist and corporatist dimensions of representation exist on a parallel level with respect to the question of who is to be represented. Representation is less a question of identifying the interests of the constituent than of identifying the constituency to be represented in a particular context. For example, the interest to be represented may be held by individuals living in the same locale, or it may be a national interest or one that relates to the good of the whole. The "classic controversy in the literature of political representation" is whether a representative should respond to specific constituents, through specific mandates or instructions, or should act independently in the country's interests.[38] An individualistic representative vision focuses on local or regional interests; collectivist representation manifested in governmental outcomes suggests a focus on the general welfare.

In the Burkean approach, the legislature is required to act for the nation as a whole, with each member judging for himself what is for the good of the nation. To Burke:

> Parliament is not a congress of ambassadors from different and hostile interests, which interests each must maintain, as

> an agent and advocate, against other agents and advocates;
> but Parliament is a deliberative assembly of one nation, with
> one interest, that of the whole—where not local prejudices
> ought to guide, but the general good resulting from the gen-
> eral reason of the whole.[39]

This leaves little room for an individual relationship between the
representative and the constituent. It exists between the entire
nation and the individual legislator (and between nation and legislature). This raises the representative above the role of pure
agent or delegate.[40] If each representative is bound by the requirement that he precisely mirror the interests of his local constituency, government action becomes a mere reflex of majority will.
Representation of the interest of the whole assumes that the public interest is greater than the sum of individual or local interests.
It demands that legislators armed with information provided by
local constituencies engage in dialogue and deliberation, and reason their way toward the good of the nation.[41]

This has implications for the role and composition of the
legislature. It reinstates the idea of the legislature as primarily
deliberative in character. The legislators only need information
from those they represent. Provided that there is at least one person in the assembly voicing each interest in society, rational deliberation will inevitably reveal the national interest.[42] Legislative
action is more than nose counting and majorities prevailing over
minorities, but entails deliberation until consensus and agreement
are reached. It matters not how many representatives of an interest are present in Congress, only that:

> all the facts and arguments be accurately and wisely set
> forth. . . . If [a group's] interest has even a single competent
> member in Parliament, it will be looked after, because it is
> not his vote but his arguments that matter.[43]

Burke asserted that even those without a member in Congress
"have an equal representation, because you have men equally interested in the prosperity of the whole, who are involved in the
general interest and the general sympathy."[44] The primary objective of elections from this perspective was to ensure that those most
capable of governing were elected. Elections should result in the
selection of the most judicious and capable people, those able to
engage in full deliberation and to discern the good of society.

The classic liberal emphasis on the individual conjures up a
wholly different set of representative responsibilities. Representa-

tion consists of activity on behalf of individual constituents, grouped together by district or region.[45] Citizens are assumed to be rational, independent, and autonomous, capable of political sophistication and of communicating their preferences to their representatives. Hence, it is their interests that matter, and not those of collectives or associations.[46]

This presents considerable challenges. As a practical matter, the representative is capable only of acting for groups of individuals. Those groupings cannot be identified by a single interest. Hence, individuals are grouped into local or geographic categories on the assumption that they share a set of roughly similar interests which are distinct from those of other regional groups. Therefore, the liberal individualistic approach compels that the representative concentrate on a local rather than national constituency.[47] The challenge is to identify from the multitude of constituents that "constituency" which he is to represent.

THE PARADOXICAL GOALS OF REPRESENTATION: UNITY AND DIVERSITY

Representation presents itself in a variety of modes. These in turn generate a set of criss-crossing activities that touch upon and involve individualistic and communal political actors, depending on the context. These multiple representative devices and theories likewise flow from a variety of specific goals and objectives. Underlying each of these sets of considerations is the paradox that is perhaps the central obstacle to a coherent model of representation. The primary challenge to sound representative structures is how to satisfy the contradictory themes of unity and diversity. On the broadest level, representation is expected to accomplish two seemingly irreconcilable concepts. On one hand, it ought to generate a commonality amongst the citizenry, a spirit of shared identity and a willingness to subordinate the purely personal to public interests. At the same time, it is expected to make government responsive to the individual. It must recognize, accommodate, and address the interests of individual citizens.

Representative structures are burdened with informing citizens of those values which they hold together.[48] If representation is expected to garner the consent of the governed, it must identify those interests common to all citizens, and yield specific governmental behavior consistent with them. Structures of representation should cultivate consensus and commonality in society, which in turn compel the citizenry's compliance with and conformity to governmental action. The corporate dimensions of representation lead to *unity*.

But representation is simultaneously trained on satisfying the diverse interests of the individuals who comprise the public. The divisions within society have increased exponentially as it has moved inexorably toward greater specialization, social diversity, and economic complexity. Countless new social interests beget a new set of political interests demanding to be heard. Not only are these interests often adverse to each other, they are often in conflict with community interests. Yet representative structures are measured by their "practical capacity for giving to the persons involved in a particular issue a due voice in the decision."[49]

Unfortunately, the attention to specific individual desires makes attainment of the common good more difficult. The challenge for democratic theorists is to strike the balance between the modes and devices of representation that will generally address these countervailing considerations. Any scheme of representation will be judged on how it performs this tightrope act; whether it is successful in composing a settlement across society of what is in the interest of the community as a whole, while concurrently enabling government to conduct those specialized activities that satisfy individual needs.[50]

The task of cultivating unity and commonality while respecting and protecting diversity dictates the need for intermediate mechanisms through which both can be achieved. Representative devices structured to pursue one goal directly or exclusively will do so only at the expense of the other. Hence the need for institutional political buffers between the individual and the national. These *subsystems of representation* are essential to mute and soften the demands of interests, and to distance them from extreme, absolutist positions to a position where they can coexist in the same space.

PARTY SYSTEMS AND GROUPS AS SUBSYSTEMS OF REPRESENTATION: THE INSTITUTIONAL LINKAGES

The need for intermediate channels in representative democracy points directly to politically active groups and organizations. Effective political representation depends on an appropriate role being assigned to, and a balance maintained between, the twin pillars of political parties and organized political interest groups.

Parties and groups are institutional structures that resolve, or at least ameliorate, the tensions between unity and diversity. As such, they are effective systematic tools of political empowerment for individuals in a large-scale democracy.

Representation theory is integrally bound up in and interwoven with the subsystems of political parties and group politics. Groups act as representative linkages within, and are overlain upon, the responsible two-party system, while the party system is pluralist in its nature and operation. Both political parties and groups are essential to fulfilling the mediating functions in democratic government.

Groups and parties serve as the primary linkages between individual citizens and the government in a *dual system of representation*. As instrumentalities of governance, they are the "effective agent[s] of political destinies."[51] Groups and political parties are two sides of the coin of representation, through which the governors and governed are bound. They are critical building blocks in:

> how the institutions of representative democracy work, and especially inquiry into the conditions under which the governors and governed are linked so that political responsiveness and responsibility are obtained.[52]

In short, politically active organizations are the requisite subsystems of representation that link citizens to their rulers.

The dual system of representation is useful in organizing and melding together the representational modes and concepts that have been discussed. It consists, on one hand, of the devices by which those who represent are chosen, and on the other, of the ways in which they are petitioned once in office.[53] Formal representation is realized through the first prong, as representative authority is granted and representative accountability assured through *elections*. Similarly, elections allow for descriptive or reflective representation, as voters choose their "type" of representative. Representation as activity, in contrast, is assured through the second prong. As citizens *petition* government, those interests, preferences, and opinions that drive representative activity are made known to the representative.

These two elements of the dual system of representation are best understood by the essential distinctions that set them apart. First, they differ as *process*. Representation in the selection of those who will govern is accomplished primarily through the electoral processes, through caucuses and nominating conventions, primaries, campaigns, and the election itself. Those institutional arrangements present in the electoral system are constitutive linkages, determining the extent to which the consent of the governed is realized through selection of the governors.[54]

Petitioning one's representative occurs via a different, largely informal, set of processes which include lobbying, letter writing, petition drives, and calling the legislator's office. It takes place in whatever processes are available for constituents to inform or influence elected officials. Editorializing, attending meetings, protesting, and demonstrating all give substantive shape to the linkages that connect citizens to government between elections.[55] It is important that one have avenues by which to bring concerns, complaints, requests, and expression of opinions to one's representative. Through these channels the governors are informed about the governed and are subjected to their consent.[56]

A second distinction is one of *timing*. The selection of leaders through elections occurs periodically. Every second or fourth year, citizens decide who will fulfill the representative function, reelecting representatives or rejecting them in favor of new ones. In contrast, the petitioning of one's elected officials is ongoing. Efforts to influence the actions of one's representative continue through that official's term. The periodic, cyclical exercise of elections suggests a static, formal representation. Petitioning of leaders recognizes the dynamic nature of the process, as the interests and opinions that drive representative activity are fluid, changing and evolving. Representation that takes place between the formal structures of elections is necessary to inform and educate legislators so that their representative activity adequately captures the shifting preferences of the represented.

Finally, the dual system of representation is delineated by considering *who is acting as representative*. To this point, we have simply assumed the representatives to be those with formal, official representative responsibilities. These are the legislators who occupy public office and are responsible, individually and corporately, for pursuing and implementing government policy. The dual system of electing and petitioning exposes a second set of representatives operating apart from the official representative relationship between legislator and constituent. These subsystems of representation are the parties and groups that mediate between the public and the elected.[57] They allow individuals to participate and gain significance through association, while simultaneously narrowing, focusing, and defining the multiplicity of interests into discernible policy positions, which ultimately shape and guide governance.

In this matrix, political parties are central to the task of leader selection. They organize and direct the electoral process, recruiting candidates, eliciting grassroots support monetary and otherwise, conducting caucuses, primaries, and conventions, consulting on campaigns, and more. Meanwhile, other political associations and organizations primarily carry out the second task of petitioning. Through the assortment of tactics that comprise pressure politics, groups present their claims to official representatives. Thus, parties and other organizations play a vitally important role in the dual representative system; parties structuring the choice of representatives, and groups representing and accommodating the vast diversity of interests in society.[58]

The respective roles of parties and pressure groups in the dual representative system are not mutually exclusive. While parties are the primary shapers of campaigns and elections, political associations and groups also carry significant clout. They weigh in on platforms, throw their support behind their favored candidate, and engage in campaign efforts. Likewise, party systems furnish an alternative route for petitioning government. Party organizations impact the behavior of public officials who belong to that party. Through the organization, party members work between elections to inform and influence party leaders and others in their party holding office.

THE REPRESENTATIONAL PARADIGM

The complexities of contemporary political representation should be apparent from this discussion. As Hannah Pitkin states, "the modern representative acts within an elaborate network of pressures, demands, and obligations."[59] The task of legislating is one of daunting complexity, in which a number of determinants are at work and must be factored into legislative decisions. Those considerations are reflected as follows:

Themes of Representation

A.   Representational Definitions

    1.   An ordering of political relations
    2.   A system of electoral devices and procedures
    3.   A condition when the acts of one vested with public functions are in accord with those to whom they are important

B.   Representational Modes and Concepts
      1.   Formal
      2.   Reflective
      3.   Relational
      4.   Active

C.   Representational Goals/Aims/Purposes
      1.   Unity/Popular control
            • Impose majority rule
            • Garner consent of the governed
            • Institutionalize values
            • Inculcate sense of common values
            • Channel opinions and preferences into policy
            • Collectively responsive government
            • Governmental accountability
      2.   Diversity/Liberal Values
            • Protect individual rights
            • Political equality
            • Admit and protect special values
            • Constituent service
            • Individually responsive government

In sum, a variety of concepts are associated with representation, of which there is no consensus or uniform acceptance. Each has relevancy and validity, depending on the context in which representation is being discussed. For example, there are situations in which representation as activity may be implausible because of irreconcilable differences between legislator and constituent or among the constituents themselves. Yet descriptive representation may still exist in a legislator who shares a constituent's values and commitments, even if they may disagree on a particular issue. Or the represented may find comfort in symbolic representation and the emotional bonds that exist despite policy differences. Finally, the citizen may take consolation in the right to ultimately participate in the removal of that legislator for failing to heed constituency wishes.

Errors arise when each concept is treated as the entirety of representation, as if it alone can provide an adequate account of representation. Each notion has something to contribute to the understanding of representation. None of the ideas discussed herein are necessarily inaccurate or mistaken, but each is insufficient when standing alone.[60] As Pitkin notes:

Political representation is as wide and varied in range as representation itself will allow. The most that we can hope to do when confronted by such multiplicity is to be clear on what view of representation a particular writer is using, and whether that view, its assumptions and implications, really fit the case to which he is trying to apply them.[61]

Thus the need for a more inclusive comprehension of representation. When considering practical problems of representation, often neglected concepts may round out our understanding of effective representation. The greater the number of ideas that come into play at a practical level, the more fruitful the structures of political representation are likely to be. Notions of formal structures and deliberative legislative bodies strike us as idealistic or outmoded. Yet they are important to achieving effective representation. When we drop them from our dialogue, or give them up as pie-in-the-sky, the aspiration of real representation suffers. Attempts to fortify representative structures require a theoretical analysis that incorporates all aspects of representation. But it must especially incorporate the systematic institutional arrangements that are the framework for formal, descriptive, and symbolic representation. Then it must scrutinize with equal care the functioning of those systems and the representative activity which flows from them.

Moreover, theories of representation must make adequate allowance for the full roster of players needed to fill the representative team. They must recognize the individualist and collectivist dimensions of representation, both in terms of who is being represented and who is doing the representing.

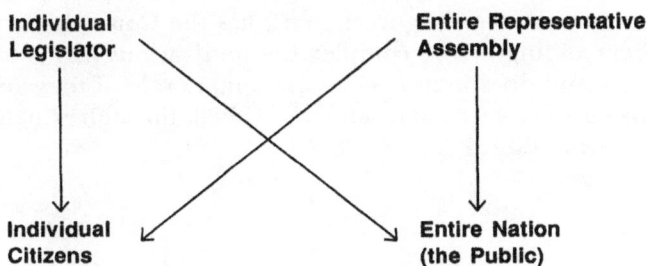

Figure 1. Representative Responsibilities

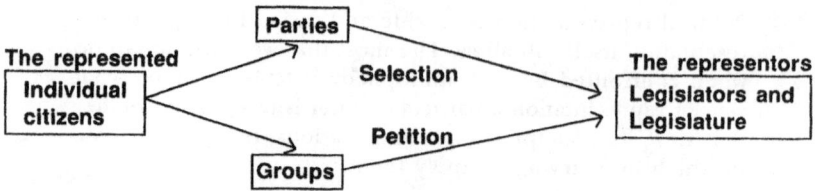

Figure 2. The Subsystems (represented and representors)

Finally, do the individualistic and corporate aspects of representation acknowledge the critical importance of the subsystems of representation? Do they leave sufficient room for parties and interest groups, as institutional forms of representation, to serve simultaneously as representatives (of the people) and as the represented (to whom representatives are responsive)? Do they acknowledge the symbiotic relationship between parties and groups as mutually supportive of each other? And do they appreciate the representative opportunities available to groups and parties in the dual system óf selection and petition?

These themes frame the remainder of this book. A host of practical problems afflict the American system of representation, which the political science and legal communities have attempted to address. This project is primarily concerned with the U.S. Supreme Court's efforts to confront and resolve the issues and dilemmas of representation. As we consider those efforts, we will repeatedly return to the theoretical and conceptual demands made upon our representative systems. To what extent have the multiple concepts of representation worked their way into constitutional jurisprudence? When faced with issues that implicate our representative system of government, has the Court demonstrated an understanding of the complexities and various forms of representation? And does it appreciate the unique role of the subsystems and linkages between state and individual through which representation is realized?

CHAPTER TWO

✤

Voting Rights and Political Representation in Constitutional Law: The Primacy of Individualism

The U.S. Supreme Court bears much responsibility for those structures and arrangements from which representation is expected to flow. It has had ample opportunity to don its hat as political theorist, and to consider issues of political representation. The explication in the first chapter of the intricacies of representation yields a standard for evaluating the Court's efforts. The Court's decisions reveal a distinct theory of representation. Unfortunately, it is a narrow one which bears little resemblance to the representational model.

The Court's theory of representation is most clearly illustrated in its attempts to define voting rights and to clarify the nature of representation stemming from those rights. The thirty-year history of federal judicial activity in voting rights, redistricting, and apportionment is characterized by two dominant themes. This chapter examines the primacy of individualism, which defined the first decade of reapportionment litigation. The Court focused almost exclusively on individual voting equality. It demonstrated little appreciation for the variable of collectives in the electoral equation, either in giving significance to individual voting rights or in engendering meaningful representation through participation. This one-dimensional view is a distant, much poorer cousin to the multi-pronged ideal, with its array of representative modes, means, players, and practices.

The following chapter will explore the gradual emergence of group identity as an important supplement to individual voting rights. The Court was forced eventually to consider groups in the electoral process, as the focus shifted from strict voting rights litigation to claims of vote dilution. With the advent of the Voting Rights Act, the Court eventually settled upon a standard for protecting racially designated groups from discrimination in redistricting and other electoral arrangements. This was to be a harbinger of future difficulties, however, as other, nonracially designated, groups sought similar legal protections to enhance their voting power.

The search for a judicial theory of representation begins at the flashpoint of the American democratic state, the sphere of voting and electoral behavior. The political consequences of electoral laws are paramount to the political status of individuals and groups. Decisions that define electoral rights go to the heart of representation. They shape the means by which electoral institutions and processes distribute political power and resources.[1] They determine who organizes and wields the legislative processes responsible for all other laws.[2] They ultimately settle who controls the instruments of power, and who influences the use of those instruments. In short, they are the first principles of practical politics, of which other issues are derivative. The extent to which the Court incorporates the numerous aspects of representation theory into issues of voting and elections is, therefore, of unparalleled importance.

The overarching theme that emerges from these various electoral contexts is one of unmediated individual political participation. Elections are viewed largely as aggregates of votes cast by individuals exercising a personal right. Absent is a recognition of groups as representative mechanisms for clarifying and augmenting individual participation. *Rarely does the Court articulate or imply acceptance of the role of collectives, either in alleviating, moderating, and tempering self-interested individual conduct, or in motivating, enhancing, and empowering individual political participation.*

The Supreme Court remains very much a child of the Progressive Era. Its vision of representation in the realm of voting and elections is skewed in favor of individuals and against collective manifestations. It holds a romanticized perception of politics as an unencumbered relationship between individual citizen and her representatives. Legitimate politics is premised on individual fairness, as judged by equal access for all individuals and processes that reflect the unfettered judgment of each.[3] The best way to make government fair and responsive is to equalize the personal influence of each voter.[4]

The corollary is a subconscious bias against those intermediate linkages of representation. The judicial mindset is one in which "groups or associations that stand between the individual and the state all too often meet with judicial incomprehension."[5] The Court is plagued with a "blind spot" when the communal dimensions of political representation are concerned.[6] Its theory of representation actually runs counter to the paradigm in which groups and parties are integral structures of representation. The less parties, groups, and other artificial institutions get in the way of the direct exchange between the governed and their leaders, the better.

VOTING RIGHTS:
EQUAL VOTES OR EFFECTIVE REPRESENTATION?[7]

The contradictory strains of representation theory are distinctly evident in the laws and institutions of voting and elections. In particular, questions of the propriety of redistricting practices suggest the need for rules that accommodate both individual and collective forms of electoral expression. Unfortunately, constitutional doctrine in voting rights settled upon an exclusive concern with individual numerical voting equality. Consequently, it accentuated the legal disconnect between individual and group, strengthening the status of the former while diminishing the latter.

The Court entered the reapportionment fray in 1962, with the seminal decision of *Baker v. Carr*.[8] In *Baker*, the Court was asked to review the malapportionment of Tennessee's state legislative districts under an apportionment statute that had operated untouched for some sixty years. For the first time, the Supreme Court determined that constitutional challenges to apportionment and redistricting questions were properly within the jurisdiction of the federal courts to decide. *Baker v. Carr* did not address the substantive legal standards applicable to the task of apportionment, but thrust the Court into an area that directly implicated the efficacy of the electoral system, and that heretofore had been off limits.[9] Within several years, the Court was deciding a series of cases that propelled it deep into the thicket of apportionment and redistricting.

In 1964, the Court tackled a bloc of districting cases that gave it an opportunity to examine electoral representation and the respective roles of groups and individuals. Those cases involved constitutional challenges to congressional districts in New York and Georgia.[10] In them, the Court took its first hard look at the severe disparities in the apportionment of state legislative assemblies, in particular those inequities between rural and urban areas. The Court examined reapportionment plans from a number of states, including New York, Alabama, Maryland, Virginia, and Colorado.[11] The series of opinions issuing from these cases contained hints that the Court might simultaneously protect individual voting rights and recognize group interests and their place in realizing effective representation. In *Wesberry v. Sanders*,[12] the Court established the "one person one vote" standard, holding that the Equal Protection Clause mandated that "as nearly as is practicable, one man's vote in a congressional election is worth as much as another's." The Court's emphasis on "equal representation . . . for equal numbers of people" indicated that a fundamental goal was to ensure mathematical equality of the individual vote.[13]

The Court went further in the companion case of *Reynolds v. Sims*, where malapportionment in Alabama had given rural legislators a virtual lock on the statehouse. The opinion set forth "fair and effective representation" as the ultimate aim of reapportionment schemes.[14] All citizens were entitled to full participation in the political system, and to "an equally *effective* voice" in the process.[15] Without specifically defining what it meant, Chief Justice Warren stressed the fundamental importance of giving every citizen a voice in the election of her lawmakers and representatives. By inference, the *effectiveness* of political participation extended beyond an equally weighted vote. Warren's references to effectiveness intimated that courts should include other considerations in their voting analysis that would endow the individual vote with greater significance in acquiring meaningful representation.

That those considerations might include acknowledgment of group affiliations was expressed by Justice Stewart in another case involving disparities in Colorado's state legislative districts. Stewart shared Warren's vision of the right to effective representation, and argued that this could be accomplished only by adding groups to the analysis. In his dissent in *Lucas v. Colorado General Assembly*, Stewart criticized equally weighted voting as:

> forever den[ying] to every state any opportunity for enlightened and progressive innovation in the design of its demo-

cratic institutions, *so as to accommodate within a system of representative government the interests and aspirations of diverse groups of people.*[16]

He offered a competing vision of representation, one more attuned to the intricacies of representation:

> *Representative government is a process of accommodating group interests through democratic institutional arrangements.* Its function is to channel the numerous opinions, interests, and abilities of the people of a State into the making of the State's public policy. *Appropriate legislative apportionment, therefore, should ideally be designed to insure effective representation* in the State's legislature, in cooperation with other organs of political power, *of the various groups and interests making up the electorate.*[17]

For Stewart, "fair, effective and balanced representation" was the overriding goal of apportionment. Voting was not the end, but was designed to yield representation in government. Representation was achieved only by acknowledging that legislators represented people with identifiable interests that coalesced in groups identifiable along regional, social, and economic lines.[18] Stewart recognized that voting rights constructed solely around the numerical value of the vote failed to account for the representative character of political groups.

The language in *Reynolds* and *Wesberry* was certainly flexible enough to incorporate these considerations, which would preserve the primary goal of roughly equal voting power. Warren warned that "[m]athematical exactness or precision is hardly a workable constitutional requirement,"[19] and acknowledged the need for neutral criteria within which group interests could be raised. These included the maintenance of political subdivisions and compactness of legislative districts.[20]

In subsequent years, however, the Court rejected a broader definition of voting rights and representation, opting for a bright line standard of equally weighted votes. The *Reynolds* goal of "fair and effective representation" receded, replaced by a principle that equated representation with equipopulous districts. Voting rights analysis focused exclusively on the numeric value of the vote, with little regard for determinants of its effectiveness. The right to vote consisted of two elements, the removal of barriers to casting the ballot, and ensuring that each person's vote was of equal weight. This required a "good faith effort to achieve precise mathematical equality" in district populations.[21] Within five years of *Reynolds*, the Court was invalidating redistricting

plans that contained the smallest of population differences between districts.[22]

Nor did the Court merely adopt a passive disinclination to
add other factors to its voting analysis. It exhibited virtually no
tolerance for state legislatures that took into account other criteria if they might cause deviations from perfect numerical equality. While paying lip service to traditional criteria, the Court struck
down plans with minuscule deviations. Communities of interests,
unique regional concerns, and other expressions of collective interests did not justify even *de minimis* departures from equal district population.[23]

The Court also left no doubt regarding the electoral status
of groups, periodically rendering unequivocal statements shunning
formal recognition of group interests per se.[24] The dominant
theme was that expressed by Justice Brennan in *Kirkpatrick v.
Preisler*:

> Missouri contends that variances were necessary to avoid frag-
> menting areas with distinct economic and social interests and
> thereby diluting the effective representation of those inter-
> ests in Congress. *But to accept population variances, large or small,
> in order to create districts with specific interest orientations is anti-
> thetical to the basic premise of the constitutional command to pro-
> vide equal representation for equal numbers of people.*[25]

For Brennan and the Court, the aims of equal voting and the
representation of collective interests were mutually exclusive, and
there was no doubt that the Court considered the former to be
far more important than the latter. Provided one's vote was equal
to that of others in the state, constitutional imperatives were
deemed to be satisfied. The result was to eviscerate the broader
implications of "fair and effective representation."[26]

A ONE-DIMENSIONAL VIEW OF
VOTING RIGHTS AND REPRESENTATION

The Court's efforts in the reapportionment arena fell short of
the conceptual demands of the representational ideal. Its obses-
sion with individual participation ignored the important role of
political actors in all shapes, sizes, and forms. Its partitioning of
representational rights along individual and corporate lines revealed an apprehension of organized political activity. Through
its definition of voting equality, the Court reinforced the tendency

toward individualism to the exclusion of a broader pluralistic, group-inclusive concept of political rights. The rights "protected against discrimination were conceptualized as rights of individuals, not of groups."[27] Individual citizens had a right to representation, while the role of intermediate groups was excluded from consideration.[28]

The Court's distinctly individualistic slant on representation returns us to the elementary task of defining representation. Does equality of representation connote an equal opportunity to participate in the political process? Is it equality in the opportunity to pick a representative? Or does it require that the actual outcomes of government be measured by some standard of equality? The crux of the issue is whether the formal assurance of equal voting power will actually produce effective representation, or whether it entails a broader substantive aim of equality in influence and outcomes.

The Court in the reapportionment decisions opted for a strict formal view of representation to the exclusion of other modes of representation. "Substantially equal state legislative representation" was ensured by giving every citizen an equal vote.[29] Provided that this process-oriented framework gave each individual a vote with precisely the same value, the Court would not concern itself with disparities in outcomes. This formal individualism eschewed broader notions of representation based on voting effectiveness.

A representational theory with the goal of political effectiveness demands more than numerical equality of the vote.[30] Voting is not a discrete, self-executing act, but becomes effective when translated into meaningful input into the system. Effective representation begins with individual voting parity, and builds upon it. If meaningful political participation connotes having a say in forming the government that tends to one's needs, then meaningful voting rights imply an opportunity to choose legislators who will represent one's interests in pursuing legislative outcomes. Effective representation is enhanced when one has the same chance to affect and influence electoral outcomes through voting.

The representational paradigm suggests serious limitations in exclusive reliance upon "one person one vote." An equal vote is an important component even in the enlarged sphere of effective and fair representation.[31] But exclusive reliance upon it yields an oppressively strict, inflexible majoritarian system. It nullifies groups of voters' prerogative to a substantively responsive government. *Qualitative* factors are sacrificed at the altar of *quantitative*

standards of equality. Group considerations are unnecessary, provided that individuals have an equal right to formally participate
in elections.[32]

The goal of "fair and effective representation" implicates
substantive notions of representation beyond formal equality, including the facilitation of group activity in politics. The broader
right forming around adequacy of representation denotes the ability to choose one's representative. This only happens collectively.
Put simply, groups of people elect legislators. Voting rights implicate the groups and interests with which one is affiliated when
one casts a vote.[33] Access for groups to legislative representation,
therefore, is a fundamental aspect of assuring significant political
participation.[34]

EFFECTIVE POLITICAL PARTICIPATION: THE LINK BETWEEN VOTING AND REPRESENTATION

The Court also struggled to make the crucial connection between
voting and representation. Voting and representation are two sides
of the same coin, the coin of meaningful, effective involvement
in the political process. Each directly affects the other, and cannot be assessed apart from it. Voting rights cannot be judged without examining the effectiveness of the representation they spawn.
Likewise, representation must be firmly rooted in the equality of
the vote. Specious distinctions that conceal this connection obscure the task of delineating a set of criteria to apply to reapportionment and other issues affecting representation.[35] The Court's
strict adherence to formal individualistic voting rights assumed the
two to be discrete and separate.[36] By focusing on equal voting
weight, the Court took a narrow view of voting which masked the
essential link between voting and representation. Its formalistic
approach disregarded the very practical issue of the caliber of the
representation resulting from the vote.

There are two fundamentally different views of the driving
impulses underlying the exercise of voting. They offer markedly
divergent solutions to resolving the twin dilemmas of voting rights:
should we include group influence in analyzing individual voting
rights?; and should representative structures be concerned with
the quality of representation?

The "liberal" understanding of the voter is as an autonomous,
independent individual for whom social bonds are secondary. She
is a self-contained political identity distinct from her institutional

ties and affiliations. The interests that motivate political participation dwell in the individual person. Shared interests are of ancillary importance. To the extent that her political identity is related to groups, it consists of a bundle of connections to a variety of groups, with often inconsistent and even irreconcilable objectives. Her interests are likely to cut across her group affiliations. Her specific policy preferences and priorities are largely subjective and fluid, changing to reflect her individual circumstances.[37]

This portrait engenders an individualistic theory of representation. In an electorate composed of self-reliant individuals voting their personal preferences with little regard for group links, it is less important that electoral mechanisms mirror diverse group interests. We need not examine representative bodies to see whether they reflect the myriad of collective attributes in the electorate, and the interests that flow from them.

The pluralist view of voting behavior is markedly different. It is one in which group affiliations constitute individuals' primary identifying features, as measures of, and as causative agents in the formation of, common ideologies, value frameworks, and world views. Unlike the paradigm of the atomistic liberal view, this voter is one whose political awareness is derivative of his social existence.[38] His political interests and preferences are formed primarily by the groups to which he belongs. Those collective bonds are the engines that drive and direct his participation in the system.

This pluralist view of voting behavior leads to a pluralist view of the political process, in which "organized groups, not individuals, constitute the only relevant political units."[39] It is the clashing and skirmishing between competing groups that generates policies in the "public interest."[40] The system must do more than simply protect individuals. Rather, it compels a scheme that affirmatively accounts for the spectrum of groups, so that the competing interests channeled through groups find adequate expression. It also triggers a disparate vision of fair and effective representation. It suggests a need for "group compensating approach[es] to representation."[41] Fair representation implicates the status and relative positions of groups, and their resources and capacity to effectively influence the system. It would examine the effect of existing electoral processes on groups' influence, and root out those practices that treat groups disproportionately or unfairly.

The comparison of these competing views underscores the shortcomings of the Court's narrow conceptualization of representation. Neither the "liberal" nor the "pluralist" school sat-

isfactorily explains the motivating force behind voting. Standing
alone, each is an abstract account which does not fit the reality of
voting. Most voters are demonstrably motivated at once by group
contacts and by personal interests and circumstances. Each of these
motives is likely to manifest itself to a greater or lesser extent in
every voter, with an infinite variety of permutations of the two
from voter to voter. Not only is each school of thought by itself
inadequate, but no single combination of the two suffices descrip-
tively to account for the voting behavior of "the electorate."

The Supreme Court, however, has relied almost exclusively
on liberal, individualistic assumptions of voting behavior. The goal
of mathematical equality of the vote reflects a singular focus on
fairness of the *process*, at the expense of "group-compensating"
factors. If voting behavior and the representation it produces are
inevitably a complex mix of the two, the Court's one-sided formal
approach is likely to be a flawed, ill-conceived definition of political representation.

The emphasis on personal political activity gets further
bogged down in the Court's tendency to consider individual and
group rights as mutually exclusive. Contemporary individualism
remains the dominant ideology in matters of inequality.[42] Hence,
when fundamental conflicts are perceived between group-regarding
and individualistic approaches, the latter is sure to prevail. When
viewed as an either-or choice, the veneration and primacy accorded
individual rights in our political and legal order submerge concepts
of group rights. Hence the Court's unwillingness to explicitly
recognize "group rights."

Moreover, the author's survey of experts' attitudes and opinions on these matters suggests that the Court's reliance on that
false dichotomy has led the legal community into the same trap.
The survey results revealed that the formal, procedural routes to
representation are as revered by the practitioners as they are by
the Court. The survey respondents mirrored the formalistic approach that has prevailed on the Court, as they overwhelmingly
considered formal means of representation to be the most important and effective structures of representation.[43]

The tendency of both the courts and the practitioners to
speak in terms of rights distorts the role of groups in the political
process. The recognition of individuals as rights-holders is extrapo-
lated to eliminate legal recognition of groups or their significance
in representation. This clouds the objective of effective representation in the voting rights and electoral arena. While groups may

not have substantive *rights*, they do have substantive *interests*. Associations that form around profession, religion, residence, and ethnicity share common political interests. Recognition of those group interests is essential to a sound theory of representation.[44] *The organizations that manifest those shared interests are critical representative linkages between individual constituent and official representative.* The neglect of these subsystems of representation impedes the Court's ability to construct a theory that preserves the centrality of individualism while accounting for the realities of group influence.

Representation cannot be distilled to purely individual terms. One can be represented only insofar as he has shared interests with others.[45] Representation as activity compels legislative attention to substantive policy preferences of constituents. This is achieved when common interests are held by a group large enough to command the attention of its representative. The legislator charts his performance in office by the collective interests of his constituents. Legislative action is taken with an eye toward its impact on groups of supporters and how they will react.

Adding quality of representation considerations to the constitutional voting analysis, however, raises the specter of a complicated morass. Unlike the process-oriented numerical definition of voting equality, qualitatively based representation suggests a results-conscious attitude toward representation,[46] one that would look to scrutinize outcomes of the electoral process with an eye toward representation of different shared interests. It dictates an assessment of how votes cast in elections translate into representation in office. In a nutshell, it suggests the need to inquire whether collective interests and concerns which constitute a cognizable political force are actually manifested and represented in electoral results.

The judiciary is understandably wary of proceeding down this path. First, the quality of representation cannot be measured until a consensus exists as to its meaning. The Court has some distance to travel before it accepts the relevancy of the numerous conceptual components of representation. Even if it could, the next step would be a complex multi-pronged analysis highly subjective in nature. Even if the Court were more appreciative of the representative contributions of political groups, it would be faced with the daunting task of managing outcomes to equalize group representation. An outcome-oriented aim of giving groups a fair share of representation is antithetical to neutral processes. It

requires subjective determinations which neither courts nor legislatures are competent to make. If the individual is composed of
assorted interests and attributes, it is problematic to decide which
ones warrant legal or political recognition. It is far less complicated to disregard group qualities and focus on individual units.[47]

Hence, the Court in the reapportionment cases was speared
on the horns of this dilemma. On one hand, it focused on a purportedly neutral process which was in fact hardly neutral.[48] The
sophisticated manipulation of districts through computer-generated
mapmaking led to a process that was neutral only in achieving
numeric equality. By subsuming qualitative, group-based considerations within the standard of strict mathematical equality, the process lent itself to the obliteration of structures that permitted some
intelligible interpretation of election results.[49] The elimination of
other factors created a vacuum in which political gerrymandering
flourished.[50] The principal casualty was political representation.
As one astute student of reapportionment explained:

> The central purpose advanced by the Supreme Court in justi-
> fying its interventions into the reapportionment process in
> the 1960s—the need to ensure "fair and effective representa-
> tion"—has not been achieved, and cannot be achieved, by
> reliance on the one person, one vote standard. Even if all
> districts are exactly equal in population, when a districting
> plan intentionally creates legislative districts in which a class
> of citizens has had its voting strength distributed in ways that
> frustrate or significantly reduce its opportunity for effective
> political participation . . . , then it cannot be said that "one
> man's vote . . . is worth as much as another's."[51]

On the other hand, the answers to the complexities and
challenges of representative arrangements seem beyond the reach
of the Court. Can the goal of effective representation be objecti-
fied to make it a useful operational standard in constitutional law?
Can voting rights and effective representation, overlaid upon the
tension between groups and individuals, be pulled together into
a cohesive theory of fair and effective political participation? Is
the Court capable of molding and meshing the numerous complementary ingredients, of groups and individuals, of voting and representation, into a coherent theory of representation?

As the next chapter illustrates, this dilemma has intensified
in recent years. Group considerations have slowly worked their
way into the Court's consciousness, as representational rights have
been extended to certain groups in specific contexts. But while

the Court has grown increasingly sensitive to group factors and needs, it has struggled mightily, but unsuccessfully, for a theoretical tool to enhance group influence while avoiding the morass of practical problems raised by formal rights to group representation. In the end, the Court remains in search of a theory of representation built on the structures and institutions that reconcile the contradictory goals of individual autonomy and collective influence.

CHAPTER THREE

Beyond Individualism:
The Group Right to Representation

The individualism that dominated the early reapportionment cases is only part of the story of the Court's search for a theory of representation. The judicial preference for unchanneled personal participatory forms of democracy has not proven inviolate. Since the 1960s, when the individual-regarding perceptions of political participation were at their zenith, the Court has shown an increased, albeit modest, awareness of the corporate dimensions of representation. In cases concerning redistricting, campaign financing, and the general right to fair representation, the Court has acknowledged the validity of collective forms of political participation, and the need to accommodate them constitutionally.

But as the Court explored the group facets of political representation, it has lacked a theoretically consistent guide to its analysis. Instead, it has extended constitutional protection to certain groups in response to political conditions and pressures, and not out of an understanding of groups as representative institutions. It has reduced representation to a "right," rather than understanding it as a melding of contending interests and preferences. It has demarcated spheres of specific constitutional rights for certain racial and political groups. Having given those rights to some, however, it is faced with other groups clamoring for similar treatment. Missing is a framework for analysis which will permit group-enhancing resolutions without sinking the Court in the mire of full-blown group "rights" to representation. In the end, the Court remains in search of a theory that will treat all relevant groups uniformly and comprehensively as representative subsystems within the context of a pluralist democracy.

BEYOND INDIVIDUALISM: THE COURT, VOTE DILUTION, AND RACE-BASED GROUP RIGHTS

The advent of vote dilution claims by racial minorities forced the Court to deal more explicitly with issues of group effectiveness in voting and representation. With the question of one person, one vote largely settled, the Court shifted its attention to issues involving the dilution of minority groups' voting power. The focus switched from assuring equal population of districts to reviewing electoral mechanisms used to stifle the voting power of certain groups, in particular African-American minorities. The Court's scrutiny of at-large elections, multi-member districts, racial gerrymandering, and slating procedures had its origins in the protection and safeguarding of the rights of racial minorities.[1] But the review of such practices also held broader implications for political groups in general to realize effective representation through legal means.

The Court laid the foundation for racial minority vote dilution claims in *Gomillion v. Lightfoot,* a 1960 decision overruling the Alabama state legislature's redistricting of the boundaries of the city of Tuskegee to exclude black voters.[2] The city had redrawn its boundaries, altering it from a square to a twenty-eight-sided figure and removing virtually all blacks in the process. The case was technically one of disenfranchisement, as the state sought to deny blacks the vote by placing them outside the city limits. Because the statute deprived blacks of the vote based on their race, the Supreme Court found it in violation of the Fifteenth Amendment. Equally significant was the Court's explicit cognizance of redistricting as a means of weakening a racial group's voting power. It carried hints of a broader future application for racial groups' claims to fair representation.

Those claims developed slowly. In *Fortson v. Dorsey,*[3] the Court upheld a Georgia statute that apportioned the state's senatorial districts along existing county lines, since it achieved mathematical parity and was neutral in its treatment of racial groups. Justice

Brennan did, however, contemplate in dicta the possible uncon-
stitutionality of other "multi-member constituency apportionment
scheme[s] ... [which] would operate to minimize or cancel out
the voting strength of racial or political elements of the voting
population."[4] The Court was clearly prepared to examine, and to
strike down if necessary, electoral arrangements that discriminated
against racial groups.

It took several years before the assertion of vote dilution
claims by racial minorities was explicitly sanctioned. In *Whitcomb
v. Chavis*, the Court upheld the justiciability of challenges to plans
that "illegally minimize [sic] and cancel out the voting power of a
cognizable racial minority."[5] Finally, in *White v. Regester*,[6] the Court
upheld a frontal attack on multi-member legislative districts in
Texas which were found to deny equal access to African American and Mexican American voters. The Texas reapportionment
plan contained a population variation of ten percent between the
smallest and largest districts, thus diluting the votes of those minority groups unconstitutionally. The Court established guidelines
to determine whether an electoral arrangement was discriminatory. It adopted a "totality of the circumstances" test which incorporated a series of possible indicators of whether a racial group's
voting power was unconstitutionally diluted.[7]

In 1982, the basis for minority groups' vote dilution claims
was strengthened when Congress amended the Voting Rights Act
to codify the guidelines for establishing a racial vote dilution case.[8]
The revised Act eliminated the need to show an intent to discriminate. Under the Act, the issue was whether, under the totality of the circumstances, "the voting strength of minority voters
is ... minimized or canceled out."[9] The 1982 amendments substantially clarified the shape of a racial group claim. While significant
questions remained, the statute lay the groundwork for expanded
voting rights claims for racial groups.

In the landmark decision, *Thornburg v. Gingles*,[10] the Supreme
Court responded in kind, further elucidating the contours of the
racially based group claim. *Thornburg* involved a challenge by black
voters in North Carolina to its 1982 state legislative redistricting
plan. Black voters argued that the plan deprived them of their
chance to elect a black representative by creating a number
of white majority multi-member districts in areas where there
were large enough concentrations of black voters to form single-
member districts with black majorities. The Supreme Court agreed,

and in the process added a judicial gloss to the Voting Rights Act. As a precondition to the factors delineated in the "totality of the circumstances" test, Justice Brennan identified three circumstances essential to successful assertion of the claim:

> First, the minority group must be ... sufficiently large and geographically compact to constitute a majority of a single-member district. ... Second, the minority group must be ... politically cohesive. ... Third, ... the white majority votes sufficiently as a bloc to enable it ... usually to defeat the minority's preferred candidate.[11]

In short, *Thornburg* provided a clear outline of a racial group's claim to fair representation. Only those minority groups with the potential, by virtue of their size and geographic concentration, to elect their candidate could prevail. Likewise, unless they were politically cohesive they had no minority interest to protect. Finally, racial bloc voting was required in the white majority which would normally defeat minority bloc voting. The ultimate inquiry was whether racial polarization and bloc voting by the majority denied the minority group the opportunity to elect candidates of its choice.

Thornburg was seen by some as an analogue to the earlier equal district population cases. By objectively measuring voting strength in a numeric fashion, it arguably put claims of racial discrimination in voting on equal footing with claims of population disparity.[12] A critical difference existed, however. *Thornburg* signified a kindling of the Court's awareness of group considerations in realizing representation through voting rights. The decision was rooted in group-based politics.[13] It accepted the rights of racial minorities to elect their preferred candidates, and it did so by setting relatively well-defined guidelines aimed at ensuring the realization of those rights.

The sanctioning of race-based challenges to redistricting which culminated in *Thornburg* was in response to a unique set of political circumstances. The Court had the benefit of a federal statute that explicitly protected the voting rights of racial groups that had suffered historical discrimination. The right was clearly limited to racial groups, but the tenor of the decision and the Court's cognizance of group-based political activity hinted at a broader application of group-conscious voting rights claims.[14] The next question was whether the Court would allow similar claims for groups defined by attributes other than race.

POLITICAL GROUPS IN CONSTITUTIONAL LAW:
THE NEW THICKET OF
PARTISAN GERRYMANDERING

The race-based vote dilution cases were rich with ramifications for group status in constitutional law. The logical extension of racial protections against gerrymandering was to other distinct groupings of voters.[15] The practice of drawing district lines to exclude or fragment voters with common interests is not confined to racial designations. The ability to vote with others sharing discernible political interests within a single district affects the caliber of representation one receives not just for racial and ethnic groups, but for religious, gender-, and geographically identifiable groups.[16] The ultimate objectives of race-based protections were political. Race-conscious voting rights were meant to enhance political rights of representation and equality. Race-based equal protection claims were attempts to compensate for *political* ineffectiveness due to past or ongoing discrimination. Consequently, it is contradictory to approve of racial identity but not political identity (which race is supposed to signify), as a relevant factor in shaping electoral structures.

Once the Court provided legal avenues to redress gerrymandering for racially identified groups, it proved difficult not to entertain similar claims for other dissatisfied political groups. The inevitable result was *Davis v. Bandemer,* in which the Court recognized general political gerrymandering claims as justiciable, even while carefully circumscribing their availability. The line of cases culminating in *Bandemer* illustrates the Court's difficulties in fitting groups into its theory of representation. While carving out a general group right to fair representation, the Court has struggled to meaningfully delineate that right. These cases ultimately reflect a superficial understanding of representation and an inability to grasp the necessity of structural representative systems which exist in the form of parties and associations. In the end, *Bandemer* reveals the fatal weakness in the Court's efforts to define political representation. It relies on a theory that omits parties and other associations as central institutional actors in representative democracy.

Gaffney v. Cummings: Parties and "Political Fairness" in Representation

The first hints that the Court might expand voting rights to include groups generally surfaced in an intriguing decision which preceded the 1986 *Bandemer* decision by a dozen years. In *Gaffney v. Cummings*,[17] the Court scrutinized a redistricting plan drawn for the Connecticut General Assembly following the 1970 census. The plan was drafted by a bipartisan board according to a "political fairness" principle designed to reflect the relative strength of the two major political parties. By attempting to create a number of safe districts for each party along with a number of "swing" districts, the plan sought to achieve election results indicative of the parties' statewide strength. Relying on previous elections, the board used partisan demographic data to create a map that would approximate the actual statewide plurality of votes in both state houses.[18] Republicans attacked the plan on partisan gerrymandering grounds.

The Court rejected the challenge, holding that the plan did not "minimize or eliminate the political strength of any group or party."[19] It lauded the Board's recognition of the parties' relative strength and its attempts to provide "a rough sort of proportional representation in the legislative halls of the State."[20] The use of partisan data was permissible because it sought to achieve fair results, not discriminatory outcomes.[21] In sanctioning this strategy, the Court left room for state mapmakers to give greater emphasis to discrete groups generally, and parties specifically, in electoral structures.

The decision appeared to reflect a newfound appreciation by the Court for collective activity, especially by and through political parties. While it did not openly address the representative function of parties, the Court implicitly acknowledged representation that occurs at the party level. Invoking the goal of "fair and effective representation,"[22] the Court determined that policies that advanced that goal warranted some latitude from the standard of precise mathematic equality. By inference, the Court conceded the relationship between the party system (as fostered by a "political fairness" redistricting standard) and fair and effective representation.[23] While not compelling states to seek rough proportional representation of parties in redistricting, *Gaffney* permitted such an approach. It opened the door for states to make affirmative use of partisan data to aid groups and parties in the linedrawing process.[24]

United Jewish Organization v. Carey: From Racial to Partisan Gerrymandering

The tensions between race-conscious remedies and more inclusive group rights to representation became more acute in *United Jewish Organization v. Carey*,[25] a fascinating prelude to the partisan gerrymandering cases. *Carey* developed out of the State of New York's attempt to ensure that its 1972 reapportionment statute satisfied the pre-clearance provisions of the Voting Rights Act. After having its first proposal rejected by the Attorney General, New York attempted to remedy the plan's shortcomings by increasing the size of nonwhite majorities in a number of districts. Under the old plan, a sizeable Hasidic Jewish community of some 30,000 had been located in a single assembly district with a 61 percent nonwhite majority and in a single senate district with only 37 percent nonwhites. Under the revised plan, the state sought to meet its goal of a 65 percent nonwhite majority by reassigning a part of the Hasidic community to an adjacent district, both in the assembly and the senate. The Hasidim challenged the plan as a dilution of their vote on account of race, and hence a violation of the Fourteenth and Fifteenth Amendments.

In *Carey*, the Court delicately sidestepped the possible extension of racial group protections to other political minority groups, primarily because the challenge was directed to a plan explicitly crafted to further racial minority voting effectiveness. The case highlighted the theoretical dilemma the Court had created for itself by establishing rights for racial groups. The New York statute at issue sought to improve the opportunities for blacks and Puerto Ricans to elect their preferred candidates by enlarging the nonwhite majorities in two districts. Those increases came at the direct expense of the community of Hasidic Jews. The plan achieved larger nonwhite majorities by splitting the Hasidim, previously located in a single district, into two nonwhite majority districts.

The Court rejected the equal protection claim, reaffirming the propriety of racial criteria in redistricting and reapportionment.[26] It approved of the deliberate drawing of lines to accomplish a percentage of districts with nonwhite majorities that "roughly approximates" the percentage of nonwhites in the county.[27] Since there was "no fencing out of the white population from participation in the political process," the plan did not unconstitutionally minimize or cancel out white voting strength.[28]

The Court was careful to avoid the troublesome implications of its decision for group representation, in particular the problem of priority of claims between groups of voters. It prudently, but somewhat disingenuously, framed the controversy as between the rights of whites and nonwhites. It reasoned that the white claimants, although fragmented into multiple districts, would still receive fair and effective representation from the white assembly.[29] This ignored the fact that the electoral interests of Hasidic Jews diverged drastically from those of whites generally.[30] Had the controversy been cast as one of competing claims between the Hasidim and the black and Puerto Rican minorities for whom the plan was drawn, the Court's conclusions would have been far more problematic. The Hasidic community held a set of interests not shared by whites generally in New York. By splitting the Hasidim into several districts, the plan removed its chance to elect its own representative and undermined the representation Hasidic Jews were likely to receive from a white representative outside their community.[31]

The ramifications of granting the Hasidim group voting rights would have been substantial.[32] It is little wonder the Court avoided viewing the case as a battle of discrete and insular minorities. Yet the decision amplified the arbitrary nature of the Court's thinking on group rights to representation. The logical extension of the protection of blacks in redistricting was to other ethnic groups, including Hasidic Jews. The political interests stemming from that group's level of monolithicity were substantial. Indeed, the Hasidism were possibly the most discrete and insular minority imaginable. Hence, *Carey* appeared to give race paramount importance over other legitimate factors that generate shared interests and sentiments—factors such as partisanship, wealth, occupation, geography, and religion. The Court easily could have found that, on the basis of its ethnicity and religion, the Hasidim was entitled to preserve its voting strength within a single district. Had this happened, the divisive tendencies of group representation would have been more apparent. The difficulties inherent in extending the group right to nonracial groups were avoided, at least momentarily.

Karcher v. Daggett: The Gathering Momentum for Group Claims to Fair Representation

Despite the troublesome issues lurking in *Carey*, there were growing signs that the Supreme Court was ready to address frontally the role of groups in redistricting, and perhaps to include them in the electoral equation. Following the 1980 decennial census, New Jersey lost a seat in the U.S. House of Representatives, thus necessitating a reapportionment of its congressional districts. In *Karcher v. Daggett*,[33] the Court ruled on the constitutionality of New Jersey's proposed reapportionment plan. Although the plan had only minuscule population deviations between the largest and smallest districts in the state, the Court rejected it on the grounds that it failed to reflect a good-faith effort to achieve perfect equality of the vote. Though it was a garden-variety vote dilution case, it provided the justices the opportunity to comment on the role of groups in reapportionment.

The significance of the case for our purposes is found in the concurring and dissenting opinions. Those opinions exposed a critical mass of justices who looked favorably upon a group right to representation. Justice Stevens's concurring opinion was harshly critical of the majority's fixation on perfect numerical equality. Contending that "numerical equality is not a sufficient guarantee of equal representation," he proposed that the proscriptions against racial gerrymandering be extended to "other cognizable groups of voters."[34] He argued that exclusive focus on individual numerical voting equality ignored whether a voter, in the casting of her vote, was combined with or separated from others sharing her interest affiliations:

> The major shortcoming of the numerical standard is its failure to take account of other relevant—indeed, more important—criteria relating to the fairness of group participation in the political process.[35]

Indeed, insistence upon absolute numerical equality could actually nullify the popular will. The *Reynolds* aim of equal representation required that a proposed plan be reviewed for its "adverse impact on an identifiable political group."[36] Identifiable groups were those belonging to a politically salient class, sufficiently ascertainable so as to be taken into account in linedrawing.

Stevens largely avoided the obvious question of which groups were entitled to the right. Groups based on political status, race, ethnicity, national origin, religion, and economic status were qualified to assert a claim. But Stevens ignored the basic issue of which political interests and identity were of such a character as to warrant recognition in electoral structures. Ethnic or national groups with no record of historical prejudicial treatment may well lack the justification for such protection. How about women? The poor? New immigrant groups? Different policy arguments exist for formally recognizing groups, some more persuasive than others. These must be confronted in granting formal representative status to groups unless the Court chooses to do so indiscriminately and without limit. Stevens sidestepped the multitude of practical problems raised by his stated goal of effective representation for politically salient groups.

Two dissenting opinions in *Karcher* contained even harsher criticisms of the standard of absolute mathematical equality. Justice White argued that strict adherence to "one person, one vote" was not neutral, but antithetical to "other interests at stake—such as the preservation of community boundaries and the grouping of constituencies with similar concerns."[37] He considered one person, one vote to facilitate gerrymandering of the worst kind, permitting those drawing the lines to minimize representation of racial or political groups.[38] Similarly, Justice Powell saw gerrymandering as "a far greater potential threat to equality of representation" than the failure to achieve precise adherence to numeric equality.[39] The disregard for political subdivisions or other natural or historical boundaries was destructive of the goal of "fair and effective representation."

> A legislator cannot represent his constituents properly—nor can voters from a fragmented district exercise the ballot intelligently—when a voting district is nothing more than an artificial unit divorced from, and indeed often in conflict with, the various communities established in the state.[40]

Powell stood ready to entertain constitutional challenges to redistricting plans that were alleged to discriminate against racial, ethnic, religious, economic, or political segments of the population. He interpreted the constitutional mandate of "fair and effective representation" as prohibiting plans that disenfranchised "identifiable groups of voters."[41]

Karcher exposed a wing on the Court that would extend judicial considerations in reapportionment cases to their impact on collective interests.[42] The *Karcher* opinions comprised a virtual invitation for someone to assert a claim that would allow the Court to consider the issue. A challenge to partisan gerrymandering seemed the most likely vehicle. The signals emanating from *Karcher* hinted that the Court might be ready to enter the new thicket of political gerrymandering.

Davis v. Bandemer and the Group Right to Representation: The Court Wades In

Three years later, the Court did precisely that. In *Davis v. Bandemer*[43] it reviewed the handiwork of Indiana Republicans in drawing the lines for state legislative districts in 1981.[44] Following

the 1980 census, the Republican-dominated Indiana General Assembly passed a reapportionment law, which Indiana Democrats
challenged as an unconstitutional political gerrymander. They
claimed that Republicans drew the new districts to solidify their
majority hold on the state assembly, in violation of the Equal Protection Clause.[45] The November 1982 elections offered compelling supporting evidence. Democratic House candidates statewide
received 51.9 percent of the total vote. Of the 100 House seats up
for election, however, only forty-three Democrats were elected.
Thus, a 52 percent Democratic share of the vote translated into
victory in 43 percent of the races. A breakdown of various multi-
member districts revealed seemingly egregious inequities far beyond the statewide numbers. For example, in two multi-member
House districts, Democrats drew 46 percent of the vote, but won
only three of twenty-one House seats, or approximately 14 percent. The Senate races revealed little disparity, the number of seats
won by Democrats corresponding with their popular vote. Democrats garnered 53.1 percent of the vote, and won thirteen of the
twenty-five seats, or 52 percent.

The Court had surprisingly little difficulty deciding that the
merits of the claim were appropriate for judicial resolution. Relying heavily upon *Baker v. Carr*,[46] the Court found no danger of
impinging on the territory of a coequal branch of government,
and expressed confidence that judicially manageable standards
could be crafted for partisan gerrymander cases.[47] When it turned
to the merits of the Indiana plan, however, the Court's first attempt to articulate those standards was an indication of the difficulty of the task.

Having found the claim justiciable, the Court confounded
many observers and participants by upholding the constitutionality of the plan. It determined that Indiana Democrats had failed
to establish a discriminatory impact resulting from the new districts.[48] The Court unequivocally rejected a standard of proportional representation (i.e., the seats won should be directly
proportional to the percentage of the statewide vote received).
Nor was it enough to merely show that a redistricting might "make
it more difficult for a particular group in a particular district to
elect the representatives of its choice."[49] Writing for the plurality,
Justice White stated:

> that the power to influence the political process is not lim-
> ited to winning elections. *An individual or a group of individu-*
> *als who votes for a losing candidate is usually deemed to be adequately*

*represented by the winning candidate and to have as much opportu-
nity to influence that candidate as other voters in the district.* We
cannot presume . . . that the candidate elected will entirely
ignore the interests of those voters.

Hence, "a group's electoral power is not unconstitutionally diminished by the simple fact of an apportionment scheme that makes
winning elections more difficult."[50]

The Court opted for a far more exacting standard. For a
gerrymander to violate the Constitution, the electoral system must
"consistently degrade a voter's or a group of voters' influence on
the political process as a whole." Anticipating the difficulty in this
formulation, the Court elaborated:

> *The question is whether a particular group has been unconstitution-
> ally denied its chance to effectively influence the political process.* . . .
> Statewide, however, the inquiry centers on the voters' direct
> or indirect influence on the elections of the state legislature
> as a whole. And, as in individual district cases, an equal
> protection violation may be found only where the electoral
> system substantially disadvantages certain voters in their
> opportunity to influence the political process effectively. *In
> this context, such a finding of unconstitutionality must be supported
> by evidence of continued frustration of the will of a majority of the
> voters or effective denial to a minority of voters of a fair chance to
> influence the political process.*[51]

The Court concluded that Indiana Democrats had not been denied a chance to effectively influence the political process.[52]

THE GROUP RIGHT TO REPRESENTATION:
FUTURE UNKNOWN

Bandemer had potentially dramatic implications for the formal status of groups and parties in matters of elections, voting rights,
and representation. It marked a discernible shift toward balancing the traditional electoral individualism with an infusion of
group-compensating considerations.[53] But it raised, without resolving, fundamental questions regarding the role of groups in American democracy. The Court's attempt to fashion a group-based equal
protection claim beyond racial grounds achieved little in the way
of consensus. The Court was badly fractured, with only a plurality
agreeing to uphold the plan on substantive grounds.[54]

The plurality was explicit in its acceptance of group-based
considerations as a supplement to the formal individual equality

that had dominated voting rights analysis. It extended Equal Protection safeguards to "groups of voters" and their ability to influence the political process. In his dissent, Justice Powell likewise asserted that the *Reynolds* guarantee of fair and effective representation could not be achieved without reference to groups. "Groups of voters elect representatives, individual voters do not."[55] Finally, the three justices who joined in Justice O'Connor's concurrence similarly understood the decision as carving out a group right to equal representation in redistricting and reapportionment plans. Indeed, this was the reason for Justice O'Connor's displeasure with the decision. She characterized the decision as recognizing "group rights to an equal share of political power and representation. . . . "[56] Making no distinction between political parties and other groups, she ominously warned that it would lead to "a requirement of roughly proportional representation for every cohesive political group."[57]

The group right to representation in *Bandemer* was an extension of the Court's efforts to cultivate the *descriptive* dimension of representation. The initial preoccupation with one person, one vote had evidenced a reliance on *formal* assurances of representation.[58] The amended Voting Rights Act and the *Thornburg* line of cases signified a heightened sympathy for representation as *reflection*. Their aim was meaningful voting and representational rights for oppressed minorities, as measured by a presence of people in the legislative body who embody their racial or ethnic identity. The fundamental presupposition of the legal restrictions on racial gerrymandering was a firm belief in the desirability of racial and ethnic groups' ability to choose representatives who were physically descriptive of them. The creation of the group right to representation in *Bandemer* extended this thinking to other (as yet undefined) groups. It implicitly accepted *reflection* as an important element of political representation. The assembly is more likely to be sufficiently representative if the groups within society have been able to place their kind in that assembly.

But the Court did little to delineate the substance of the "group right" to representation or those groups encompassed by it. It left untouched a series of fundamental issues that must be confronted to give the group claim some definition. First, to what groups does the right apply? The Court avoided the central question of how to identify groups for purposes of parcelling out representation. Justice White did not address the nature or character of those groups that warrant acknowledgment in redistricting or in electoral schemes relating to representation. But his focus on "identifiable political groups" seemed to extend well beyond limited groups of voters or party partisans, seemingly contemplating something broader and more inclusive. This led Justice O'Connor to assume in her concurrence that the right applied to all political groups, and that it would consequently inundate the Court with a tide of litigation following every round of redistricting.

This issue must be directly addressed for the group right to representation to have any significance. But the task of identifying minority groups for purposes of representation is inherently problematic. While voters who support a political party can be counted up and registered:

> One cannot speak so casually about other kinds of minorities ... without making a number of crucial and (as it often turns out) quite arbitrary, question-begging assumptions. These assumptions concern how members of the group in question actually think of themselves in political settings, how uniform and labile their voting patterns and intensity of preferences are, what kinds of political alliances they enter into and on what terms, and many other factors.[59]

Those assumptions skirt the central issue of whether group affiliation is a valid benchmark for gauging the political interests of those who associate with it. Various characteristics of a group determine its capacity to accurately represent its members. These traits determine the strength and legitimacy of its claim to recognition as an official representative entity in activities that have electoral consequences. The Court neglected the derivative nature of the group right and the challenge of delineating the requisite group character that justifies bestowing the right. Such distinctions are essential to demarcating a meaningful group right.

A related set of questions involve the legal standard for the group claim, and the proof required by it. The Court paved the way for the assertion of claims by groups that have been locked out of the political process. The phrase triggering the claim is an "*electoral system ... [that] consistently degrade[s] a voter's or group of voters' influence on the political process as a whole.*"[60] This suggests a complicated, multivariate analysis, entailing a host of factors regarding the group's standing electorally, in the political process, and in society at large. The references to the "electoral system" and the "political process as a whole" affect more than the redistricting plans or elections. They require a group to show it suffers from pervasive discrimination throughout the political process.[61]

This could ensnare the courts in detailed subjective inquiries. For example, does the group asserting the claim have access to political resources that are determinative of influence? Is it rich or poor in media exposure, money, human resources, and other influential political assets? Is it hindered in its ability to enter into political coalitions with other groups? Does it have the means to avail itself of informal avenues of political influence? Does it have the organization and resources to pursue lobbying and other interest group activities? Does it suffer from stigmatization in society which impedes its political effectiveness? A group's inability to influence the political process would presumably require consideration of these questions.[62] The Court skirted these difficulties, either unaware of the need to resolve them, or reticent to undertake that daunting task. These questions illustrate the conundrum facing attempts to implement formal group representation. Lest the group right degenerate into the scenario depicted by O'Connor, a standard for distinguishing must be imposed. Unfortunately, this would entail a lengthy and complex scrutiny of each group that asserts a claim, something in which the Court is rightly loath to get involved.

Third, while marking a renewed respect for the goal of "fair and effective representation," the Court did so without comment on the nature or limits of that standard. Depending on how it is defined, fair representation can be frustrated in innumerable ways, only one of which is gerrymandering to block a group's choice of its own representative. Does the fact that a group's chosen representative is incompetent in office deprive his constituents of effective representation? Does a group represented by a first-term congresswoman have as effective representation as a district represented by the chairwoman and senior member of a powerful committee? What barriers to representation are precluded by the rubric of "fair and effective representation"? Do these scenarios compel a constitutional standard by which legislative outputs correspond with specific policy goals of groups within the state? Imbuing a group with a right to representation opens up a Pandora's box of claims outside the redistricting and reapportionment context. The Court's disinclination to consider the possible repercussions left groups a vague shadow in the horizon of electoral politics.

Hence, the waters of the group right to representation remain largely uncharted. In light of the Court's avoidance of basic questions, the group claim set down in *Bandemer* could proceed in a number of directions.

SHAW AND *MILLER:* A POSTSCRIPT

The contradictions in the Court's analysis on voting and representational rights have converged in its most recent decisions, *Shaw v. Reno*[63] and *Miller v. Johnson.*[64] Those decisions have exposed a Court grappling with the connection between districting and the representation it generates, and the implications for individuals, groups, and parties. *Shaw* involved the North Carolina state legislature's reapportionment of U.S. House districts following the 1990 census. The initial plan, which created a single black majority district, was objected to when submitted for preclearance under the Voting Rights Act. A revised plan added a second black majority district of a decidedly irregular shape, which threaded 160 miles along the Interstate.[65] White residents alleged a racial gerrymander.[66]

The Court upheld the claim, imposing limits on the affirmative use of race. It imposed three criteria for assessing race-based redistricting: 1) was the redistricting so irregular on its face that it could only be an effort to segregate the races for purposes of voting; 2) did the plan heed traditional districting principles; and 3) was a compelling justification offered.[67]

The Court took its reasoning in *Shaw* a step further in the *Miller* case, which arose out of Georgia's redistricting efforts following the 1990 census. After the U.S. Justice Department objected to the initial plan, which created a second black majority-minority district, Georgia offered a plan adding another majority-minority district, raising the total to three. White voters living in that third district brought suit, alleging a Fourteenth Amendment equal protection claim. The district at issue connected black urban neighborhoods in Atlanta to poor rural black coastal areas some 260 miles away. By a narrow five to four majority, the Court found race to be "the predominant, overriding factor" in explaining the shape of the district. Since the state was unable to articulate a compelling governmental interest justifying this use of race, the Court concluded that the plan violated the Fourteenth Amendment.[68]

Both decisions reflected the theoretical puzzle of reconciling racial considerations with broader group-based representation. The Court retreated noticeably in its regard for race-based remedial gerrymandering. It echoed criticisms levelled by others at race-conscious remedies, for deepening racial cleavages, generating majority backlash, and obstructing the formation of biracial coalitions.[69] The majority in *Shaw* lent official credence to criticisms of race-based remedial redistricting, revealing an ambivalence as to the divisive potential of that approach.

The majority explicitly adopted several arguments frequently forwarded by opponents of the Voting Rights Act and the *Thornburg* line of cases. Employing provocative language, Justice O'Connor analogized the excessive use of racial distinctions in mapdrawing to "political apartheid." She faulted it for accentuating racial differences while excluding other legitimate differences that have political consequences and that cut across racial lines. She opined that even a positive racial gerrymander may "exacerbate the very patterns of racial bloc voting that majority-minority districting is sometimes said to counteract."[70] She rued its adverse consequences for the efficacy of representation:

> When a district obviously is created solely to effectuate the perceived common interests of one racial group, elected officials are more likely to believe that their primary obligation is to represent only the members of that group, rather than their constituency as a whole. This is altogether antithetical to our system of representative democracy.[71]

Justice Kennedy's opinion for the majority in *Miller* echoed those contentions.[72]

At the same time, both decisions revealed the Court to be much more cognizant of other interests which might be recognized through districting. *Shaw* contained further signs that the Court would entertain claims to representation for groups identified by something other than race. By inference, Justice O'Connor almost put other group influences on a par with racially motivated districting considerations. While race was significant, so too were considerations of age, economic status, religion, and political persuasion. Dissenter Stevens likewise contemplated an expansion of group considerations beyond race, though for much different reasons. He considered it permissible to draw lines to facilitate the election of a member of any group lacking power due to underrepresentation in the legislature. This applied to groups defined by political affiliation, economic interest, or by religious, ethnic, or racial characteristics.[73] While O'Connor invoked the salience of other groups as a basis for narrowing race-conscious linedrawing, Stevens favored broad affirmative use of districting to advance the interests of a variety of groups. Likewise, in *Miller*, the Court was increasingly concerned about the "actual shared interests" and "common thread of relevant interests" that ought to be recognized in the districting process.[74] The Court was increasingly aware of the need to accommodate group identities and shared interests within electoral schemes.

But most significant in *Shaw* and *Miller* was the Court's reliance upon the traditional, neutral criteria of redistricting to reconcile the fears of racial polarization with the need for a group-compensating approach. To the Court, "reapportionment is one area in which appearances do matter."[75] In this sense, these decisions are a reflection of the contradictions in the law of redistricting. Race-based remedies assume the need to accommodate racial groups victimized by past discrimination to ensure effective present representation. Remedial steps toward this end have included easing territorial criteria, sometimes dispensing with them altogether. But this ignores the fact that traditional geographic requirements incorporate group considerations. Thus, representational benefits to racial groups were achieved at the expense of broader, more diffused political groupings. The *Miller* majority found the challenged district objectionable because it "fractured political, social, and economic interests" to create a black majority.[76] As such, it was a "tale of disparity, not community."[77]

One perspective on the Court's recent decisions, then, is that they stand as an attempt to strike a balance between competing group considerations. Unfortunately, the Court missed the opportunity to articulate the theoretical basis for retaining traditional redistricting criteria as inherently worthy. O'Connor emphasized compactness, contiguity, and respect for political subdivisions "not because they are constitutionally required—they are not . . . but because they are objective factors that may serve to defeat a claim that a district has been gerrymandered on racial lines." In short, they were only evidentiary benchmarks to establish or disprove ulterior motives in the redistricting process.[78]

This misses the essence of the geographically based system of districts. Redistricting based on territorial considerations is grounded in principles of representation that are by their nature group-based.[79] Territorial considerations are not merely arbitrary means of categorizing numbers of voters. Rather, they designate areas likely to have "legitimate collective interests arising from the identity of citizens within real places and areas."[80] Traditional factors (communities of interests, political subdivisions) reveal patterns by which people gather into identifiable groups. Geography anticipates the social, religious, and political habits of its residents, albeit imperfectly and incompletely. One need only look at the map of the North Carolina district at issue in *Shaw* to understand the challenge to the conscientious legislator seeking to diligently represent his entire constituency. Common interests besides race that are encompassed by territorial boundaries are obliterated by the district.

The Court in *Shaw* and *Miller*, however, obscured the value of traditional districting practices. It nonchalantly levelled charges at race-based linedrawing, and treated territorial considerations only as a means of policing that activity. Consequently, the Court managed to delegitimize the value of both prongs. The need to aggressively pursue remedies for dispossessed minorities remains. But race-conscious districting taken to an extreme demolishes means of incorporating group concerns that transcend purely racial interests. This suggests the need to keep remedial racial redistricting within the constraints of neutral territorial considerations. It ensures that group influences generally are respected, and the representational rights of all groups in society advanced.

But while a geographic basis for representative districts is a useful measure of certain shared interests, its utility is not unlimited. Geography may have little to do with a raft of opinions and preferences that comprise the political presence demanding representation. People in contemporary society affiliate with groups that are disconnected from physical proximity. In a complex, industrialized society, issues cut across geographic lines, or are unrelated to them altogether.[81]

For this reason, the traditional mode of territorial districting is overlaid upon partisanship.[82] Broad-based, coalition-building parties attract interests that do not fit neatly into geographic units. Herein lies the key to a representative scheme sensitive to both racial and relevant nonracial groups in the electorate. The pluralist reality of group influence compels subsystems and structures that are not identified solely along the lines of race or ethnicity. It demands intermediaries that go beyond racial characteristics while including them. Parties, as civic educators, as melders of cross-cutting groups, and as advocates and incorporators of race-based interests, are one distinct possibility. They blend racial minority concerns with other legitimate political interests. Parties have the capacity for responding to racial groups, but they are not defined exclusively by them. In sum, party structures allow the pursuit of racial political equality, while tempering the divisive tendencies of purely race-based remedies.

CONCLUSION

Bandemer, Shaw, and *Miller* reflect the absence of a theoretical framework for implementing group considerations. Sensing the need to supplement individual voting rights with an attunement to group voices, the Court is rightly apprehensive over the polarizing potential inherent in formally recognizing those collective interests. The group right to representation remains undetermined, as the Court struggles for a theory by which it can position groups within the complex system of representation.

The challenge is to broaden and inform the Court's narrow conceptualization of representation. This requires a thorough understanding of the group theory of political activity and the pluralist definition of democracy that it has propagated. The solution to the perplexing problems of group representation lies in the pluralist account of government and the weaknesses in the theory and practice of pluralism. Before the Court can constitutionally situate politically active groups and parties in the labyrinth of representation, it must have the requisite understanding of group theory and pluralism, and the dilemmas they raise. It is that task to which we now turn.

CHAPTER FOUR

Group Theory and the
Pluralist Challenge to Representation

The theoretical portrait of political representation is a labyrinth, comprised of a myriad of forms and shapes, accomplished through an assortment of practices and processes, and executed through a roster of political actors. The Supreme Court's constitutional theory of representation has failed to capture the intricacies of representation. It initially relied upon a one-dimensional, individualistic, formal notion of representation which slighted the essential representative character of groups and associations. More recently, the Court has become conscious of the importance of collective political behavior, but has lacked a structural framework for incorporating group politics into its definition of representation.

The Court is in need of a constitutional definition of representation that grasps the essential nature of group activity and is more indicative of the complex reality of representation. The answer to that search lies in theories of group politics and the derivative group-inclusive description of pluralist democracy. In this chapter, we briefly review the group theory of politics, tracing its growth from its early twentieth-century roots into a full-fledged pluralist account of operational government.

That review points to the pluralist dilemma that confronts the Court in its search for a group-conscious theory of representation. That dilemma exists between two observations that characterize American pluralist democracy. The first rests on the group theory of political effectiveness, which holds that individuals realize political influence only when they associate with politically active groups. The efficacy of individual political participation in a large-scale democracy hinges on the effectiveness of the groups to which one belongs. Consequently, individual political equality cannot be attained without a semblance of parity among political organizations.

But attempts to construct a group-constituted scheme of government get hung up on a number of practical and functional realities: undemocratic associations, unequal dispersion of political resources, constricted avenues of group access to spheres of power. As inequities inevitably appear in a pluralist system, some groups dominate while others go unheard. Hence the dilemma: if group politics conditions individual equality upon group equality, how is meaningful individual participation to be assured in light of the disparities between groups? Recast in terms of representation, the dilemma is how to arrange representational structures to permit equal opportunity for political groups without obliterating the primary goal of enhanced representation for the individual citizen. A critical assessment of pluralism in practice exposes the theoretical problem at the heart of pluralism; *can collective political participation be managed and equalized so that it furthers the end of individual political effectiveness without violating the sacred traditional liberal values of individual equality.* This paradox ultimately must guide the search for a theory of representation in constitutional jurisprudence.

ARTHUR BENTLEY AND THE ADVENT OF THE GROUP THEORY OF POLITICS

Arthur Bentley's work serves as the launching pad for the study of the role of groups in American politics. Bentley was the first, and most forceful, advocate of the group theory of politics in this century. Searching for a tool by which to better understand and analyze the workings of government, he settled upon groups as the "raw material" of politics.[1] Bentley concluded that everything acting in or upon government could be distilled down to group interests at work. Society was nothing other than the complex arrangement of the groups of which it was composed. There were "no political phenomena except group phenomena."[2] Hence, "when groups are adequately stated, everything is stated."[3]

Bentley's devotion to groups was all-encompassing, to the exclusion of alternative forms of political activity. Individual autonomy was nonexistent as a source of political awareness. One's political preferences grew out of group affiliations and identifications, and the demands and expectations engendered by those associations.[4] Likewise, Bentley sought to ascribe virtually every aspect of the public sphere to group forces. Legal processes and outcomes, political parties and interest groups, public opinion, and government itself were all outgrowths of group forces at work. Be it the formal institutions of government or the players who sought to wield political influence on those institutions, the political process was one of groups interacting with other groups.

Consequently, government agencies were best understood by studying the variety of groups working in and through them.[5] The legislature, the executive, the bureaucracy, even the judiciary, primarily operated as mediators between the group interests pressing in upon government. The public sphere was a tension between the pressures emanating from a host of groups; government institutions were the means of adjusting and reconciling those interests.[6] The legislative process was one of group dynamics, involving formalization of group objectives and the struggle of groups with a stake in the outcome.[7]

Bentley foresaw the pluralist view of government as a state of constant group activity, pushing and pulling, cooperating and competing, merging and splitting, reforming and adapting, acquiring new alliances while abandoning old ones, in the end somehow producing policy in response to public needs.[8] In this political arena, serious students of government were required to contemplate the character of such groups and their ultimate impact on governmental process. This moved Bentley to consider the array of politically active groups, from political parties to policy organizations and interest groups, to public interest groups and civic associations. Parties occupied a central position in this group-oriented political universe. They were *representative* of groups, as "organization[s] of voters, brought together to act as a representative of the underlying interest groups in which these voters . . . present themselves."[9] They provided group interests a means of securing electoral results that would advance their interest.[10] Parties functioned as "a group among groups, a group which mediates between others, and which reflects others with varying degrees of adequacy."[11]

The defining attribute of any group was its representative capacity. Ultimately, a group's influence in the political arena depended on the nature and extent of its capacity to represent some underlying interest.[12] Likewise, the sufficiency of government required examining the people and interests represented by groups, and the processes by which those groups advance the public interest.

GROUP THEORY IN THE MID-20TH CENTURY: DAVID TRUMAN AND *THE GOVERNMENTAL PROCESS*

Now regarded as one of the truly original works of political science in the twentieth century, Bentley's discourse went largely unnoticed by his peers. Not until a group of scholars in the 1950s warmed to group politics did the theory postulated by Bentley take hold. The most prominent of them was David Truman, who picked up where Bentley left off, tracing the role of groups from Madison's early preoccupation with factions to their growing importance in the increasingly complex society of the mid-1950s.[13]

Like Bentley, Truman considered groups the primary interpretive looking-glass through which individuals viewed world and society. "The group experiences and affiliations of an individual are the primary . . . means by which the individual knows, interprets, and reacts to the society in which he exists."[14] Society was a mosaic of groups, each representing the "habitual interactions of men," formulating and guiding the attitudes and behavior of its participants.[15]

But unlike Bentley, who focused on describing government action in group terms, Truman stressed the groups themselves, and what he considered their critical characteristics. He underscored their organizational traits and the extent of their "democratic" character. Organizational attributes served as a benchmark of a group's cohesiveness and solidarity in principle or objective,[16] reflecting both the nature of the group and the situation it was created to address. Political analysis, therefore, depended on careful and accurate group classification, and recognition of the fluid, dynamic content and context that reflected the reality of groups.[17]

Truman harbored a benign view of groups in politics, stemming from his idealized vision of their democratic nature.[18] He assumed groups would naturally adopt a structure in the democratic mold, lest they remain fractured and ineffective. In turn, group cohesiveness produced well-defined conflicts between narrowly focused groups, from which political cleavages and alliances were formed, and out of which sprouted the general interest.[19] The democratic underpinnings of political groups, consequently, were central to Truman's vision of pluralism.

In this vision, the overriding objective of politically motivated groups was to influence governmental decisionmaking.[20] Policy outcomes were the result of groups weighing in at various points in the process. Logrolling, horsetrading, and alliance-building in Congress were reflections of group forces at work. Swapping of votes and legislative give-and-take in response to constituent demands were the techniques by which group claims were aired and resolved. These were legitimate, even desirable, means of adjusting the collective interests in society.[21]

In sum, Truman envisioned groups as the participatory tools through which individuals sought political power. Groups were the hub of governmental process at all levels, in the formal agencies and offices of government, in intermediate entities such as political parties, and in the private organizations, associations and interest groups seeking to influence government action. In this group-constituted public sphere lay the seeds of the positive pluralist account of government. Group politics presupposed that multiple points of access to government decisionmaking for a diversity of groups would ultimately yield a stable, desirable policy-making mechanism.[22]

GROUP THEORY INTO POSITIVE PLURALISM: THE TENETS OF THE PLURALIST IDEAL

Once Truman and others picked up the mantle of group politics, they did so with unrestrained zeal. Whereas collective associations were once neglected, everything was now reduced to groups. Earl Latham's statement was illustrative: "The chief social values cherished by individuals in modern society are realized through groups."[23] Associations were tools of power to achieve the societal ends of common value to their members.[24] At the same time, groups were the crucial cog in the machinery of government. Government outcomes flowed from a free-wheeling market of group-driven forces, refereed by government to ensure that all interested groups could participate.[25] Earl Latham, Truman's contemporary, described the group theorists' political universe as:

> an aggregation, a collection, an assemblage, a throng, a mov-
> ing multitude of human clusters, a consociation of groups, a
> plurality of collectivities, an intersecting series of social or-
> ganisms, adhering, interpenetrating, overlapping—a single
> universe of groups which combine, break, federate, and form
> coalitions and constellations of power in a flux of restless
> alterations.[26]

This view of the political world inevitably led to a pluralist
account of the democratic order, the makeover of group theory
from abstract principle into the functional tool of analysis envisioned by Arthur Bentley.[27] V.O. Key set the stage for the practical application as a descriptive analysis of American politics and
political institutions:

> At bottom, group interests are the animating force in the
> political process; an understanding of American politics re-
> quires a knowledge of the chief interests and of their stake
> in public policy. The exercise of the power of government
> consists in large part in the advancement of legitimate group
> objectives, in the reconciliation and mediation of conflicting
> group ambitions, and in the restraint of group tendencies
> judged to be socially destructive. Hence, an examination of
> pressure groups and of the interests from which they arise
> throws light on the material that politicians must manage, and
> the problems with which they must cope.[28]

It is pluralism, group theory's practical embodiment, that
holds the key to the puzzles of representation theory. The dilemma
the Court must confront exists amid the core tenets of pluralism
and the criticisms it has received. The first, self-evident, assumption requires little elucidation in light of the foregoing discussion. It simply acknowledges that the political system is
group-constituted, and the public order a function of the interplay
between contending group forces.[29] Distribution of political power
and formulation of policy stem from "a more or less unstable
equilibrium among competing interests."[30]

Second, pluralism recognizes the *inherent limitations of formal
democratic processes, namely elections.* Elections are designed to uncover majority preferences in the electorate, but do little to assure that policy decisions will coincide with those majority
preferences. As Robert Dahl commented:

> We cannot correctly describe actual operations of democratic
> societies in terms of contrasts between majorities and minori-
> ties. *We can only distinguish between groups of various types and*

sizes, all seeking in various ways to advance their goals, usually at the expense, at least in part, of others.[51]

In this light, policymaking and governmental decisions are "the steady appeasement of relatively small groups."[32]

Third, the demands of a pluralist society are satisfied through *group interaction and competition.* Consensus is attained through complex processes involving a multiplicity of issues, groups, memberships, resources, and points of access, all converging in a confluence that captures the public good.[33] A particular set of issues yield a particular coalition of groups.[34] That state of equilibrium changes when a group forms, or an existing group asserts itself, or otherwise evolves or adjusts to address a situation affecting its interest.[35] A new issue generates a clamor for political remedies, arousing dormant groups or stimulating the formation of new ones, and prompting other collective interests to enter the fray in opposition.[36] Pluralism is at work when "one class or group becomes discontented with existing conditions, and the processes of politics go into operation to create a new equilibrium."[37]

The pluralist political arena is *dynamic,* with groups thrusting and parrying in response to current situations, government action, or other group activity.[38] Policy-making, the implicit goal of which is to more accurately reflect new societal circumstances, is perpetually buffeted by group forces. In sum, *public policy is the result of a floating balance between multiple groups seeking access to the public authority.*[39]

This pluralist view of group forces hinges on *open and dynamic, not closed and static, decisionmaking processes.* It compels that politics be easily penetrable by concerned groups. Hence Robert Dahl's confident assurance that "the independence, penetrability, and heterogeneity of the various segments of the political stratum all but guarantee that any dissatisfied group will find spokesmen in the political stratum."[40]

Moreover, this system is of little practical significance unless politically interested groups have means to enter through the door. Pluralism assumed a system of *widely dispersed resources,* with power and influence distributed broadly among a range of groups.[41] No group would dominate the decisionmaking process, nor would any group ever totally lack influence.[42] This dispersion of power lay at the center of a feasible system of pluralism. The pluralist vision was of a congeries of hundreds of special interests, with concededly different power bases, but with a variety of techniques for exercising influence relative to the decisions of importance to them.

Nor were interest groups and associations the only salient units in this group-constituted political arena. Rather, they existed in an environment of other groups and institutions.[43] In particular, the relations between parties and groups were a key to understanding the role of groups in politics. *Pluralism was to operate only within the context of the party system.* Groups attained an elevated political position due to the need to fill the gaps in the political system in an increasingly complex, specialized society.[44] As such, they were *supplemental,* not substitutionary, instruments of public policy. As Key put it:

> *A striking feature of American politics is the extent to which political parties are supplemented by private associations formed to influence public policy.* These organizations . . . promote their interests by attempting to influence government rather than by nominating candidates and seeking responsibility for the management of government. . . . Pressure groups, as they seek to influence the exercise of public policy, play a distinctive role: *They supplement the party system and the formal instruments of government by serving as spokesmen for the special interests within society.*[45]

This relationship and balance between parties and groups led Sartori to label it "party pluralism."[46]

This meant that interaction between parties and groups was critical to striking the right equilibrium. The "lines of cleavage" that determined the balance between groups were drawn by parties dependent upon groups for constructing winning coalitions.[47] Motivated to win elections through group coalitions, parties selected the issues and formulated the responses so as to maximize the vote from their respective groups.[48] This provided groups with leverage to pursue their objectives, through nominating candidates, drafting platforms, supporting campaigns, and ultimately influencing policy decisionmaking once the party is successful.

This symbiotic relationship between groups and parties also ensured access for all political interests. A penetrable power structure rested upon the mechanisms of elections and competing parties.[49] A party that neglected potential sources of support put its electoral success, and perhaps its survival, at risk. As new elements in society emerge, "existing or aspiring party leaders will see and seize opportunities to enhance their own influence by binding these new elements to the party."[50] The parties ensured that few social elements will be neglected for long by the political market.[51]

The pluralist model also rests upon a series of assumptions as to how groups operate within and in relation to other groups.

Groups are allowed a primary place in pluralist democracy because they are *representative* in character, and consistent with our democratic tradition of representative government. A group's legitimacy is derived from its ability to act as a conduit for the views of its members. Group leadership and organization are necessary to discern the opinions of members, shape them into consensus, and act as a mouthpiece for bringing those preferences into the public forum.

Similarly, groups that occupy strategic positions in the hierarchies of private power are tolerable only if they are publicly *accountable*.[52] They serve their representative purpose only when subject to control by their members and the general public through internal democratic structures. Especially as groups become larger, elections and other self-imposed democratic practices are necessary to ensure that the members will retain control over the leadership of the organization.[53]

Public control is also necessary to allay the self-interest that drives any group to political involvement. By virtue of their admission to the policy playing field, groups have a responsibility to modify their self-interest when it is adverse to the public good. In the pluralist model, this check comes from other group players. The mutual antagonism between opposing groups is a natural restraint built into the system. "The broad conception of countervailing power is that the giants pit their strength against each other and the public incidentally benefits from the resulting balance and stalemate."[54]

The other check on group power is the "threat of state intervention which could deprive them of their authority or regulate the manner of its exercise."[55] Government is the moderator of group conflict, ensuring that they play within the rules and work toward ends that benefit the public. When a group fails to operate within those guidelines, or when its interests are patently adversarial to the public interest, government must intervene with its formal powers of coercion.[56]

A final check on group activity comes from *overlapping memberships*.[57] The recognition of multiple affiliations is "the distinguishing trait of a pluralistic structuring."[58] The bundle of interests wrapped up in each individual translate into multiple affiliations with different groups, each pursuing different purposes. The consequence is to muffle the narrow self-interest of a particular group. Since individuals are associated with groups with dissimilar or even inconsistent objectives, group cohesion is reduced and compels internal democratic decisionmaking.[59] In this way, the individual's overlapping memberships contribute to a process of adjustment and compromise within groups.

Moreover, the multiple groups within one's range of interests prevent any single group from dominating its members.[60] Cross-cutting associations "prevent one line of social cleavage from becoming dominant, and they constrain associations to respect the various affiliations of their members lest they alienate them."[61] By dulling the sharpness of a particular group's demands, multiple memberships are an important building block in the pluralist argument.[62]

This anticipates one final conclusion, *the centrality of individualism as the foundation for pluralism.*[63] American pluralism is derived from a liberal, individualistic set of values and beliefs.[64] The group is not of intrinsic value, but is a tool of empowerment for those who belong to it. It focuses less on group status than on the cultivation of groups to ensure individual independence. *Its aim is the empowerment of the individual through the balance of group forces.*

CRITICISMS OF PLURALISM AND THE GROUP THEORY OF POLITICS

That these core tenets of pluralist doctrine were the key to a healthy and just political process was assured. But the neatness of the pluralist reduction of all politics to groups invited critical responses.[65] It provoked a heated debate over the capacity of the system to accommodate all relevant group voices in policymaking, such that governmental outcomes are just and fair to the entire society.

E.E. Schattschneider and the Mismanagement of Conflict

E.E. Schattschneider was the first of a modern generation of political scientists to take critical aim at group politics and the pluralist mode of policymaking. Schattschneider strove not to knock pluralism down, but to ensure it retained its proper balance, especially within the context of political parties. In Schattschneider's appraisal of pluralist democracy, two aspects of the world of interest group politics undercut the neat group formulations of Truman and his followers. One was the narrowness of the scope of the political conflict and the number of players who influenced it. "The range of organized, identifiable, known groups is amazingly narrow; there is nothing remotely universal about it."[66] Second, group influence was heavily slanted in favor of upper-class and business interests and neglected the interests of the poor and disadvantaged.[67] Thus, conflicts were badly skewed in favor of particular interests to the exclusion of others.

Schattschneider did not reject the basic postulates of group theory. The pluralist vision of linking the public to ultimate policy outcomes through groups—namely political parties and interest groups—was an accurate characterization of politics. Democracy was "a competitive political system in which competing leaders and organizations defined the alternatives of public policy so that the public can participate in the decision-making process."[68] But he refused to accept Truman's idyllic view of group-driven politics. His critique of pluralism was rooted in his understanding of the dynamics of democratic politics. Politics was a function of conflict, "the central political fact in a free society."[69] The outcomes of political conflict were contingent on its scope and "the extent to which the audience becomes involved in it."[70] The more confined and privatized the scope of a conflict, the less public preferences would be reflected in its outcome.

Democratic government was intended to achieve the opposite result; its goal was to expand and socialize conflict to involve all parties and ensure that all pertinent interests were reflected in the final outcome.[71] Government was the engine for enlarging the conflict and disrupting the privatization of power. All political participants, the branches of government, political parties, and interest groups were to be judged by their capacity to manage and publicize conflict to extend its sphere.[72]

But in an organized pressure system so skewed toward business and upper-class elements of society, it could not be assumed that all interested groups would naturally coalesce or surface to argue their case.[73] "The flaw in the pluralist heaven is that the heavenly chorus sings with a strong upper-class accent."[74] Schattschneider, therefore, was highly skeptical of attempts to explain all politics in terms of groups. Rather than widening or socializing the conflict, pressure group politics was dominated by special interests with small numbers of individuals who could be easily mobilized around their exclusive interests. It was selective rather than inclusive, balanced in favor of small, intensely interested minorities, and ill-designed to serve the more diffuse interests of the public.[75]

Schattschneider, the great advocate of political parties, saw them as the only remedy. Parties were absolutely essential democratic institutions of organization and leadership. Political strategy, as exercised by the parties, centered on the exploitation, use and suppression of conflict. The control of conflict, by substituting, displacing, and prioritizing issues, was the essence of their political power: "The definition of the alternatives is the supreme instrument of power."[76] This set party politics apart from pressure groups, which were incapable of socializing and publicizing conflict. Political institutions were necessary to channel and prioritize conflict.[77]

Schattschneider anointed the parties to perform that task. Only they could organize political conflict by managing its visibility, intensity, and direction. Motivated by the desire to win office, parties defined issues and created cleavages to attract voters and forge the strongest, largest coalition.[78] Their failure to satisfactorily discharge this responsibility was a primary weakness in American democracy. Low rates of participation evidenced their failure to address the issues of importance to the public. "Abstention reflects the suppression of the options and alternatives that reflect the needs of the nonparticipants."[79] Identifying the issues and framing the responses simply failed to involve the entire community.

Such poor levels of participation had serious deleterious consequences. Government in the hands of small, self-interested groups resolving conflict privately ran the risk of losing the requisite support of the public.[80] It failed the basic test of pluralism, the enhancement of the political presence and influence of the individual in a large-scale democracy. A skewed pluralism dominated by certain interests did precisely the opposite, pushing people from the system.[81]

Grant McConnell and Private Power and American Democracy: *Groups as Models of Democracy*

Another stern critic of the positive pluralist ideal was Grant McConnell.[82] McConnell thoroughly dissected the assumptions as to the supposedly democratic character of private associations upon which positive pluralism rested. Noting that large segments of policy had been co-opted by private associations, McConnell was willing to accept this condition only if those associations exhibited the liberal democratic tendencies and structures that were characteristic of or analogous to the state. More often than not, he concluded, those groups wielding private power exhibited undemocratic forms. As a result, they served less as means of empowering individual citizens than as tools of oppression and conformity, favoring elites to the exclusion of other groups, discouraging public values, and neglecting public interests.[83]

McConnell recognized the primacy of private associations in American democracy. Private power was so pervasive that it was perhaps the most readily identifiable form of power on the contemporary scene.[84] In short, private control of governmental agencies meant "the rise of a scheme of representation alternative to the machinery of Congress, legislatures, President, and governors."[85] It constituted "a reformulation and redistribution of [the] authority" of the state.[86]

This was hardly worrisome to pluralists, for whom small groups were the most democratic, and hence the most preferable, implements of public policy. McConnell, however, was willing to concede the propriety of associational power only if organizations exhibited traits consistent with the goals and objectives of liberal democracy.[87] A closer look at the internal governing structure of various associations led him to conclude that they did not.[88] First, organizational activity often was plagued by a divergence between the interests of group leadership and those of their members. Echoing Michels's "iron law of oligarchy,"[89] McConnell observed the tendency of associational leaders to pursue different interests than the rank and file, as they became more concerned with the preservation of the organization and the perpetuation of their leadership. Organizational activities, therefore, often did not mirror the interests within the group.[90]

Nor did McConnell find the level of homogeneity within associations that is presumed by pluralism. There was far more diversity and disagreement than commonly believed. At the same time, the governance of organizations stifled dissent and encouraged forced consensus.[91] Private groups lacked the requisite "guard[s] against tyranny and injustice to minorities and individuals" to qualify as genuinely democratic.[92]

In short, the presumed democratic nature of organizations was highly dubious.[93] Their shortcomings were troublesome in light of government's failure to place limits on private power that groups refused to impose upon themselves. The pluralist ideal of government as manager of group conflict did not comport with reality. Instead of government acting as mediator, government itself was fragmented and beholden to particular interests.[94] Indeed, it was the failure of the state to monitor group imbalances at which McConnell launched his most withering

criticisms. The absence of formal legal standards to control
agency action:

> magnifies the danger of arbitrary and discriminatory action.
> It is not mere coincidence that largely autonomous agencies
> of government have developed close informal ties with par-
> ticular constituencies and have failed to develop clearly de-
> fined standards to guide their actions. The problem of criteria
> and power are ultimately connected.[95]

Only through external, objective criteria could government
control the exercise of power and assume responsibility for governing. The absence of standards meant the loss of control over
agency action and the forfeiture of power to undemocratic organizations with narrow interests. This capitulation made a:

> mockery of the [pluralist]vision by which one interest opposes
> another and ambition checks ambition. The large extent of
> autonomy accorded to various fragments of government has
> gone far to isolate important matters of public policy from
> supposedly countervailing influences.[96]

The ultimate consequence was the unequal exercise of private
power to the exclusion of the public interest.

Theodore Lowi and Interest Group Liberalism: Perverted Pluralism

Theodore Lowi followed McConnell's critique with a scathing indictment of contemporary pluralism embodied in the administrative state.[97] He laid bare the notion that pluralism naturally and
automatically worked to produce policy results for the common
good. On the contrary, he painted a picture of a bureaucratic
structure incapable of acting in ways responsive to the public.

Lowi criticized pluralism on both the theoretical and applied
planes. He argued that the theoretical underpinnings of pluralism had been twisted by contemporary pluralists. The original
pluralism of Madison was one in which government was constrained, as an enlarged republican sphere created a multiplicity
of offsetting, competing factions. In contrast, the new pluralism
considered government a positive good, to which all groups were
entitled entry.[98] This benign view of a perfect, self-regulating pluralist politics eliminated the skepticism over government which
was once a very American trait.

Its practical consequence, "interest group liberalism," bore
the brunt of Lowi's condemnation. The interest-group liberalism

label referred to a perverted pluralism characterized by the avoidance of law and the "parceling out to private parties the power
to make public policy."[99] Groups were at the center of policy-
making, but in a way that undermined the very legitimacy of the
modern democratic state. This vulgarized pluralist mutation rested
upon several false assumptions. First, organized interests were not
necessarily homogeneous or easily defined. It could not be assumed, therefore, that effective representation of interests would
inevitably emerge from all corners of society to counteract existing interests.[100] Moreover, even if groups did surface, a compromise or bargain resulting in the public interest was by no means
assured. The administrative state was simply too poisoned by unequal levels of group access.[101] Pluralism was far more likely to be
an accommodation of specialized group interests than a competition between them, due largely to government's failure to ensure
equal access for all interested groups.[102] Ultimately, the pluralist
paradigm idealized groups. It ignored the latter half of Madison's
definition, of factions as "adverse to the right of other citizens, or
to the permanent and aggregate interests of the community."[103]
No longer a necessary evil to be regulated, groups were to be
accommodated and indulged.[104]

The consequence was the enervation of democratic government on an operational level. The parcelling out of power to the
most interested parties eliminated those not specifically organized
around a particular issue or program. "The people" were shut out
of the policy-making process, from the agenda-setting phase on
through to the actual legal outcomes. It was administration and
policy-making without public control or accountability. In the end,
interest-group liberalism was a means of creating and maintaining privilege.[105] It was sponsored pluralism, conservative in its resistance to change and its desire to uphold the existing order of
agency-group relations.[106] The victim was political representation.
Interest-group liberalism reduced the number of competitors, favoring the organized and limiting political "participation to channels provided by pre-existing groups."[107]

Pluralism: Unifier or Divider?

A final criticism of pluralism is its threat to a unified public consciousness. Robert Dahl was fairminded enough to acknowledge
that pluralism might deform, rather than inform, civic attitudes.[108]
The practical outgrowth of groups organized to press a particular
interest was the fragmentation of public concerns. Organizations

are formed to achieve consensus and solidarity within, and to produce conflict without. The inevitable result was to move group
members to equate their segmental interests with the common
interests of society.[109]

Ironically, the theoretical justification for pluralism was that
it would work in the other direction. It was to endow one with a
sense of community by keying him into groups that would amplify his political voice. Group involvement was to create a sense
of enhanced political efficacy, from which one's interests would
be refined and reconciled with those of society.[110] Pluralism at its
core was a theoretical exercise to empower individuals by making
people's voices discernible in politics. But as a functioning democratic system, it was to serve the country and work toward the
public interest.

Pluralism assumed that multiple group affiliations would develop a refined understanding of minority rights, compromise, and
the primacy of the public interest.[111] When that assumption gave
way to the possibility of a dominant group with which one identifies her political interests, the potential of pluralism to dampen
self-interest was twisted into a tool of division and compartmen-
talization. In *The Disuniting of America*,[112] Arthur Schlesinger, Jr.
described a "cult of ethnicity" in which greater civic participation
was sought through group separation and differentiation. He recognized the contradiction in trying to achieve a unified culture
through essentially divisive means. Schlesinger bemoaned the country "not as a polity of individuals but as a congeries of distinct
and inviolable cultures."[113]

This is the challenge to pluralism. "Sanctification of the
group" endangers the goal of a shared commitment to common
ideals, making the creation of a nation with a distinct identity
more difficult.[114] Group politics must keep "divisions from dissolving the society into which they enter—of keeping such a highly
differentiated society fundamentally sound and whole."[115]

THE PLURALIST DILEMMA:
REPRESENTATION OF GROUPS OR INDIVIDUALS?

The pluralist democratic challenges must direct the Court in its
search for a group-conscious theory of representation. Legal responses to perceived pluralist shortcomings must be scrutinized
with an eye toward how they address these issues. Are the policy
decision-making processes and outcomes they produce in the gen-

eral interests of the country? The critiques of Schattschneider, Lowi, and others suggest they are not. And if not, is it because the processes of decisionmaking that generate public policy are not open to all groups? Does every group that is interested in a policy matter have a legitimate opportunity to make itself heard? Or are groups so unequal that some can dominate policy while others are effectively precluded from exerting influence?

Second, are the imperfections of modern pluralism the result of its theoretical limitations? If group equilibrium in the policy realm does not flow from self-corrective, self-regulating group forces, can it be achieved by the imposition of outside regulatory mechanisms? Are the political interests in a complex, advanced society ever fixed, identifiable, and stable enough to permit this? Can group interests be catalogued and classified so as to make management of group forces feasible?

Third, is group-constituted pluralism appropriate, in light of the skepticism over the democratic nature of groups? Are organizations as representative as assumed? To serve as legitimate tools of representation, groups must authentically reflect the needs, preferences, and desires of their members.[116]

Finally, what is the suitable position for groups relative to other political institutions, in particular political parties? Are pressure groups and organizations still most desirable when working to supplement the parties, or have they superseded parties as the primary vehicles of policy formation? Is positive pluralism realized when organized interests operate within the party system, or when they bypass it?

All of these questions are sub-parts of the fundamental question which is the paradox of representative democracy, the tension between individual and collective standing in attaining political equality. This, then, is the pluralist dilemma; how is the central objective of individual political equality to be reconciled with group or organizational inequality?[117] According to group theory, formal political equality of individuals will not yield real equality if the groups to which one belongs are inferior to other organizations. One side of the dilemma, therefore, is that individual political equality cannot be realized without some semblance of parity in the efficacy of groups and organizations.

The objections to pluralism are variations of this theme. A bias toward business organizations is a form of group inequality that impedes the individual clout of those belonging to non-business collectives. The same consequence flows from unequal distribution of group resources, the failure of political institutions to manage and enlarge conflict, and the indictment of sponsored interest-group liberalism. Each one thwarts the primary goal of individual political efficacy.

The other horn of the dilemma is whether organizational equality can be achieved without compromising the sacred creed of individual equality. Simply put, can group inequities be remedied without gutting individual equality? Can laws simultaneously guarantee all citizens equal access to democratic processes and effectively regulate political resources to equalize the influence of organizations? Group theory points to groups as functional units of political regulation. But can the universe of groups be reduced to a common ground that will permit their management and elevate them as devices for attaining individual equality?

Groups vary in a multitude of ways, in size, assets, degree and type of organization, leadership, size and complexity of agenda, political resources, and the degree of permanency of their existence. Democratic values correspond to these differences and have implications for how groups are treated for purposes of securing individual equality. A group with highly refined democratic features arguably warrants more generous treatment than a severely autocratic organization. A group with a comprehensive, multi-issue program may warrant treatment more favorable than that granted a narrow, single-issue group. Even more problematic is the question of how to gauge nonmonetary resources or intangibles such as leadership, group status and prestige, goodwill, skill, or other ethereal political resources. In short, only the number of members in a group is easily quantifiable. Even this may prove difficult, given the fluid nature of groups and the ease with which individuals enter or exit. These questions underscore the challenge of remedying organizational disparities while preserving sacrosanct principles of individual equality.

The pluralist dilemma is one of reconciling these fundamental principles. *The crux of the theoretical problem is how to reconcile the underlying principle of individual equality, as reflected in principles like "one person, one vote," with the representation of collective interests or organizations, which vary widely in the factors affecting political efficacy.* Can the inviolable principle of individual equality be squared with that elusive equality among organizations and groups? This is the central question facing the Court in issues of representation. A guiding element in American constitutional law has been the "evolution of a political system in which all the active and legitimate groups in the population can make themselves heard at some crucial stage of the process of decision."[118] The functional flaws in pluralism imperil that objective.

We are now prepared to consider how the Court might resolve this fundamental problem. We first examine judicial efforts to overcome organizational inequities by altering the processes through which groups participate. This neopluralist approach seeks to level the group playing field by monitoring and equalizing the influence of groups in the political arena. It bestows formal advantages and special constitutional consideration upon certain groups, while burdening others. The goal is to craft constitutional guidelines that level "the status and power of the particular groups who gain or suffer by their operation."[119]

The Quest for Representation in a Pluralist Democracy: Group-Centered Representation (or the Neopluralist Response)

This, then, is the dilemma facing the Court. The labyrinth of representational modes and means compels the existence of structures sensitive to collective voices. Group theory and its pluralist offshoot similarly presuppose the centrality of group participation in achieving effective individual political activity. However, disparities between groups, which muffle or exclude collective voices in the political arena, undermine these suppositions. Hence, representation theory requires structures that facilitate group politics and alleviate group inequities, while simultaneously enhancing individual political effectiveness.

One response to this dilemma is to conclude that groups are simply tools to perpetuate existing individual inequality, and to abandon the goal of collective equality in favor of direct participatory activity by individuals. At the core of the Progressive movement was an idyllic notion that the best democracy was built around unadulterated, unmediated interaction between citizen and government. But group theory indicates that while forms of direct participation may increase the individual's sense of import as political actor, the practical consequence in a mass democracy is a disconnect between the rulers and the ruled.

Instead, the Court must delineate a group-regarding alternative that promotes group influence rather than stifling it. In this chapter, we examine what has been termed the neopluralist approach. It focuses directly on groups and associations, striving for political effectiveness by according them official representative status. Schemes of group representation range widely, as the thinkers we sample illustrate. But all share a common desire to equalize groups' political influence through conferral of formal legal status. Campaign financing laws provide a striking example of how the legal structure of group representation might look. The Court and Congress have pursued a regulatory scheme aimed at parity of group representation through categorization of groups and equalization of the resources they can expend.

In the next chapter, we shall consider the theoretical and practical obstacles to group representation, then turn to a party-systems alternative. Ultimately, the neopluralist approach falls short of the representational paradigm, abandoning the complex representative ideal in favor of a one-dimensional descriptive imitation.

GROUP/INTEREST REPRESENTATION:
THE PROMISE OF THE NEOPLURALIST RESPONSE

Proposals to confer formal representative status upon particular groups or interests are a logical response to group theory and the flaws of the pluralist system. Formal recognition of groups assumes group identity to be of central importance, and individual political identity to be constituted by group affinities.[1] Proponents of group representation, therefore, react to the pluralist dilemma by enhancing the legal status of unequal or disadvantaged groups.

Iris Marion Young and "Democratic Cultural Pluralism": Group Representation for the Oppressed

Iris Marion Young has articulated the theoretical foundation for group representation. At its core is a reconstructed, group-based vision of justice and political equality. Justice is the primary objective of democratic processes. Deliberative democracy is most likely to arrive at just outcomes when it invites the participation of all groups and interests affected by its decisions.[2]

If group affinities are central to defining individual identity, then democratic processes must be structured around that realization. The recognition of group differences is at the heart of political equality. Young proposes a "democratic cultural pluralism,"[3] whereby equality among socially and culturally differentiated groups is achieved by affirming their differences, rather than submerging them. "Radical democratic pluralism," which acknowledges social group differences, "ensur[es] the participation and inclusion of everyone in social and political institutions."[4] Participatory democracy requires an acknowledgment that groups differ and "that some groups are actually or potentially oppressed or disadvantaged."[5]

Moreover, social justice requires public interaction that is cognizant of group particularities and differences. It should underscore the public as a heterogeneous collection of differences to be respected and acknowledged.[6] This compels *open and accessible public spaces and forums*, in which to encounter differing perspectives, experiences, and affiliations. The collective activity characterized by Lowi's interest-group liberalism is manifestly inadequate.

Though group-constituted and particular, interest-group liberalism is neither publicly conducted nor public-minded. The group players have no responsibility to listen or attend to the claims of other groups. Rather, they privately advance their concerns and maximize their position. In a society of disparate resources and unequal access, this ignores the needs of marginalized groups, elevating the interests of some groups while denigrating or disregarding those of others.[7] "[G]roup domination through formally equal processes of participation can be avoided" only when all groups can express their interests publicly and equally in relation to other groups.[8] Justice and democratic legitimacy demand group autonomy for the empowerment and development of group-specific voices and perspectives.[9]

These criticisms merge into Young's call for a "group-differentiated participatory public," in which groups are acknowledged by policy-making institutions through specific group representation. She advocates "specific representation of those oppressed groups, through which those groups express their specific understanding of the issues before the public and register a group-based vote."[10] Only such a group-constituted democracy will insure that the "distinct voices and perspectives of those of its constituent groups that are oppressed or disadvantaged" are heard.[11]

Young's work is most important as the theoretical buttress for claims to interest or group representation. As to its practical implications, group representation:

implies institutional mechanisms and public resources supporting (1) self-organization of group members so that they
achieve collective empowerment and a reflective understanding of their collective experience and interests in the context
of the society; (2) group analysis and group generation of
policy proposals in institutionalized contexts where decision-
makers are obliged to show that their deliberations have taken
group perspectives into consideration; and (3) group veto
power regarding specific policies that affect a group directly."[12]

Young does not advocate a full-fledged system of group representation, but limits it to marginalized groups. Political equality does
not require formal recognition of those groups that already pos-
sess ample resources and organization, but only of those oppressed
or disadvantaged groups.[13]

This is Young's answer to concerns that group representation will generate an infinite number of groups approaching the
altar to receive a special dispensation of representation. Limiting
formal representation to oppressed groups will avoid the unman-
ageable proliferation of groups. A group suffering any one of five
"faces of oppression" would qualify for representative status: (1)
exploitation in the labor market to maintain the power and wealth
of other groups; (2) *marginalization* of groups of people that the
labor force will not use; (3) *powerlessness* in authority, status, or
policy decision-making; (4) victims of *systemic violence*; and (5) *cultural imperialism* through which dominant societal mores stigma-
tize a group.[14]

Young's attempts to restrict the proliferation of groups is
undercut by her own litany of qualifying groups, which includes
"women, blacks, Native Americans, Chicanos, Puerto Ricans and
other Spanish-speaking Americans, Asian Americans, gay men, lesbians, working class people, poor people, old people, and men-
tally and physically disabled people."[15] She also utilizes a definition
that amplifies the problem of identifying groups worthy of recognition. Most proponents of group representation suggest that
group identity is a function of its interests. Young specifically excludes groups classified by interest. Those that matter are *social
groups*, whose members share an "affinity" for each other.[16] Young
would differentiate between social groups according to those cultural norms and practices that lead to the feeling of affinity.

Young identifies three benefits of formal group recognition.
One is greater procedural fairness in determining the public
agenda by eliciting the needs of all groups. This increases the

likelihood that all relevant interests and perspectives will be addressed in democratic deliberation. A second is promotion of a public debate that casts group considerations in appeals to justice rather than self-interest. Third, it should foster just outcomes by maximizing the information available to policy-makers.[17] In sum, justice demands a democracy in which people are involved in the discussion and decisionmaking that affect them. When political and social institutions favor some groups over others, they must be adjusted to ensure representation for the less privileged groups.[18]

Lani Guinier and the Representation of Interests

The neopluralism of Iris Marion Young is not merely some esoteric academic theorizing. The experience of Lani Guinier aptly illustrates just how potentially explosive the political dimensions of group representation can be. Guinier is a leading neopluralist scholar who, until 1992, had been toiling in relative obscurity as a law professor at the University of Pennsylvania law school. That changed abruptly when Bill Clinton, an old friend who had recently acquired new responsibilities as the President of the United States, selected former civil rights litigator Guinier to head the Civil Rights Division of the Department of Justice. Her brief, and ultimately unsuccessful, foray from academe into practical politics provided a somewhat tragic, but nonetheless powerful, reminder that those who dare to move against the sacred creed of American individualism do so at their own risk and at great peril.

Guinier's nomination sparked a tempestuous national debate that was both remarkable and disconcerting. The level of public discussion and interest generated by her views on such "scholarly" issues as interest representation, redistricting, and apportionment was unparalleled. At the same time, the substance of the debate reflected a rather discouraging lack of deeper understanding of the issues at hand. The choice of Guinier provoked a firestorm of criticism from a number of corners. Those who claimed to have read her numerous law review articles on ways to enhance minority representation in politics (heretofore unnoticed by the broader audience) issued distorted doomsday warnings of how radical her ideas were. She was caricatured as a racial minority "quota queen," who as Civil Rights chief would raze our system of majority rule. President Clinton, in full retreat in the face of venomous opposition from numerous Guinier detractors, quickly torpedoed the nomination, thus setting off another political squall.

Unfortunately, the President's decision to abort prior to the congressional hearing stage deprived the country of a potentially enlightening and valuable civics lesson on representation and our electoral system. But even as Professor Guinier resumed her place in the ivory tower (albeit in much less obscurity), the supercharged atmosphere surrounding the fiasco underscored several important points. First, it attracted widespread attention to issues of effectiveness of representation and the role of groups. It brought the discussion out of the abstract and theoretical into the real world of practical politics. Moreover, it illustrated in stark fashion that theoretical arguments over majority rule and minority group representation have very real practical ramifications. They go to the heart of how we define ourselves politically, and to the character of the society which is in large part a product of our political system. In the end, it demonstrated how important it is that reforms ultimately fit within the deeply entrenched philosophy of individualism and majoritarianism that is the foundation of our political culture.

What were Guinier's core ideas that prompted such a virulent reaction? As one of the clearest examples of contemporary neopluralist thinking, they warrant a closer look. It is misleading to casually portray proponents of "group representation" as a unified or cohesive voice. The label does not adequately convey the variety of approaches held together only by the desire to alter the system so as to better reflect collective preferences within society. It includes not only group representation advocates, but also those who propose interest or preference representation.[19] "Group representation" and "interest representation" are often used interchangeably to refer to attempts to incorporate mechanisms for recognizing collective voices presently without access to the public forum. The common theme is the desire to remedy disparities by giving political presence to corporately held views heretofore excluded from the public realm.

The contrast between Young's writings and those of Guinier illustrates the diverse ways of accomplishing this. Young's ultimate goal is to ensure that the particular concerns of disadvantaged groups are heard and considered in public decisionmaking channels. Guinier goes a step further in pursuit of government outcomes that actually reflect minority interests. Her notion of political equality is not satisfied merely by giving groups a voice.

It demands that political results reflect the multiplicity of interests in society. Formal political equality is insufficient. Groups currently ignored by the system are entitled to tangible results. The group right to "full and effective participation" requires equality in governmental outputs.[20]

Thus, Guinier is critical of the notion that exclusive reliance upon voting rights litigation will enable minorities to elect their own representatives. This is a flawed strategy based on the naive assumption that integration of the legislature will naturally lead to consideration of all interests. She rejects the "descriptive" representation underlying minority districting tactics, which only "transfers the problem of disenfranchisement from the electorate to the legislature."[21] She flatly rejects the existence of deliberative legislative character, which underlies descriptive remedies.[22] "Racial polarization . . . in the legislative body destroys the reciprocity/virtual representation principle and buries it within racially fixed majorities, thereby transforming majority rule into majority tyranny."[23] She rejects representative ideals whereby a legislator might accommodate the interests of minorities within his district, or virtually represent oppressed minorities outside his constituency.[24]

Ironically, the survey of practitioners revealed that they share Guinier's dissatisfaction with descriptive ideals of representation, though they would likely disagree with her characterization of legislatures as inherently racist. The canvassing of political leaders and lawyers involved in voting and redistricting disputes exposed surprisingly strong negative attitudes toward descriptive or reflective representative goals. It suggested that legal and political practitioners are similarly disillusioned with the notion of descriptive representation that underlies voting rights litigation.[25]

Guinier departs from the survey subjects in her rejection of parties as a means of bringing groups into the system. A rigid two-party system, operating within the framework of the district system, stifles third parties, which Guinier considers critical to minority interests.[26] She holds no hope that minorities will gain access as part of an electoral or governing coalition. "Racism excludes minorities from ever becoming part of the governing coalition, meaning that the white majority will be permanent."[27]

Electoral processes that enable a group to elect a proportionate number of its representatives are inadequate measures of minority representation. They equate political power with electoral success, at the expense of policy responsiveness.[28] Representation requires a proportional stake in legislative outcomes.[29] Disadvantaged groups are entitled to a government responsive in its actions to their preferences, as identified by their collective consciousness and activity.[30] This leads to Guinier's solution of interest representation.

In Guinier's view, political representation is doomed unless it includes a qualitative gauge that examines the justness of legislative outcomes. Its aim is to allow those at the low end of the political pecking order to have their policy preferences satisfied.[31] Guinier would replace fixed geographic districts with "voluntary interest constituencies."[32] Group representation would exist on two fronts, in the selection of officials and in governmental outcomes. The enhancement of the descriptive quality of the legislature would be supplemented with a proportionality principle of legislative decisionmaking. Guinier would restructure the policy process along the lines of jury panels, to ensure true deliberation. She would likewise bolster the deliberative process through rules reducing the votes on proposed legislation and seeking consensus and compromise instead. The goal ought to be to "desegregate the white majority by minimizing the 'threshold of representation' and the 'threshold of exclusion' for exercising political power."[33] By breaking up winner-take-all voting mechanisms, politically cohesive minority interests otherwise submerged in majority interests can be recognized. *The ultimate objective is not only to give each group a right to have its interests represented, but to give each group a right to have its interests satisfied a fair proportion of the time.*[34]

Robert Grady: Restoring Real Representation *Through Functional Group Representation*

Young and Guinier would extend group representation only to marginalized or disadvantaged groups. Other proposals contemplate a broader schematic arrangement that applies to all relevant collectives within society. An illustrative example is Robert Grady, who champions "functional democratic constituencies" as an alternative to traditional geography-based representation.[35] Grady considers territorial representation no longer useful in determining political interests in contemporary society. Rather, shared interests congeal around those "functional associations" in which people are involved. Unlike geographic criteria, functional associations are the "jurisdictions of meaningful political participation and the source of shared values."[36]

Grady's preference for democratic functional constituencies is grounded in an intense dissatisfaction with interest-group liberalism.[37] As the predominant theme in contemporary American political theory, interest-group liberalism is a cheap imitation of representation consisting of a mostly symbolic relationship between voters and government.[38] Grady's remedy is not to forsake pluralism, but to impose democratic restraints upon it. He contemplates assigning decisionmaking authority to functional bodies, provided two democratic ideals are met. First, the grant of power must be in the public interest. The legitimacy of decisionmaking by functional constituencies is rooted in the standards pursuant to which authority is assigned. Therefore, delegations must be made pursuant to explicit public interest standards arrived at through open, thorough legislative deliberation. Furthermore, liberal values require that the functional unit be governed internally by democratic procedures to ensure that it represents the interests of the members and not the leadership.[39] Finally, the actual decisions of the functional organizations must heed those public interest guidelines.[40]

Despite Grady's evident disapproval of interest-group liberalism, his solution is consonant with positive pluralism and group theory. Functional constituencies strike at the core of traditional liberalism and its individualist assumptions. Functional demarcations are fundamentally at odds with the liberal notion that individual political values and interests cannot be predetermined by functional categories.[41]

Like other advocates of group representation, Grady is faced with the difficult question of how to determine the relevant functional units. He forthrightly recognizes the perplexing nature of that task. Grady's recommendations are driven by workplace units, but he readily admits that one cannot easily pick and choose between potential bases of group representation.

> Which functional interests have greater priority over others for inclusion in an arrangement that provides for group representation? If a legislative body attempts to incorporate functional interests within a scheme of representation, it cannot avoid simultaneously designating specific functional interests. Virtually by definition, the concept of functional representation entails types, classifications, categories.[42]

He concedes that this is an inherently messy task. Group representation requires a functional prioritizing of the interests worthy of representational status. Nor is the system self-operative once those distinctions are made. The fluid nature of groups necessitates an ongoing evaluation of the status and claims of groups and interests. Legislative bodies accustomed to the art of interest-group politics would be hard put to make the distinctions initially or to exercise the necessary ongoing oversight and supervision.[43]

GROUPS AND CAMPAIGN FINANCE REGULATION IN CONSTITUTIONAL LAW: THE COURT'S EXPERIMENT IN NEOPLURALISM

Proposals of formal group-based representational arrangements are more than the abstract pinings of dreamy reformers. On the contrary, the group leveling rationale at the heart of such proposals has become increasingly prevalent in constitutional analysis. In particular, the Supreme Court's review of mechanisms for regulating campaign financing has come to rest firmly upon neopluralist arguments. It is the starkest example of a judicial strategy to enhance group representation by monitoring, managing, and equalizing the expenditure of group resources. The campaign finance decisions provide a glimpse of neopluralism applied, and the problems it presents.

It is significant that the most adventuresome experimentation in neopluralism should occur in campaign finance, in light of its role in American politics. Politics is largely animated by the influence of money. As the "mother's milk of politics," money is the primary political resource through which individuals, groups, and parties seek access to power. Its central role in expensive modern-day electoral campaigns provides a golden opportunity for political actors of all types. Those willing to financially nurse a candidate, a cause, or an organization will probably realize a voice in the political arena which they would otherwise not enjoy.[44]

For the same reasons, campaign financing also has the greatest potential to distort the representativeness of political activities and institutions. A single wealthy individual can wield as much influence as a sizeable group of people with modest means. Much of the inequity at the heart of pluralist critiques is traceable to financial disparities. Those groups with inordinate political influence are business, trade, and professional associations of higher socioeconomic status; in short, those with more money.

The prominence of money in political campaigns, and unease over its influence, has made it the subject of repeated regulatory efforts. Congress and the courts have struggled to establish rules that might cure the distorting effect of money while preserving the speech and associational rights of those affected. In the name of limiting corruption and undue influence, Congress has pursued statutory efforts to equalize the financial input of a variety of political players. In reviewing the constitutionality of those regulatory efforts, the Court has followed suit. As a result, campaign financing provides a conspicuous illustration of group representation, as Congress and the Court have actively participated in neopluralist linedrawing aimed at a fair system of group politics. They have become increasingly receptive toward legalized efforts to "level the playing field" for various group voices. Robert Dahl once concluded that problems of authority in America could never be solved "unless resources are distributed much more equally."[45] These cases exhibit a striking attempt by the Court to do exactly that by equalizing resources along group lines. *This area of constitutional jurisprudence, therefore, offers the clearest example of the Court's opting for a group-based neopluralist approach at the expense of the party alternative.*

FECA, Buckley *and the Individualistic Origins of Campaign Finance Regulation*

The campaign finance cases, stretching from the landmark 1975 decision of *Buckley v. Valeo*[46] to the present, have been marked by two notable parallel movements. Those movements mirror the Court's theory of representation generally. The statutory regulations reflected a desire to redress inequalities in individual access to the political process, a goal with which *Buckley* was largely consistent.[47] The Court initially adopted a highly individualistic approach to regulating money in campaigns, at which time it explicitly repudiated legal attempts to equalize group voices. But in the two decades that followed, the individualistic assumptions of *Buckley* were cast aside in favor of group considerations.

The modern era of campaign finance regulation began with the 1974 amendments to the Federal Election Campaign Act (FECA). Those amendments to FECA represented a sweeping set of campaign finance reforms undertaken during the post-Watergate era in response to unseemly activities engaged in by the committee to reelect President Nixon, and to bring campaign financing out of the shadows into public view. Among other things, those reforms did the following:

1.   limited the amount that individuals could contribute to candidates to $1000 per election and $25,000 cumulatively;

2.   similarly limited the amount that individuals could spend on candidates as "independent expenditures";

3.   limited the amount that political action committees could contribute to a candidate to $5000 per election, with no cumulative limit;

4.   limited by formula the amounts that political parties could spend on behalf of House and Senate candidates.[48]

Shortly thereafter, a coalition of politicians with diverse interests challenged the constitutionality of the FECA regulations. The plaintiffs opposed the statutory limitations imposed on campaign contributions and independent expenditures, arguing that they placed impermissible burdens on First Amendment rights of political expression and association. The result was a fragmented Supreme Court statement in *Buckley v. Valeo,* holding that the independent expenditure limitations violated First Amendment speech rights but that the contribution limits were justified.

At the core of *Buckley* one could find the same individualistic perception of politics that pervaded the voting rights cases at the outset. While the Court reaffirmed the fundamental nature of the rights of political association and expression, it cast them in essentially individualistic terms.[49] This was most evident in the disparate treatment accorded campaign contribution limits and limits on independent expenditures. The Court strove for individual parity in political input, upholding the limits on what individuals could contribute to candidates or committees. But its rejection of the proposed limits on independent expenditures reflected an implicit bias toward individual input over associational activity.[50] In elevating independent expenditures over campaign contributions, the Court determined that money spent directly on behalf of a candidate was purer political speech than contributions made to a party, committee, or campaign organization. The ruling diminished the importance of associational contacts as a means of individual political expression. It discounted the reality that one's money can be used more effectively when put to use by an organization, party, or association.

Money spent independently, however, is not likely to be as effective as when put to use by a political organization. Campaign organizations are run by political experts, media professionals, consultants, pollsters, strategists, and others whose responsibilities and expertise include how to maximize the message made possible by contributors' financial resources. Independent expenditures are unlikely to be as effective in transmitting the desired message. Monies spent independently may even run counter to the strategy of the campaign itself. Nevertheless, the Court was willing to limit the associational use of money, but not independent individual efforts.[51]

The individualist thrust of *Buckley* was further evidenced by the Court's explicit rejection of group-regarding regulatory measures. It renounced the suggestion that the capacity of groups to exert political influence should somehow be equalized:

> It is argued, however, that the ancillary governmental interest in equalizing the relative ability of individuals and groups to influence the outcome of elections serves to justify the limitation[s] . . . *But the concept that government may restrict the speech of some elements of our society in order to enhance the relative voice of others is wholly foreign to the First Amendment.*[52]

The Court repudiated the idea that the political playing field could be levelled by handicapping or equalizing group expenditures. Provided that individual opportunity was roughly equal, the Court would not try to give various group voices an equal chance to be heard through political spending. As one commentator stated, "the Court was prepared to take a substantial risk of collective inequality to satisfy a desire for individual fairness."[53]

The individualistic perspective underlying *Buckley* remained intact in *California Medical Association v. FEC.*[54] The FECA limits on individual contributions also applied to what could be given to multicandidate committees, of which the California Medical Association was one. In this 1981 decision, the Court upheld those limitations, which the CMA had knowingly violated by accepting amounts over the maximum. In doing so, the Court offered a cramped concept of political association, which consisted solely of the rights of the contributor to the exclusion of the recipient association. Provided the "rights of a contributor" were not impaired, limits on committee contributions were permissible.[55] The Court exhibited disdain for associational activity by treating expenditures as pure speech but donations to associations as "speech by proxy" entitled to something less than full First Amendment protection. It showed no inclination to admit that individuals might attain heightened political effectiveness through participation in associations. Its narrow formulation of speech and associational rights suggested a "one-dimensional sum-of-its-parts view of political association"[56] which ignored the unique functions and rights of the recipient associations. *The Court was seemingly oblivious to the representative benefits realized through organized, institutionalized political behavior.*[57]

Buckley *Begone!: Judicial Levelling of the Group Playing Field in Campaign Finance*

That was soon to change, as the Court departed drastically from the individualistic assumptions of *Buckley* and its declared denunciation of attempts to balance group voices. More recent cases expose an embrace of neopluralist reasoning by the Court, as it has drawn legal distinctions between types of groups based on their representative capabilities. These decisions legally differentiate between groups in their right to collect and spend money for political purposes. They reveal a Court endowing groups with varying degrees of associational rights and rationalizing those differences on the basis of the groups' representative character. As such, they offer a preview of how the Court might address group-based claims to representation in a broader context.

Dramatic changes in the direction of campaign funding that occurred following the 1974 FECA amendments and *Buckley* left the Court with little choice but to entertain challenges involving the propriety of various aspects of group involvement. An unintended consequence of FECA, as interpreted by *Buckley*, was the rapid proliferation of political action committees, especially in the realm of business and industry.[58] The full advantage to which the business community used PACs increased the anxiety among many that those with too much influence were achieving even more. The dominant perception was of campaign finance rules that aided rather than restrained wealthy groups' capacity to drown out other voices and dominate the political policy-making arena.[59]

Congress responded to the hue and cry for greater regulation of PACs by amending FECA to define and categorize more carefully various group elements. As those regulations inevitably invited constitutional challenge, the Court was drawn into the perilous course of considering associational character as a determinant of the rights of groups to participate financially in campaigns. As had been the case with the Court's establishment of minority group rights in redistricting, it again found itself reacting to a perceived political crisis rather than being guided by an

overarching theory of representation. The Court's move into
neopluralist group equalization was driven by a political consensus that campaign financing in the real world had gone badly awry,
not by an understanding of group theory.

The first rumblings of group-based differences surfaced in
FEC v. National Right to Work Committee.[60] FECA prohibited corporations from using general treasury funds to pay for campaign
support activities. Instead, corporations and unions were required
to establish segregated funds for political activities, for which they
could solicit donations from designated categories of employees
and members. Only those with some connection to the corporate
structure could be solicited for funds. The National Right to Work
Committee (NRWC) was a nonprofit corporation established for
the stated purpose of protecting the working rights of employees
who chose not to join labor organizations. The NRWC was prosecuted by the FEC when it sought and received contributions to
its segregated fund from nonqualifying nonmembers.

The High Court rejected NRWC's constitutional challenge,
invoking the *Buckley* rationale of avoiding corruption to restrict
NRWC's associational rights. However, the Court added a justification that ran counter to its earlier disavowal of group equalization efforts. For the first time, it employed the doctrine of political
association as a legal tool for gauging group influence. It accepted
Congress' judgment that the special characteristics of corporations
compelled prophylactic measures in campaign finance regulation.
The statutory purpose was:

> to ensure that substantial aggregations of wealth amassed by
> the special advantages which go with the corporate form of
> organization should not be converted into political 'war chests'
> which could be used to incur political debts from legislators
> aided by contributors.[61]

The Court rationalized that differing organizational structures
and purposes required "different forms of regulation in order to
protect the integrity of the electoral process."[62] Corporate wealth
that dominated the political forum threatened the integrity of the
process. Since corporate forms had greater political resources at
their disposal than did other associational forms, they warranted
additional restrictions. In short, the Court condoned legislative
attempts to "restrict the speech of some elements . . . to enhance
the relative voice of others . . . ," something it had refused to
tolerate in *Buckley*. The departure from *Buckley* signified a
marked shift from an exclusive focus on individual equality to an

endorsement of legislative manipulation of group input to accomplish a fair political playing field.[63]

In *FEC v. NRWC*, the group distinction upheld by the Court was between corporate and unincorporated associations. In *FEC v. National Conservative Political Action Committee*,[64] (*FEC v. NCPAC*) the Court went a step further, as it differentiated between types of incorporated organizations. *FEC v. NCPAC* pertained to FECA limits on how much independent political committees could spend on Democratic or Republican Presidential candidates who received public funding.[65] NCPAC was a conservative, nonprofit corporation registered as an independent political committee and subject to FECA. It planned to spend substantial amounts in support of President Reagan's 1984 re-election bid. NCPAC's contributors were solicited through direct mail and had no input into how their contributions were spent. When NCPAC exceeded the statutory dollar limitation on independent expenditures, it was sued by the FEC.

In striking down the limitations as applied to NCPAC, the Court demonstrated a heightened awareness of the import of group involvement. It praised PACs as an unparalleled means by which "large numbers of individuals of modest means can join together in organizations which serve to 'amplif[y] the voice of their adherents.'"[66] More significantly, it relied upon inequalities between groups as a basis for judging the constitutionality of the provision. It found the statute overbroad, since its prohibitions applied "equally to an informal neighborhood group that solicits contributions and spends money on a presidential election as to the wealthy and professionally managed PACs involved in these cases."[67] The Court objected to the failure of the provisions to treat wealthy PACs more stringently than the "informal discussion groups that solicit neighborhood contributions to publicize their views."[68] The legislature was not neopluralist enough to please the Court.

Though the NCPAC was incorporated, it did not present dangers of undue corporate influence sufficient to warrant restraining its political activities. Established for the express purpose of participating in political activities, it differed from traditional corporations organized for economic gain. The evil of "traditional economically organized corporations" was absent.[69] The Court warmed to the task of group classification, railing against the statute for indiscriminately lumping in poorer, smaller associations with large, for-profit corporations.[70]

Justice Marshall was even more explicit in his support for group distinctions. He espoused the need to level the resources of differently situated groups, stating that:

> The limitations on independent expenditures challenged in [*Buckley*] and here are justified by the congressional interests in promoting 'the reality and appearance of equal access to the political arena.'[71]

FEC v. NCPAC marked another advance in the emergence of a group-based typology for governing campaign finance.

In *FEC v. Massachusetts Citizens For Life*,[72] (hereinafter *FEC v. MCFL*) the Court took another stride away from the group neutrality of *Buckley* and toward group classification. It made increasingly subtle distinctions between corporate forms to explain dissimilar constitutional treatment of groups. MCFL, a nonprofit corporation engaged in a variety of pro-life activities, was required by FECA to make any independent campaign expenditures on political activities from a segregated fund. The FEC prosecuted MCFL when, without first establishing the requisite segregated fund, MCFL published and disseminated a special newsletter exhorting its members to vote pro-life in an upcoming election.

The Court held the restrictions to be unconstitutional as they pertained to MCFL, finding that the character of the organization did not justify placing limits on its spending of general corporate funds on political activity. The justices donned their political scientists' hats, as they weighed the purported justifications for the regulation against MCFL's representative qualities and its contributions to the democratic process. In freeing MCFL from the FECA segregated fund requirement, the Court highlighted several essential features of the organization. The most important was MCFL's purpose for existing, which was solely for political purposes and not for business activities.[73] It posed no threat to the electoral process that the regulation of corporate activity was meant to remedy, namely the potential for unfair deployment of corporate wealth to advance its political causes.[74]

On one hand, the Court reinforced the rationale for differentiated group treatment based on the "corrosive influence of concentrated corporate wealth."[75] Restrictions on corporations were justified to "protect the integrity of the marketplace of political ideas."[76] The tenor of the case confirmed the Court's full-scale abandonment of the *Buckley* line that had eschewed attempts to aid some group voices by muting others. But the Court also demonstrated a greater cognizance of the complexities of the connection between money and political speech. It did not simply disparage financial resources as an inherent evil. Rather, it attempted to distinguish between those circumstances when money was a valid benchmark of an association's representative character and when it was not. The Court rightly noted that some resources were legitimate gauges of the popularity of ideas advanced by a group, while others were simply amassed in the economic marketplace without any connection to those political ideas.

Organizational wealth, in itself, did not necessarily compel regulation, since the "[r]elative availability of funds is . . . a rough barometer of public support."[77] It was not necessary that "all who participate in the political marketplace do so with exactly equal resources."[78] But it was objectionable when a corporation gained a political advantage by spending monies that bore no relation to the ideas being advanced. The Court sought to weight group resources so that they were representative of the intensity and strength of support for the underlying ideas. The Court was intuitively guided by the notion that the expenditure of group resources should roughly correspond to the level of support underlying that group's preferences.

This was the basis for the requirement that corporations create a segregated fund, so that solicited monies could be linked to a specific political agenda. General corporate funds unfairly "make a company a formidable political presence" when those funds are in no way an indication of the popular support for the company's political ideas.[79] MCFL did not present this danger. It was formed to advance political ideas, not to amass capital. Its resources were "not a function of its success in the economic marketplace, but its popularity in the political marketplace."[80]

FEC v. MCFL featured a full philosophical embrace by the Court of enhancement of group representation through equalizing group influence. The Court assessed group activity based on whether it accurately reflected the intensity of the political ideas it represented. The money collected and spent by MCFL was presumed to be a valid measure of the strength of pro-life opinions among its members. As such, it was "representative" in character, and legal regulation of its spending less justified. *The decision confirmed group rights for politically active associations based on their capability to function as representatives of members' preferences and to publicly express those preferences.*[81]

The future of group-differentiated constitutional jurisprudence in campaign spending remains to be seen. Certain members of the Court reject the neopluralist flavor of the recent cases
and oppose judicial efforts to categorize groups. The philosophical differences on the Court surfaced in *Austin v. Michigan Chamber of Commerce*,[82] a 1990 decision that exposed the conflicting
attitudes toward attempts to regulate group influence. *Austin* involved a challenge by the Michigan Chamber of Commerce to a
state statute regulating corporate spending on statewide elections.
Like FECA, the Michigan state law required the establishment of
a segregated fund to support political activities by corporations.
The Chamber was prosecuted for violating that requirement when
it used general funds to place an ad supporting a candidate in a
special election for the Michigan House of Representatives. It
claimed its nonprofit status should exempt it from the state law.
The Court denied the Chamber's challenge, characterizing it as a
business association, not a political advocacy group.[83] As such, it
was properly subject to the regulatory measure.

The majority opinion elicited a strong anti-neopluralist dissent from Justice Kennedy, who doubted the Court's ability to make
sophisticated distinctions that would actually advance the elusive
goal of political equality. He described the statute as "value-laden,
content-based speech suppression that permits some nonprofit
groups, but not others, to engage in political speech."[84] The notion that government could "shap[e] the political debate by insu-
lating the electorate from too much exposure to certain views"
was incompatible with the First Amendment.[85]

Justice Scalia lodged a more strenuous dissent, rejecting the
idea that government was capable of assuring the fairness of political debate.[86] He accused the Court of wrongly endorsing the
principle "that too much speech is an evil that the democratic
majority can proscribe."[87] He facetiously proclaimed the effect of
the majority opinion this way:

> To assure the fairness of elections by preventing dispropor-
> tionate expression of the views of any single powerful group,
> your Government has decided that the following associations
> of persons shall be prohibited from speaking or writing in
> support of any candidate: _____.[88]

Scalia described as "illiberal" the premise that expenditures must reflect actual support for the political ideas espoused,

scornfully calling it a "one man-one minute" proposal contrary to *Buckley*.[89] While conceding the noble objective of equalizing the political debate, Scalia concluded that "establishing the restrictions upon speech" was something government "cannot be trusted to do."[90]

CONCLUSION

Whether the consequences are as dire as Scalia predicts, the combined legislative and judicial efforts in campaign financing mark the boldest experiment to date with neopluralist strategies for ameliorating political inequality. FECA, with its judicial gloss, is an effort to erect a group-constituted system of financing elections. It aims at parity of group influence by regulating and controlling the volume of group voices in the public forum. Focusing on the aims, structures, strategies, and resources of political associations, Congress and the Court have created tiers of groups with differing sets of rights in the realm of influencing elections. They are formalizing what had informally comprised the second prong of the dual representative system, that of intermediate interest group representation. By monitoring and administering group spending, Congress and the Court are attempting to guarantee that group influence is sufficiently "representative" of the size and strength of the preferences held by group members.

The Court's distinct turn toward neopluralist constitutional jurisprudence was less attributable to the conscious pursuit of a well-balanced theory of representation than it was to political pressures to control the level of influence exercised by new collectivities. Is this neopluralist trend an adequate response to the challenges of representation and the pluralist dilemma? Analyzing the Court's neopluralist efforts from this perspective raises a host of questions. For example, if the ultimate goal is equality of influence, then the logical extension of these decisions is to apply them to other political resources.[91] Should we not also neutralize groups with advantages in organization, political expertise, access to the media, and prestige? Similarly, the goal of equal representation suggests that we look at other possible benchmarks of a group's representative character, such as organization and leadership, substantive interests, scope of agenda, decisionmaking procedures, member roles, and so on.

Once the law moves into neopluralist remedies, it is in danger of sliding down the slippery slope into a legal morass.[92] Legal structures aimed at equalizing the influence of groups raise a raft of questions that indicate it may be a futile enterprise. They underscore fundamental objections to theories of group representation generally. These objections warrant careful consideration before we are immersed in a quagmire of group representation from which we cannot be extricated.

CHAPTER SIX

❧

Party Subsystems as a Response to the Neopluralist Argument

Congress and the courts have begun a largely untested social science experiment in the realm of campaign financing to equalize the political influence of all relevant groups. It is unlike race-based redistricting, which sought to enhance group representation selectively. Those dalliances were meant to be temporary and remedial, for historically disadvantaged or oppressed minorities. In campaign finance, the Court's objective is broader, its means more pervasive. The goal is to modulate and temper the political input of some political groups to achieve equal influence for all. This approach has far-reaching implications for representation, and compels a careful evaluation. The standard for assessing it is twofold. First, does it coincide with and incorporate the multifaceted paradigm of representation? Second, does it confront the individual and collective sides of the pluralist dilemma, the paradoxical goals of unity and diversity? In the end, group-based representation is susceptible to criticisms on both fronts. Its weaknesses point to an alternative, that of party subsystems.

On a theoretical level, formal group-based structures of representation appear incapable of satisfying the inherent pluralist tension between individual and collectivism. Based on principles of group-specific separatism and segmentation, they may be incapable of generating sound, broad-based, publicly interested policy outcomes. On a practical level, implementation of group-constituted schemes of representation presents insurmountable challenges. It is beyond our institutional capacity to erect a system of group representation that mirrors the paradigm of representation while treating groups in a principled, logical, and consistent manner. Ultimately, we must look elsewhere for the answer to the puzzle of pluralist representation. That answer lies in party structures and organizations.

The variety of modes and concepts of representation reveals daunting complexities in political identity and in the task of representing it. The pluralist operation of group forces in an open political market, while concededly imperfect, nevertheless provides countless outlets for the expression and representation of political identity. Formalized group representation, in contrast, institutionalizes, rigidifies, and ossifies those political identities, most likely in an inaccurate and simplistic way. As a result, it makes effective representation more difficult to actually achieve.

What is needed are subsystems of representation that permit these fundamental questions to be resolved politically rather than "scientifically." Those systems are present in the representation paradigm in the recognition of political parties as institutions of representation. Party systems provide a compelling alternative to the representative challenges of pluralism. Parties are uniquely constituted and situated to reconcile the contradictory goals of individual political autonomy and the need for group influence. Party subsystems enhance group influence indirectly, as group facilitators, diffusers of faction, and balancers of majority rule and minority rights. Recognizing parties as functionally distinctive in their representative capacity, this alternative seeks to invigorate parties and enhance their ability to operate as vehicles of group effectiveness. *In the end, a set of political subsystems in the form of parties and groups is better equipped than a legal system of group representation to consolidate the network of representational forms and practices, and to secure a more effective system of political representation.*

THE GROUP RIGHT TO REPRESENTATION: BALKANIZATION THROUGH LAW?

Group representation proposals must confront a central theoretical objection: whether the basic aims of a liberal democracy can be attained by accentuating group differences. Unity and the general welfare are not exclusive ends in themselves, but are also means to the realization of liberal values of individual equality, liberty, and dignity. Feelings of solidarity stem from a shared civic identity, a sense of being bonded together. Those passions instill in individuals and groups a larger perspective, a respect and concern for the welfare and well-being of individuals and groups who do not share the same particularized concerns. This interconnectedness between groups and individuals permits a heterogeneous people to settle on a collective definition of the common good.[1]

Group representation intuitively points in the opposite direction. The setting of group against group inherent in the neopluralist strategy may only fragment our politics.[2] Its focus is on the particularized interests of groups, and it emphasizes categories of peoples. Its tendency is to condition people to think in terms of their group's perspective, circumstances, and interests. Instead of cultivating an appreciation for others' welfare, it reinforces and hardens the separatist pull of diversity and the natural instinct of self-interest.[3] The result is a system of discrete, distinct interests held and advanced by groups. Its outcome is a compartmentalized society of peoples who feel deprived of meaningful political input until the system takes explicit cognizance of them. As Cynthia Ward puts it, group representation makes it:

> less likely that citizens will take seriously their duty to regard and treat each other as equal human beings who have the capacity to agree on, and work toward, common societal goals. . . . In short, group representation is deeply destructive of successful republican community. It derives from . . . the pluralist notion that diversity can be acknowledged and empowered only through constant political battle pitting the races and genders against each other in a never-ending contest for recognition and public benefits.[4]

Proponents of group representation minimize the threat of separatism by limiting their proposals to historically oppressed minorities.[5] But even selective reliance on group representation may have the same result. The logic of its underlying behavior is that those who are "like us" must act exclusively "for us." But the flip side is that those who are unlike us will feel free to ignore our interests. Even limited forms of group representation may lead majority groups to segregate minority groups on policy issues, to sequester and ignore their interests.[6]

These objections are not merely the abstract musings of ivory tower types theoretically opposed to group representation. They are shared by lawyers and political activists working at the most

practical level. The canvassing of legal and political leaders un-
covered serious reservations about the tendency of group representation proposals to increase the division and tension between
groups.[7] The deep skepticism of those most involved in matters
of representation at the operational level is strong reason for pause
as we contemplate further resort to group representation. All
group representation proposals, therefore, are plagued by the
nagging question of how to avoid the disposition toward social
and political fragmentation. They must convince us that they will
produce legitimate policy in the public interest, and not just a
screech of clamoring self-interested groups.

GROUP REPRESENTATION: OBSTACLES IN IMPLEMENTATION

An even more daunting challenge facing interest/group representation reformers is to devise a workable design based on rational
distinctions as to which groups qualify for official representation.
The practical problems of constructing a scheme of group representation help explain the Court's traditional adherence to individualistic modes of constitutional adjudication in matters of
political rights and participation. Individualism lends itself far
better to the establishment of neutral, workable principles of constitutional jurisprudence than do group considerations. The individual is a distinct, definable empirical unit. Standards that are
gauged by the individual can be measured and applied with clarity. When groups are added to the equation, that simplicity and
clarity are lost.

Group categorizations reveal formidable practical challenges.[8]
Do fixed groups or interests actually exist? Are they quantifiable
and verifiable? And which ones are deserving of preservation in a
system of formal representation? Interests or groups might be catalogued by organization, scope of activities, political or monetary
resources, functions, or any of a host of other determinants. Each
carries with it a perplexing set of ramifications for questions of
establishing representation.[9]

Consider, for example, the basis for the decisions in campaign finance, the typing of groups pursuant to political resources.
Creating a typology around political resources to equalize group
influence would be no easy task. It is not enough simply to equalize monetary resources. Electoral and organizational resources may
be equally important to political effectiveness.[10] Moreover, while

political resources such as membership size and financial assets are easily quantifiable, intangibles such as prestige, organizational strength, cohesion, and leadership, are more nebulous and difficult to quantify. Furthermore, the importance of each in assigning representation is murky. Is a group rich in these resources less in need of formal representation? Should a group that exhibits political savvy and the ability to engage in the necessities of politics be penalized for its effectiveness? In short, classifying and handicapping groups according to political resources quickly becomes complicated. Selecting and defining the proper benchmarks of measuring political equality in resources among groups is extremely problematic.

Other typologies are equally challenging. How does one assess the pertinence of organizational traits to representational issues? Different organizational aspects have different consequences for the validity of group claims to representation.[11] What are the members' roles, responsibilities, and relations with other members and the group leadership? How is the leadership constituted? Is the decisionmaking process of the organization authoritarian or democratic? Does the organization evidence a capacity for entering into coalitions with other groups? How formal and permanent is the organization? The answers to these questions have repercussions for conferring representation.

Equally perplexing questions could be raised for a typology based on a specific subject or interest area, group function, motive, or something else.[12] Each typology presents a myriad of complex determinations, which exceed the rational capabilities of our governmental institutions. Furthermore, to consolidate or incorporate multiple typologies would magnify those complexities exponentially. Moreover, the determination of group status occurs in a dynamic environment, not a static one. Groups and interests are fluid and ever-changing. They emerge, evolve, or fade away with each policy debate. Institutional arrangements would compel constant adjustment of the assignments and weighting of group representation.

In sum, a model of group representation faithful to the democratic ideal of individual equality appears to be empirically unattainable. Group representation presupposes that systematic inequalities in individual influence can be neutralized by taking note of group status.[13] This is possible only if we operate from the flawed premise that all individuals within a group are in precisely the same posture.[14] This oversimplifies group structures and

ignores the complexities of multiple affiliations and disparities in
intensity of group association. Regardless of how the group is
defined, its members are positioned differently. Consequently, according official representative status will give some in the group
too much and others not enough. Group status "cannot be determined independently of the degree of disadvantage of the individuals who are and are not members of the group."[15] This is
empirically impossible to execute. Group rights are:

> grossly unjust as applied to specific individuals within those
> groups. Application would almost certainly be both over-
> inclusive and underinclusive, granting significant benefits to
> many who did not need or deserve them and discriminating
> against many who badly merited greater solicitude.[16]

If the goal of pluralism ultimately is to foster individual equality, then the goal of group equality as an end becomes difficult to
justify, and worse, the empirical obstacles become fatal. Nor are
the empirical difficulties avoided by limiting the scope of group-
based representational arrangements to dispossessed groups
blocked out of existing structures. Group claims based on a history of discrimination have assumed that inclusion in the group
is sufficient evidence of a socially determined disadvantage. But
the goal of individual equality still demands that we take into account specific individual disadvantages.[17]

Selective group representation only raises a different set of
problems. How do we determine which groups are oppressed?[18]
The system has always been armed with filters that allow certain
groups in, while restricting others. Politics is the triumph of certain groups at the expense of others. The exclusion of groups is
made on any number of grounds, the propriety of which is not
always clear. While there is near-universal consensus that exclusion based on race or sex is inappropriate, other groups may be
barred for seemingly legitimate reasons. Limiting the scope to
suppressed groups still requires a determination of what constitute valid grounds for suppressing groups.[19]

But what is the basis for courts and legislatures to make these
distinctions? Is there a moral framework, whereby who is admitted or banned depends on the moral worth of their underlying
claims or characteristics? And does the state have the authority or
ability to decide which group claims are more deserving? These
decisions have generally been left to the operation of the free
markets of politics, except where the basis for group exclusion is

so clearly unjustified and blatant as to warrant government intervention. Lack of influence may be self-inflicted, the result of organizational flaws or shortcomings, poor leadership, inactive
membership, or poor marshalling or use of resources. It may be
the consequence of the group's failure or refusal to engage in
practical politics, or to do it well.[20] It may even be a conscious
group strategy to bypass political channels, and opt instead for
legal avenues to achieve their objectives. Groups often choose to
wage their battles for legitimacy in courts instead of in legislatures or the realm of public opinion.

In sum, discerning the real sources of political ineffectiveness
and deciding whether they warrant a remedial form of group representation requires a depth and subtlety of analysis beyond the
expertise of legislatures or courts (or political scientists, for that
matter). It wrongly assumes that equality of group influence can be
reduced to scientific determinations. Proposals of group representation forget that certain basic questions are essentially political and
not susceptible to scientific or objective analysis. Basic criteria of
fairness and representation depend largely on the attitudes and
actions of citizens. As such, the "basis of people's right to choose
'their own' representatives . . . can be decided only in the political
(and constitution-making) arena, not at the analysts' desks."[21]

The pluralist operation of group forces in an open political
market, while concededly imperfect, nevertheless provides countless outlets for the expression and representation of political identity. A legal construct of group-based rights to representation, in
contrast, ossifies and hardens those political identities, making
effective representation more difficult to achieve. Unlike the "scientific" distillation of group rights, subsystems of representation
permit these fundamental questions to be resolved politically.
These systems are premised on the unique ability of parties to
reconcile the contradictory goals of individual political autonomy
and the need for group influence. It is those theoretical attributes
of parties to which we now turn.

PARTY SUBSYSTEMS AS INSTITUTIONAL
REPRESENTATIONAL LINKAGES

The pluralist dilemma demands systematic means of facilitating
the advancement of a range of group interests, while simultaneously protecting against imbalance in the influence of those

voices. The two basic criticisms of neopluralist strategies, the theoretical weakness tending toward separatism and the practical problem of feasibility, suggest the same conclusion, the need for intermediate systems of representation. These flaws are alleviated by representative subsystems that operate on two levels: as absorbers and refractors of *interests,* and as molders and reconcilers of *influence.* While pressure groups intensify individual preferences and offer a partial perspective, intermediate subsystems enlarge the partial perspective through aggregation, consensus, compromise, and civic education. At the same time, those substructures correct inequities between collectivities. The same associational traits of compromise, of enlightening and broadening particular interests, and of enlarging the interests pursued, give voice to interests that deserve to be heard.

Our purpose is not to attempt a formal theory of political parties, the organizational structures that have traditionally fulfilled that role.[22] Nor is it to suggest that parties are the ideal solution to the pluralist dilemma. They are highly imperfect and erratic in their performance, which is reflected in the low standing of parties among the electorate. But having issued that admonition, we now explore those aspects of party theory that support their primary importance in meshing individual, group, and state into a representative pluralist democracy. Party subsystems enhance group influence indirectly, as group facilitators, diffusers of faction, and balancers of majority rule and minority rights. Despite their flaws, party systems are essential to accommodate the competing strands of representation, and to engender a richer, more effective system of representation.

Political Parties as Group Facilitators

The case for party subsystems rests on a symbiotic relationship between political parties and pressure groups. Groups are not excluded from party systems, but are essential to them and channeled through them.[23] Parties and political associations depend on each other as intermediate representative linkages between individuals and government. Party structures bind the parties and other politically interested groups, whereby political benefits flow to lesser groups via energized, vitalized political parties. Not only are the parties themselves manifestations of collective activity, but they are a vital channel through which groups of voters with shared interests can influence the process. It is groups working through parties that maintain a balance between the dual representative functions of selection and petition.

The importance of the relationship is evident in the problems that arise in its absence. Groups wield political clout outside the parties framework through a series of activities registered at points outside of the electoral process, and directly impacting policy. Without an electoral system that accommodates collective interests, groups make their case directly to legislators. As American parties have eroded, groups have pursued this strategy relentlessly. Unfortunately, the disparities in group influence and resources are amplified when group activity is unfiltered and unchecked.

The imbalance between party-group relations also explains the correlation between the declining prominence of political parties and the increased demand for formal group-based representation.[24] As long as parties played a primary role, first in getting candidates elected, and subsequently in enabling those individuals to actually govern, group claims for direct representation were muted. Groups could count on a degree of satisfaction through strong, dynamic, and influential parties. But as parties' influence diminished, direct group claims on government rose. Through lobbying and resorting to the courts, groups increasingly have attempted to achieve legislative results or legal status that parties are unable to provide.[25] Rather than reconciling their claims with other interests through political parties, groups now demand direct representation for their particular claim.

This requires that the electoral system be responsive to the preferences and interests of cognizable political groups. Responsible parties are the theoretical tools for accomplishing that.[26] Just as individual voters gain voice by banding together with others who share their preferences, so group participants find electoral expression through parties. Just as individual votes acquire significance when exercised as part of a collective choice, parties are the means by which groups band together to wield electoral power. Parties serve as prisms through which a spectrum of group interests are combined and melded into political power. Through party affiliation, groups organize and amplify their political strength to exert influence on the system.

The symbiotic relationship between parties and other groups stems from a fundamental distinction in their respective motives and organizational character. Parties are motivated by a desire to gain control of power by winning public office through elections.[27] That desire generates their policy positions. Groups are motivated by an interest in particular policies. They seek influence so that their policies will be enacted. Their desire for policy outcomes drives their political behavior.[28] These divergent motivations create a set of systems in which parties and associations are necessary to the accomplishment of the goals of each other. The relationship is one of mutually beneficial support. The parties provide a path to influence for groups because of their goal of winning elections. The parties' primary goal is to draw enough groups of ample size and strength to construct "an election-day partisan coalition."[29]

Voters with common interests find their voice in the system through their value to the parties' efforts to build that coalition. To garner votes from a variety of groups, parties are forced to air their concerns, through policy proposals, platforms, or doling out influential positions in the party or the governing administration. The parties' intellectual component reflects the ideology, philosophy, and policy stances of the groups in their coalitions. Even when parties behave only roughly in this fashion, they provide a partial solution to our neglect of "the intermediate institutions that stand between the individual and the state."[30] As structural buffers between citizens and the impersonal bureaucratic state, cohesive parties have an unparalleled facility for articulating the concerns of all groups in society, legitimizing the political system in the process.[31]

The party-centered system does not operate as a mutually exclusive alternative to direct political activity by groups. Groups still occupy a crucial role in enriching and attaining representation. Even the most vital parties cannot satisfy completely the need for, or the needs of, other intermediate entities. The pluralist vision of politics and society makes it unlikely that parties can satisfactorily accommodate the full array of group forces. The public is neither an undifferentiated whole nor comprised purely of discrete, atomistic individuals. It is actually many publics, each more or less organized, identifying its political interest, and pursuing it. The more complex the society, the greater the number of publics that comprise *the public*, and the greater the challenge for parties as representative organizations. Parties must pick and choose, prioritizing the importance of various groups to their coalition, and consequently excluding many altogether. Thus the need for groups to still act outside party systems, to seek access directly when the parties are unable to meet that need. But in the dual system of representation, groups supplement rather than replace parties in representing otherwise unrecognized interests.

Groups acting in the *petitioning* mode of representation perform important functions. First, they allow individual citizens to aggregate their voices. Individual voices, so diffused as to be undiscernible if unmediated, are clarified and amplified in group form. Second, collective activity gives the legislator a means of involving citizens in the policy process. Individual preferences expressed in group form can be gauged by the legislator to determine their place in policy considerations. Finally, groups facilitate the flow of information between legislator and constituent, information necessary to the performance of official representative duties.[32]

Groups, therefore, wield leverage within and outside the parties. They are influential in recruiting and supporting candidates and in getting them elected, and help the public express itself electorally.[33] But this is the vaguest, most minimally comprehensible form of public communication. The representative also is affected and persuaded to act through the level of organization within his constituency. The political organizational life in the district informs and directs legislative action.[34] The confluence of activity by well-organized groups in the selection of leaders, and in pressure politics bearing on those leaders, is a critical element of connecting the governed to their governors.

But this is a supplemental, not a primary, mode of representation. When direct influence is the principal form of group activity, the collective inequities at the core of the pluralist dilemma are accentuated. Parties as group facilitators counterbalance overly influential groups, providing a forum for groups with competing interests. An equilibrium in group influence is possible only when party subsystems provide political entry for a greater number and diversity of groups.

The Answer to Faction

The potential for increased tensions in schemes of formal group representation points to a second benefit of party subsystems. Parties are uniquely positioned to dampen the factional tendencies of intensified group participation. Excessive factionalism has long been thought to present a substantial danger to effective governance.[35] Madison's primary fear was of a particular faction dominating the political landscape, garnering political power far beyond its numbers, and threatening both the will of the majority and the concerns of other minorities.[36] That fear has been displaced by apprehension over fragmentation of the public interest into competing demands of countless self-interested factions.

Talk of enhanced sensitivity to group interests fuels such visions of group conflict. It conjures up images of a free-for-all between collective interests, creating a political arena characterized by excessive conflict and marginal accomplishments. Detractors of interest groups and PACs paint a picture of public servants handcuffed by the pressure imposed on them by powerful private groups. In contrast, party structures disposed to granting recognition to groups have the constructive effect of bringing to the surface group conflict which already exists, but at a level often out of the eye of public scrutiny.

The contemporary political process is rampant with group influence. PAC funding of campaigns and intensive lobbying are at the heart of contemporary politics. These are legitimate forms of political participation, not necessarily inconsistent with Madison's attempts to diffuse factions by playing them against each other. The contemporary pluralist spin on Madison's treatment of factions recognizes competition between groups as a positive democratic force. But it is tempered by the qualification that the groups granted access to the playing field be diverse and representative of society. The capacity to generate sound policy is contingent on a wide range of groups being heard. The greater the spectrum of ideas and preferences brought to bear on policymakers, the sounder the policy outputs will be.[37]

This is precisely the prospect that stirs the fear of fragmentation. Just as unmediated individual participation is criticized for diffusing electoral behavior so that it is indecipherable[38], so the group equivalent is vulnerable to similar critiques. The fear is that the unchanneled input of too many collective voices will cause a level of dissonance that renders political consensus and compromise impossible.

At this point, the unique capacity of party systems to mitigate the tensions of pluralism becomes clearer. Parties provide a release for the pressures of competing groups on the system. They become the conduit for focusing and reconciling the competing claims of groups. The struggle is moved off the center stage of policy-making and into the side arenas of partisan politicking, through caucuses, conventions, and platforms. Group claims within party organizations are not an either-or proposition, as might be required at the policy-making stage. Rather, platforms and party proposals permit a comprehensive program sensitive to the diverse needs of different groups.

In this way, parties act as a palliative, moderating and diffusing group conflict.[39] Group activity need not mean warfare between purely self-interested groups bombarding the policy-makers. Rather, parties push conflict to an earlier point in the process, avoiding ultimate resolution between competing claims, and instead accommodating various groups within the context of a cohesive program. Ralph Goldman explains:

> The process for the most part requires leaders who know how to be political brokers, groups that know how to compromise, and institutional forums and procedures, such as legislatures or party conventions, in which leaders and followers may communicate. The election system must compel them to communicate, and *parties must organize the competing constituencies to achieve the election outcomes required if they are to control the government.*[40]

An additional reason for focusing on parties as the center of group politics is the avoidance of the raft of difficult questions as to how to delineate those groups that warrant recognition. Those troublesome questions are alleviated through party systems. Groups acquire voice by successfully making their case to a political party. They command attention by organizing and maximizing their electoral clout and demonstrating to the party their value as part of the coalition. Thus do they merit recognition and gain influence within the party structure. The model, therefore, is one of competition between representative groups within the framework of the party system of representation.

Parties and the Balance Between Minority Voice and Majority Rule

Parties also are the key to resolving the critical tension between unity and diversity, and the contradictory demands of individual and collective. That tension is manifested in the counterweights of majority rule and minority voice.[41] Our electoral system of territorial districts and "one person one vote" is predicated upon majoritarian values and principles.[42] Yet our pluralist heritage presupposes a sensitivity to minority interests and concerns. It seeks to elevate the individual voice to a discernible level even when one belongs to no majority.

These contradictory themes imply the need for legislative outcomes that are simultaneously legitimized by majority support and sensitive to unique minority concerns. The goal is "parity between votes and representation sufficient to ensure that minority voices are heard and that majorities are not consigned to minority status."[43] It seeks majoritarian government, but through representation that captures the diversity of interests in society.[44]

Party subsystems are essential to reconciling these competing pulls. Popular majorities select a government through elections. Those majorities are rallied by the parties, which are loosely formed combinations of minority voices.[45] Parties mobilize and represent a definable majority, and translate it into a governing regime. That party which successfully reflects the majority is rewarded with the tools of governance. The parties are organized to govern and take responsibility for that power. It is this character that transforms majority preferences into majority rule.

But parties also accommodate diverse interests. While officially tools of unity and majority rule, they unofficially are pluralistic, promoting direct democracy and inviting diversity. Through their collective structure and representative nature, parties at once give coherence to majoritarian government and voice to minority interests.[46]

DO PARTIES REALLY ACT LIKE THIS?: A CAVEAT

One important caveat must be injected. This discussion admittedly presupposes a view of the political parties that fails to comport with reality in significant ways. Parties are susceptible to a variety of criticisms questioning their abilities to function in ways that are consistent with the party systems model I have set out. For one, they are prone to anti-democratic tendencies. Groups operating within the party system still must be large and mobilized enough to make their presence felt. Legitimate group interests that cannot meet that threshold of electoral clout may be neglected or drowned out, and go unrepresented in a party-based system.

Moreover, the parties' present characteristics and modes of operation are a far cry from the party systems ideal. History confirms the danger of parties that are too democratic. They may become diffused to the point of impeding the realization of a cohesive intellectual program (e.g., the Democrats in 1984). Likewise, a highly motivated, organized group may acquire influence within the party not justified by its numbers (e.g., the Christian Right and the Republicans in 1992). Both circumstances present challenges to the parties' representative character.[47]

Finally, the discussion suggests a level of intellectual clarity and cohesion which the parties have not achieved in recent years, if ever. Parties have been much maligned for perceived shortcomings in their substantive makeup. For decades, they have endured criticism for lacking the intellectual coherence and programmatic character that would allow a responsible two-party system to work as envisioned.[48] Hence, the perception of the two major parties as "Tweedledee and Tweedledum," without a dime's worth of difference between them. Not until the Republican takeover of Congress in 1995 had there been any persuasive evidence to the contrary. The new Republican majority has proven, at least in the short term, to be remarkably cohesive, disciplined, and programmatic; in short, it has come close to matching the "responsible party government" model. It remains to be seen whether this programmatic character can be maintained, or whether the Democrats will follow suit.

These weaknesses have contributed to the parties' lack of standing with a variety of constituencies. Their declining salience within the electorate is well documented, and is attributable, at least in part, to their failure to offer a convincing substantive portrait of themselves to the voters. The case for parties as key representative devices in pluralist democracy rests on their ability to act responsibly and democratically. The parties often fail to exhibit those characteristics.[49]

The public's disenchantment with parties is shared by other important segments of society. Both the media and the politicians themselves routinely castigate the parties for their inability to perform effectively. Even more sophisticated observers share these concerns to a degree. The experts and practitioners surveyed as part of this project expressed the same concerns. They are inflicted with a certain ambivalence regarding the parties' capacity to perform in the manner described herein.[50] Nevertheless, this did not deter the experts from generally being desirous of ways to amplify the influence of political parties on the policy-making process.[51]

Hence, the Court must be constantly mindful of the inability of parties to fit the model, and the low regard for parties which their failings breed in various circles. The public sentiments and the attitudes of legal and political practitioners serve as dampers on what we can expect to accomplish. While they ought not to deter the Court from the all-important task of searching for optimal structures of representation, they shape the ways in which we seek to accomplish that goal, and the rate at which we proceed.

Enthusiasm for the party systems alternative should be tempered by the acknowledgment of parties' lack of popularity and acceptance among many Americans. The ideal way for parties to empower individuals is to entice them into action at the grassroots level. Yet it is at this level where parties are suffering their greatest decline. One must query how effective changes in constitutional doctrine will be as long as parties are on the wane on the most fundamental and personal level for most Americans.

Having offered that disclaimer, the weaknesses of the parties can be ascribed to, and are understandable in light of, their theoretical position in pluralism. If the political galaxy exists in, and is derivative of, a complex, group-constituted society, one must question how programmatic and substantively well-defined the parties can be, and still fulfill their pluralist role of integrating and mediating a broad array of groups. To maintain their viability and remain competitive, parties must incorporate as many groups as necessary to win. This can be accomplished only by dulling the sharp ideological edges of the parties and dampening the ideological bent of any single group.[52]

The threnody over the present state of the parties fails to appreciate their dual functions of amplifying and muffling group voices, providing a forum for groups, but also checking group activity. Alfred de Grazia describes the inherent tension between party pluralism and pure group pluralism:

> Since each party must treat its samples of the political cosmos family in order that they may be adequate samples, the voice of each as an *interest* tends to become weaker while its voice as a group of *interested individuals* tends to grow stronger. American party pluralism, in other words, tends to sap the vitality of essential pluralism and that is why proper pluralists have never been happy with party pluralism.[53]

Hence, our unhappiness with the parties may be because they are performing their role within the pluralist model too well.

Political parties do perform the necessary functions, albeit crudely and clumsily. They are representative and democratic, though in an imperfect form. They exhibit a penchant for self-correction that, while often slow to respond, eventually pushes them in the right direction. In the absence of other players on the political landscape that can bring to the game those qualities that political parties imperfectly embody, we have no alternative but to accept them, warts and all. Despite the flaws in our contemporary parties, a vigorous party system is better equipped to accommodate the range of competing strands of representation and to engender a richer, more effective system of representation.

CONCLUSION

The set of political subsystems in the form of parties and groups is better equipped than a legal system of group representation to consolidate the network of representational forms and practices, and to secure a more effective system of political representation. The pluralist dilemma points to the singular functional qualities of party subsystems. The tensions between collective political involvement and individual political existence which characterize pluralism are answerable only through parties. Mediating parties palliate the inherent contradictions of representative democracy in a way that factions and groups cannot.

Party subsystems also provide the answer to the riddles and complexities of political representation, belonging "first and foremost to the means of representation."[54] They express the demands and desires of people and groups, while simultaneously channelling those desires.[55] As *expressors* and *channellers* of popular opinion, their functional character is unmatched by other groups. As a result, they are singularly constituted to weave together the patchwork of representational threads and cloths.

One may be dissatisfied with the dissimilarity between the model and the reality of parties. That disparity is certainly relevant when considering legal responses to the dilemmas of representation. But the purpose of the model is not to describe reality, but to bring into prominence basic features that might otherwise get lost in the complexity of descriptive accounts.[56] We must now assess whether the Supreme Court adequately accounts for party systems in its theory of representation. In patronage disputes, ballot access issues, and in gerrymandering cases, the party systems model set forth in this chapter has been too often ignored or disregarded by the High Court.

CHAPTER SEVEN

The Law of Reapportionment:
Party-Poor Theories of Representation

We now turn to the final element of the Court's constitutional theory of representation, its treatment of party subsystems of representation. To this point, we have noted three aspects to the Court's theory. The first was a dominant individualistic perception of politics reflected in one-person, one-vote and mathematical equality of the vote. The second was a growing awareness of the role of group politics in achieving representation, and the gradual incorporation of group considerations in the law of reapportionment. The third was a neopluralist experiment in formal group representation in campaign financing, as the Court sought to equalize the influence of groups by monitoring and controlling their financial input.

Each of these aspects reflected a deficiency in representational theory. The dominant individualism slighted the functional representative significance of collectives. The subsequent inclusion of groups in the equation occurred without a structural tool that would uniformly and consistently recognize the representative capacity of all groups. The neopluralist approach in campaign financing, while well-intended, falls prey to the insurmountable theoretical and pragmatic challenges of formal group representation.

The preceding discussion of party systems indicates that each of these imbalances could be rectified by giving greater credence to party structures of representation. We now turn to several areas of constitutional law to explore the extent to which the Court has relied upon party structures to enrich its conceptualization of representation. Unfortunately, a careful examination of the Court's decisions reveals a consistent neglect of party structures as structural components of representation. The Court lacks a vision that includes political parties' institutional role in realizing representation.

This oversight is evidenced by a haphazard, inconsistent treatment of parties in different contexts. In some instances, such as campaign finance, parties are notably absent from the entire discussion. At other times, parties are included, but are either indistinguishable from or subordinated to other groups. Finally, in areas involving the weighing of state regulatory rights with the representative roles and rights of parties (ballot access, party autonomy), the result is a jumble of cases in which parties have no clearly defined representative function.

Taken in their totality, these cases suggest the Court is less guilty of adopting an overtly anti-party theory of representation than of adopting a theory in which the parties are simply absent. In short, they indicate that the Court has no coherent theory of political parties. Absent a heightened appreciation for party systems in representation, the Court has no mechanism for *constraining* and *facilitating* the influence and effectiveness of groups.

THE SUBORDINATION OF PARTIES IN REDISTRICTING LAW

We first return to the key reapportionment decisions, in which the Court had begun to delineate spheres of specific rights for limited groups and associations. These cases reveal the Court's tendency to treat parties as simply another interest group, sometimes even subordinating them to other groups.

This was first evident in *Gaffney v. Cummings*,[1] in which the Court scrutinized a 1970 redistricting plan drawn for the Connecticut General Assembly. The purpose underlying the plan was to roughly reflect the proportionate strength of the two major political parties in the state. Based on demographic data from previous elections, it was drawn to approximate the actual statewide plurality of votes in both state houses.[2] The Court rejected a Republican challenge to the plan that had alleged an unconstitutional partisan gerrymander. Instead, the Court approved of gerrymandering used affirmatively to ensure fair treatment of both parties.

In one respect, the decision was sympathetic to parties, as the Court lauded the recognition of the parties' relative strength in seeking a rough sort of proportional representation in the legislative halls of the state. In sanctioning the affirmative use of partisan data, the Court left room for state mapmakers to give greater emphasis to the role of parties in representative government. The opinion did not explicitly address the representative function of parties, but implicitly acknowledged the political representation that occurs at the party level. Invoking the *Reynolds* goal of "fair and effective representation," the Court inferred the relationship between the party system (as bolstered by a "political fairness" redistricting standard) and that objective.[3]

But the text of the decision contained little evidence of a deeper appreciation for parties as systems of representation. In fact, dicta reflected an assumption that parties were no different in their representative capacity than other groups. The Court expressed approval of plans that reflected the "political strength of any *group* or *party*,"[4] voicing its disapproval of plans that fenced out "racial or political groups" from the political process.[5] The significance of Connecticut's efforts pertained to "racial or political elements," not to political parties per se. The decision did not mention the positive attributes of political parties, or why the Connecticut approach was a worthy one. It spoke of parties in neutral, value-free terms and language. It neither encouraged nor discouraged the "political fairness" approach to parties, but merely validated it. The *Gaffney* Court neither rejected nor required rough proportional representation of parties in redistricting.[6] It passively accepted the state's use of partisan data to ensure fair treatment of the parties.

The Court's tendency to categorize parties together with other political collectivities, evident in *Gaffney*, continued in *Bandemer*. Recall that *Bandemer* involved a Fourteenth Amendment equal protection challenge by the Indiana Democratic Party, alleging that the plan drafted by the Republican majority unconstitutionally impaired the Democrats' right to fair representation. As such, it directly implicated the formal status of parties, and offered the Court a rare opportunity to clarify their place in matters of representation. On one hand, the Court responded with a discernible shift toward balancing the traditional electoral individualism with an infusion of group-compensating considerations.[7] But at the same time it gave the parties short shrift as tools for incorporating those group considerations.

The Court again casually lumped parties together with other political groups. Its focus was not on gerrymandering discrimination against a political party per se, but against a political group that just happened to be a party. The claim found to be justiciable was not specific to parties, but involved the right of "each *political group* in a state [to have] . . . the same chance to elect representatives of its choice as any other *political group*."[8] The issue at stake was not party-specific, but "whether a particular *group* has been unconstitutionally denied its chance to effectively influence the political process."[9]

Justice O'Connor's concurrence similarly treated parties as interchangeable with other groups. She found the plurality's result unpalatable precisely because she could not perceive of parties differently than other political groups. She cautioned that:

> If members of the major political parties are protected by the Equal Protection Clause from dilution of their voting strength, then members of every identifiable group that possesses distinctive interests and tends to vote on the basis of those interests should be able to bring similar claims. Federal courts will have no alternative but to attempt to recreate the complex process of legislative apportionment in the context of adversary litigation in order to reconcile the competing claims of political, religious, ethnic, racial, occupational, and socio-economic groups.[10]

In O'Connor's view, political parties were indistinguishable from any other political group.[11] She saw no theoretical or functional grounds for treating parties dissimilarly from religious, economic, ethnic, or professional groups.

More importantly, the practical effect of the Court's resolution of the group claim in *Bandemer* demonstrated a subconscious bias in favor of other political groups to the detriment of political parties. The Court was willing to find a constitutional violation only when there was a "lack of political power and the denial of fair representation."[12] This necessitated a showing that the group had been essentially shut out of the political process on a statewide level.[13] The practical effect of this standard was to effectively render the group right to representation a nullity with respect to the major political parties.

If other courts were to adhere to a literal interpretation of *Bandemer* (as a California district court did in *Badham v. Eu*[14]), it is difficult to imagine when the two major parties might ever prevail on a gerrymandering claim. The standard articulated by the

Court in *Bandemer* requires a total "lack of political power" and
proof that a party has been *wholly shut out of the process.* Even in
the strongest single-party state, the minority party occupies legislative seats and exercises a marginal degree of influence. Neither
party will be "locked out of the process" to a degree that would
allow it to establish an actionable gerrymander.[15] The statewide
"lack of political power" requirement renders the constitutional
restrictions on political gerrymandering of little utility or applica-
bility to the parties in the contemporary political landscape.[16]

   Bandemer was something less than a ringing condemnation
of political gerrymandering.[17] In comparison to the potentially
wide-ranging impact the decision might have for political groups
generally, its application specifically to political parties is clearer.
It holds no special place for the parties as beneficiaries of a group
right to representation. In a solitary reference, Justice White acknowledged that "the individual voter gains significance in elections only through collective strength as supporter of party."[18] The
remainder of the opinion failed to demonstrate a deeper understanding of why and how that is indeed the case.

PARTY SYSTEMS: MISSING LINKS IN THE COURT'S THEORY OF REPRESENTATION

The Court's failure to acknowledge the value of party structures in
elections revealed a fundamental flaw in its understanding of political representation and how it is attained. The explicit objective
of *Bandemer* was "fair and effective representation." But did the Court
move closer to that goal, in light of the representational paradigm
previously set forth? Was it cognizant of the many sides of representation? Or did it obfuscate the goal of effective political representation by espousing simplistic assumptions that failed to comport
with political reality? Ultimately, it rendered an incomplete portrait
of representation, relying upon conflicting, unrealistic, and incomplete assumptions as to the nature of representation. The Court's
refusal to rein in gerrymandering with regard to the parties specifically ignored the parties' institutional value in assuring principles
and precepts at the center of democratic government.

The Court's Understanding of Collective (Party) Representation

Bandemer subtly demonstrated the neopluralist strains that exist in
the Court's theory of representation, and that operate to the
exclusion of party-regarding considerations. The decision was

constructed around the flawed axiom that parties and other political associations are fungible and indistinguishable. The utilization of a standard that dismissed the singular role of parties in elections and governance illustrates the serious theoretical and practical pitfalls for democratic efficacy and legitimacy that exist when parties are not properly accounted for.

Representation is multidimensional, with individualistic and collective facets. The choice of representatives occurs individually (through the casting of equally weighted votes) and corporately (through an electoral scheme that permits groups of voters with shared interests to band together to select their preferred representative). Likewise, representational activity occurs individually (as individual legislator represents individual constituents) and collectively (as individuals and groups are represented by the legislative body as a whole). These individual and collective dimensions are conciliated through the active participation of intermediate representative structures, namely political parties and interest groups.

Both the corporate and individual aspects of representation surfaced in *Bandemer*. In *Gaffney*, the Court had evidenced a tacit appreciation for the collective dimensions of representation as measured by party strength statewide. In *Bandemer*, the Court focused on groups of voters' influence statewide, and the plan's impact on "the voters' direct or indirect influence on the elections of the state legislature as a whole."[19] Those alleging impairment of their influence were required to show "lack of political power and the *denial of fair representation*."[20] Not only did this standard understate the role of parties as intermediate systems of representation, but it neglected the importance of collective legislative action in achieving representation.

The consequences of the Court's blurring of the distinctions between parties and other associations are subtle, but significant. They are made clearer by a closer examination of the Court's linking of fair representation to a group's statewide political power. In *Bandemer*, this meant that, despite egregious gerrymanders within several of Indiana's multi-member House districts, the Democrats' failure to present more compelling evidence of *statewide* discriminatory effect doomed their claim.[21]

While the benchmark of statewide power might make sense for political groups generally, with respect to parties it submerges the critical role of parties-in-government. To pass constitutional muster, a plan need only assure party *presence* statewide, and need not be concerned with party *strength* (as measured by the number of seats in relation to votes received). Party presence recognizes parties as tools for *influencing* policy-makers, but ignores their role as instruments for *controlling* policy-making within government. It treats party presence statewide as a guarantee of effective influence on policy outcomes. This slights the role of parties as representative agencies within government that control policy processes and in large part dictate their outcomes. In a majoritarian system, this is a serious oversight.

If one measure of representation is a system that produces results in response to people's needs and desires, recognition of parties as principal players within government is essential. The parties have continued to maintain a degree of vitality and importance within government that they have been unable to sustain amongst the electorate itself.[22] This is currently on display in the impressive cohesion of the new Republican Congressional majority as well as the spirited opposition of the Democratic Party. Parties remain a "durable means for organizing and conducting congressional business,"[23] as evidenced by party-line voting and party cohesion within Congress.

This means that majority party status is crucial to legislative success. The likelihood of translating a policy agenda into legislative outputs depends on party control of the legislature. Again, consider the complete transformation of the legislative priorities once the Republicans took control of Congress in January 1995. Majority status greatly enhances the odds of success, while the minority is relegated to opposition status, sustaining vetoes, and generally adopting an obstructionist role. Since party control of government is central to directing government, statewide *presence* of a party does little to achieve that. For partisan voters who comprise a majority in the electorate but only a minority in government, statewide *presence* falls far short of *control* of policy.

The Court overlooked other essential differences between parties and other political associations. While other groups petition government, parties alone fill the institutional role of assuring that government is actually responsive to those petitions. *Bandemer* implicitly acknowledged parties as mirrors of political interests. But it rejected the vital representative function of parties in government, as tools for organizing legislative action, setting agendas and determining alternative responses, and controlling the use of power and distribution of political resources. In a representative form of government, this is a serious oversight.

If equal protection implies that "the laws and other products of the representational process correlate in some manner with the legislative goals of groups and individuals within the state,"[24] parties must be attributed due recognition as tools of governance.

Bandemer *and Individual Representation*

Bandemer is predicated upon an equally distinctive perception of the individual representative relationship, one with little basis in contemporary reality. The Court baldly asserted that winners of elections will not disregard or ignore the interests of those who supported the loser. Even those who voted for the defeated candidate could count on being "adequately represented by the winning candidate" with as much opportunity to influence the legislator as his supporters. This assumption is highly dubious, resting on a nonexistent representative ideal.

The portrait of legislators who represent all constituents equally denotes an abstract ideal of representation hardly descriptive of reality. Implicit in the Court's statement is an assumption of representatives as high-minded guardians of the public trust rather than agents merely mirroring the wishes of the constituents.[25] The legislator conscientiously gathers diverse views and opinions of all his subjects, objectively weighs them, and ultimately chooses that which will further the long-term interests of his constituents and the country. The elected official will adequately represent all constituents, since he seeks the common good to the benefit of all.[26]

Under this theory of representation, partisan gerrymandering, even if wildly successful, is unobjectionable. It minimizes the need to ensure a voice for various group interests. Representation is guaranteed by the selection of capable and judicious legislators. Group concerns will be accounted for, within the context of the common good, by well-intentioned, altruistically motivated representatives.

This ideal does not fit the contemporary legislator. The behavior of modern legislators falls somewhere between delegate and trustee. The description of legislators as "singleminded seekers of re-election," motivated primarily by their desire to win their next election,[27] is an overstated caricature. But legislators are highly sensitive to the political consequences of their actions. They are not spurred to action purely by the inherent worth of some policy, but as much by the potential for gain in public approval. The public interest, from the legislator's perspective, is not simply that which is for the good of society, but also that which satisfies the greatest number of the voters in one's district, maximizing the legislator's opportunity for electoral gain.[28]

This reality is not necessarily a debasing of our politics. It increases the responsiveness of legislators, at least to segments of their constituents. But it calls into question the Court's view of winners and losers as having equal input and influence. People vote in elections precisely because who wins has consequences. The victor, once in office, will favor his supporters with greater access and by giving priority to their preferences. The prudent legislator interested in retaining office will curry the favor of those who elected him and pursue action that will solidify their support. He will be hard pressed to pursue the agenda of those who did not vote for him, and risk alienating his supporters.

The theoretical justification for periodic democratic elections is that they serve as expressions of majority preference for one program or set of ideas over another. No politician will interpret the results as requiring that she give equal attention to the losers. Rather, she will act as she would expect a majority of her constituents to. This is the essence of representative government. Only Justice Powell in his dissent readily acknowledged this:

> It defies political reality to suppose that members of a losing party have as much political influence over state government as do members of the victorious party. Even the most conscientious state legislators do not disregard opportunities to reward persons or groups who were active supporters in their election campaigns. Similarly, no one doubts that partisan considerations play a major role in the passage of legislation and the appointment of state officers.[29]

It distorts political reality to say that who wins has little to do with the representation, respectively, of winning and losing voters.[30] The Court's resort to this skewed view only heightens the barriers to an accurate understanding of representation.

Party and Representation: An Alternative View

A contrasting theory of representation was found in Justice O'Connor's concurrence. O'Connor categorically rejected the plurality's reliance on statewide party representation. Yet she erred in the opposite direction, grounding representation solely in a personal relationship to the exclusion of collective party representation.

> The new group right created by today's decision is particu-
> larly unjustifiable in the context of the claim here which is
> founded on a supposed diminution of the *statewide* voting
> influence of a political group. . . . *To treat the loss of candidates*
> *nominated by the party of a voter's choice as a harm to the indi-*
> *vidual voter, when that voter cannot vote for such candidates and is*
> *not represented by them in any direct sense, clearly exceeds the limits*
> *of the Equal Protection Clause.*[31]

O'Connor's narrow view of representation was firmly rooted
in the classic liberal mold. She rejected the notion that a party-
affiliated voter is represented by other elected members of her
own party. Individual voters are represented directly by the legislator elected from their district. In contrast to the plurality's preoccupation with group influence statewide, O'Connor dismissed
altogether statewide dilution of party influence as a factor. While
the plurality slighted the importance of party control of government, O'Connor virtually discarded parties within government
altogether.

O'Connor's view of representation offers a deficient picture
of party influence. Despite the enfeebled nature of contemporary
parties in the electorate, the efficacy of representation remains
tied to a party that promotes a program of governance with which
the voter agrees.[32] A voter may not be *directly* represented by legislators in his party who hail from other districts. But the *indirect*
representation he receives is no less important than personal representation in achieving desired policy results. Those who support
losing candidates are forced to rely on their party statewide for
meaningful representation.

This is true whether one belongs to the majority or minority
party statewide. For those in the majority, party representation in
government is critical to legislative success.[33] For those in the minority, expression of opposing viewpoints and the ability to act as
a check on the majority rests on the minority party's statewide
strength. Political gerrymandering that discriminates against the
statewide presence of either, therefore, eviscerates the effectiveness of collective representation crucial to meaningful voting
rights. Statewide party representation must be included in the
representational equation.

Concepts of Representation in Gerrymandering Law

Much of the wrangling over the politics of linedrawing is precisely
that, partisan whining by the minority party, which invariably con-

siders itself the ill-treated victim of underhanded politics. But objections to gerrymandering have a far deeper basis, striking at the theoretical assumptions that legitimize our form of government. Those legitimizing theories include rational public choice, competition, and popular control of government. Consequently, the partisan gerrymandering controversy offers a stark lesson in the importance of a broader understanding of political representation. The Court's neglect of the party role in representation undermines the accountability and responsiveness of government, and threatens the very legitimacy of the state itself.

Weakening Formal Representation Through Gerrymandering: Parties as Tools of Authority and Accountability

The *Bandemer* slighting of parties is ironic, in light of the Court's traditional preoccupation with formal modes of representation.[34] Parties are instrumental to the achievement of meaningful forms of representation. Concepts of formal representation rest on the twin pillars of *authority* and *accountability*. Representation is assured when citizens can choose their representatives (electorally bestowing authority) and hold them accountable (through subsequent elections). The opportunity to cast a ballot and equality of the weight of one's vote are essential factors in realizing accountability and authorization between individual and constituent. But when unmediated, they cannot furnish the requisite authorization for a representative body to act, nor can they hold it accountable when it fails to. In this sense, *party systems are the group-compensating forms that permit collective authority and accountability essential to fair and effective representation.* The Court's effective preclusion of parties makes achievement of these goals much more difficult.

Parties are critical to *authorizing* representatives to act. Elections are the single point at which the public bestows its authority, registering a collective opinion on who should govern and those matters that they should address. Election results, however, are susceptible to numerous interpretations. (Some would posit that they are not susceptible to meaningful interpretation at all.) A legitimate democratic system presupposes that the public will, as reflected in the choices communicated through the electoral medium, should be manifested in the electoral consequences. Stated another way, those candidates who share the views of the electoral majority should occupy a majority of the seats in the legislature.

An electoral process that distorts those choices deprives the governors of the requisite authority to act. Choice suggests a system that is stable, systematic and competitive, criteria which the parties share. Opposing parties develop competing programs of governance, upon which the public renders its judgment in an election.[35] Although this idealizes the electorate's capacity to digest highly programmatic campaigns, parties nevertheless provide a crude mechanism for assuring democratic choice and making electoral processes intelligible. The best chance for a campaign between contending ideas that might translate into a guide to governance is still a spirited contest between energetic political parties. Regardless of how one might feel about the substance of the Contract with America that served as the Republican congressional platform for the 1994 elections, it had the undeniable effect of sharpening the issues and the party differences when Republicans chose to run on it and Democrats made it the focal point of their opposition. The 1994 election was a clear reminder that parties do provide alternatives and permit majority preferences to prevail.

Blatant gerrymandering of parties can jeopardize this critical element of democratic legitimacy. It hampers the electorate's ability to engage in rational choice. It stifles the means by which the intellectual component of parties is recognized as the source of governance. By precluding competition through manipulation of the mapmaking process, it threatens the ability of the public to exercise choice.

First, unbridled gerrymandering undercuts individual choice, eroding the ability of each voter to express a preference for a particular candidate with a fair and realistic chance that his candidate may win. The creation of safe districts in gerrymandering obliterates meaningful choice for minority party voters in that district. It undermines the exercise of electoral choice for the voters in that district who are registered with the opposing party. Real competition is seriously impeded, and sometimes eliminated altogether. Votes for the minority party in a safe district are cast without a realistic opportunity to choose their representative.[36] In the absence of real competition within a district, those voters' choices are rendered meaningless. The creation of noncompetitive districts emasculates the right to a meaningful ballot.[37]

A successful gerrymander also eliminates choice on a collective scale. When a majority vote for one party but receive a minority of the seats, their collective choice is thwarted. By frustrating the public's ability to reject a party at the polls, gerrymandering seriously limits public choice.[38] When it submerges the majority of the voters (as it did in *Bandemer* and *Badham*), it undermines the electorate's ability to render the most basic judgments through elections. If the public cannot render such judgments, it cannot authorize the elected to act. Without formal authority from the majority, legislative legitimacy is compromised, and the credibility of the entire system put at risk.

Representative government is likewise grounded in popular control and consent of the governed. It connotes institutions whose legitimacy rests upon their *responsiveness* and *accountability* to the will of the public. It is essential, therefore, that representative democratic institutions reflect and react to significant shifts in public opinion. Again, parties are active agents in ensuring that responsiveness. The two-party system is the primary tool of accountability. The principal role of party in government allows for a reasonably coherent program for governance. If the majority party pursues an irrelevant agenda or is simply ineffective, the opposing party stands ready to challenge, and to provide an electoral alternative.

The fundamental objection to partisan gerrymandering is its ability to slow or forestall representative responsiveness to the changes in the current of public sentiment.[39] Pervasive gerrymandering reduces all but the most extreme shifts in voter preference to having only minimal effect on the makeup of legislatures. The result is to nullify the public's ability to hold its governors accountable, hence discrediting the governmental actions and outcomes which follow.

The facts underlying *Bandemer* and *Badham* illustrate the point. In Indiana in the late 1970s, Republicans were voted in as a majority of both state houses. In 1982, Democrats received fifty-two percent of the vote for congressional seats, but were rewarded with just forty-three percent of the House seats. In California, the tables were turned. Democrats comprised the majority of the state legislature at the time of the 1980 census. In 1984, Republicans received over fifty percent of the vote statewide for congressional seats, but collected only forty percent of the seats. In both instances, the public initially registered its support for one party by virtue of an election. In each case, public sentiment appeared to change, as the opposing party received a majority of the statewide vote in the subsequent election. The partisan vote suggested that the public wished to hold its elected officials accountable by removing their party as the majority party. In the interregnum between elections, however, the majority party was fortunate enough to have the opportunity to redistrict. By sophisticated exploitation of that task, it avoided the transposition of the apparent shift in public opinion into a change in the composition of government. Though Indiana Democrats and California Republicans won a majority of the votes, they remained minorities in their respective legislatures, and by substantial margins.

In both cases, gerrymandering stifled the responsiveness of electoral outcomes to shifts in opinion.[40] The suppression of changes in public preferences extinguished accountability, and compromised the legitimacy of the legislatures and their accomplishments. It thwarted the very purpose of voting, which is to enable people to express their collective will, in the hope that it will result in the election of their candidates. Gerrymandering which has this effect is indefensible.[41] Districting plans that impose a partisan imbalance through gerrymandering techniques violate the "fundamental tenet of American democracy that a representative government be responsive to the changing will of the electorate."[42]

Group Rights: Elevating Reflective Representation, Minimizing Representative Activity

Bandemer also marked the continuing ascendancy of judicial sympathy for reflective modes of representation. In contrast to the formalism of one-person, one-vote and mathematical equality of the vote, the Court's expansion into political gerrymandering generally, and racial gerrymandering specifically, added the dimension of **descriptive** representation. The Voting Rights Act and the line of cases culminating in *Thornburg* denoted sympathy for representation as **reflection**. Their aim was meaningful representation for oppressed minorities. The means to that end was through the election of people who embodied the relevant racial or ethnic identity. The fundamental presupposition was the desirability of racial and ethnic groups' ability to choose representatives who are descriptive of them, who are "like them," who reflect their physical traits.

Bandemer's creation of the group right to representation was an extension of this thinking to other (as yet largely undefined) groups. It implicitly accepted **reflective** representation as an important element of effective political representation. It was important that the legislator embody or mirror those whom he represents, and that the representative assembly reflect the tangible, physical characteristics of society.

The Court's enhancement of reflective representation came at the expense of its concern for representation as activity. The failure to offer parties greater legal protection from gerrymandering practices frustrates the most important aspect of representation, that of *activity*. Representation as activity is premised upon a correlation between specific policy preferences of the represented and the ultimate policy outcomes by the representors. The stronger the relationship between outputs and preferences, the more legitimate the democratic processes which generated them. The stronger the nexus between public wishes and government action, the more representative those actions in the public's mind.[43]

Parties are necessary to achieving this. In short, they are the mechanisms by which voter preferences are translated into public policy.[44] Therefore, when the interests of an electoral majority are consigned to minority status in the legislature, the legislature and its actions become suspect. A partisan legislative majority that received less than a majority of the votes is likely to pursue policies which deviate from those held by the majority of voters who supported the opposing party. Its legislative outputs will differ from those that would have resulted had the other party garnered a working majority. Those outcomes lack the requisite democratic foundation that entitle them to full legitimacy and respect.

Some semblance of proportionality between parties and votes is crucial to safeguarding against this.[45] The Supreme Court, therefore, was on tenuous footing in *Bandemer* when it required proof of discriminatory impact in several elections for a group of voters' influence to be "consistently degraded."[46] A single skewed election result that deprives the majority of control is open to challenge on grounds of democratic legitimacy and accountability, and effectively weakens representation for that legislative term.

CONCLUSION

The partisan gerrymandering controversy was particularly significant for two reasons. First, it exposed the Court's disregard for party structures in the important area of voting and representational rights. While recognizing the need to incorporate group voices and shared interests, the Court glossed over the parties as the means to that end. As a result, parties are legally submerged in the very electoral institutions and practices from which democratic society springs.

Moreover, *Bandemer* demonstrated the threat to the efficacy of the democratic process that results when party structures are not considered. These gerrymandering disputes illustrate the perils of overlooking the unique contributions of political parties. In refusing to seriously constrain gerrymandering practices that hamper fair competition between the parties, the Court overlooked the crucial interplay between parties and other groups, and the capacity of each for turning voting into effective political participation. The result was a legal standard that inadvertently compromises the fundamental underpinnings of the democratic system. Unfortunately, this is not an isolated area of neglect. The following chapters confirm the Court's inability to recognize the importance of parties to the vitality and legitimacy of the electoral process.

CHAPTER EIGHT

Parties and State Regulation of Access to Elections: Association without Organization

The previous chapter revealed a judicial lack of understanding of political parties as integral structures of representative politics. When faced with a choice between uncurbed individual participation and a party-centered approach, the Court invariably opts for the first. When it intuits the need for collective dimensions, it mollifies those needs with neopluralist strategies to the neglect or exclusion of parties. Party structures are critical to easing the inherent tensions in the theory of representation. The Court, however, has failed to carve out a place in its constitutional theory of representation for parties as institutional bridges to the enhancement of individual and group influence.

In this chapter, we examine the rights of parties in relation to the propriety of state action to regulate elections. In particular, two categories of state laws especially impact party organizations; those defining the rights of voters to participate in primary and general elections, and ballot access guidelines determining who can run for office. Once again, the Court's attitudes in these areas reflect a legal shunting of parties as institutional channels for individuals and groups of voters, and as organizational representative linkages within government. The result is the obfuscation of fair and effective representation.

As custodians of the electoral process, states have the power to regulate voters' access to the polls, the access of third party or independent candidates to the ballot, and the behavior of the major parties. Once again, party perspectives on ballot and voter access restrictions pull in an opposite direction from individual voters' perspectives. On one side, the interest in expanding the individual's right to vote dictates removing electoral laws that limit or restrict that vote. It suggests that individuals should be free from residency requirements, party affiliation requirements, and waiting periods to vote in party primaries and general elections as they wish. It also intimates that there should be unbounded access to the ballot for any candidate in order to maximize the choices available to voters.

Juxtaposed against this are considerations designed to enhance the meaning and significance of the ballot. Mass democratic participation requires institutionalized means of focusing public opinion and determining and implementing majority preferences.[1] Limits on who can run for office and vote in party primaries are intended to clarify and shape ballot choices. Proscribing the numbers of candidates in general elections, and the labels under which they run, narrows electoral choices and gives meaning to the votes cast. It reflects a legitimate interest in ensuring a comprehensible, orderly electoral process.[2]

The decisions regarding access to elections endeavor to strike a balance between these countervailing considerations. Constitutional disputes revolve around the question of whether individual voters' freedoms should be constrained to increase the quality of the vote. The tension is between expanding choice by increasing the number of candidates from which to choose, and ensuring a more meaningful vote by limiting the size and shape of the ballot.[3]

That tension has implications for the place of parties in elections. These cases offer another stern test of the Court's ability to perceive parties as institutional building blocks of representation. Unhampered individual participation is at odds with a party-based system of regulation. The unfettered electoral participation of individuals is accomplished at the expense of the parties' ability to select and elect candidates who embrace the party label and program. Similarly, making the ballot accessible to all independent or minor party candidates detracts from a focused ballot between competing party programs and candidates.

The Court's resolution of these cases is less straightforward than in other areas we have examined. Its handling of access issues has been unsteady, as it first leaned heavily in favor of the individual right to vote, but it has since become increasingly aware of the need to mediate voter participation in order to give it significance. It has sporadically upheld ballot access requirements that rely on the two major parties to fill that need. Still, it has had difficulty seeing the parties as indispensable structural counterweights to unmediated individual democratic participation. *Ultimately, the Court has not consistently recognized parties as the institutional equipment necessary for the performance of the crucial representative functions of aggregation and mediation.*

WHO GETS TO PARTICIPATE?: THE PARTIES' RIGHT OF ASSOCIATION

The doctrine of associational rights furnishes the legal context for issues of who may participate in elections. The connection between the theory of group politics and the right of association is self-evident and all-important. Not only do people have the constitutional right to express views on political candidates and issues, but association is necessary to that end. Associations affect both the views of the public and the expression and representation of those views. *The transformation of the assortment of views and preferences into a meaningful picture of the aggregate or composite of the public is not possible without association.*

Irony resides in the doctrinal core of the Court's elucidation of associational rights. Political association suggests a cognizance of, if not a focus upon, the organizational models that represent collective political action. But the Court's individualistic explication of the right has obscured the organizational character of collective political activity. It has overlooked the relation between the participatory rights of individuals and the associational rights of the groups to which they belong, especially parties.[4] Instead, the association is "but the medium through which its individual members seek to make more effective the expression of their own views."[5]

The Court's "sum-of-its-parts" view of the right of association ignored the amplifying effect of organized political activity. Once an organizational threshold is reached, the political effectiveness of that organization exceeds the mere sum of its members. Individual influence is magnified by involvement in a political organization. Consequently, political association that is manifested organizationally should trigger constitutional protections which apply to the organizations as well as the individuals seeking realization of their political aims through them.[6]

From the outset, the Court's ruminations on political association have paralleled the dual themes present in its theory of representation. On one hand, the doctrine is thoroughly imbued with an individualistic conceptualization of political participation.[7] On the other hand, the Court's increasing tendency to infuse its analysis with group-conscious reasoning is hampered by a lack of a structural framework within which to address collective political activity. The Court initially grounded political freedom in the individual right of every citizen "to engage in political expression and association" for the purpose of advancing beliefs and ideas.[8] Those rights dwelt not in the associations, but with the individuals affiliated with them. Hence, interference with the organization was significant only as an interference with its adherents.[9]

Despite the individualistic origins of associational rights, the potential benefit for parties was substantial.[10] Those rights provided party members with new opportunities for challenging the constitutionality of a host of state regulations.[11] In recent years, parties have taken full advantage of these legal avenues, asserting their associational rights in a variety of situations to oppose state efforts to regulate them. As a result, the judiciary has had occasion to clarify and reshape the legal status of parties within the constitutional contours of the political process.

VOTER AND CANDIDATE ACCESS

The right of association was first invoked in the context of candidate access to the ballot in *Williams v. Rhodes*,[12] a case stemming from George Wallace's independent candidacy for President in 1968. Wallace and his American Independent Party had been denied a place on the ballot in Ohio under a state statute that barred independents from running and allowed new parties on the ballot only if they could petition fifteen percent of those voting in the previous election. Wallace easily surpassed the petition requirements by garnering over 450,000 signatures. The state required the petition to be filed, however, in February of the election year. Wallace did not establish his organization in Ohio until January, and obtained the requisite signatures only long after the deadline had passed.

In striking down the Ohio statute, the Court enunciated the two rights at stake in ballot access restrictions, "the right of individuals to associate for the advancement of political beliefs," and the right of qualified voters "to cast their votes effectively."[13] But while it resolved the constitutional question by reference to a distinct right of association, that right was narrowly circumscribed by the Court's earlier voting rights analysis. The result was associational rights with a markedly individualistic hue. In rejecting the petition requirements as an unfair advantage to the established parties over "new parties struggling for existence," the Court concluded that such restrictions unconstitutionally burdened "the right to vote and the right to associate."[14] The rights were held by voters and individual party members, not by the organizations themselves. What mattered was the impact on the individual's right to vote, not the candidate's or party's associational rights.[15] By placing obstacles in the path of aspiring parties and candidates, the restriction limited the right to choose between a greater array of options on the ballot.

The Court strayed from that adherence to the enlargement of voting rights in *Jenness v. Fortson*.[16] *Jenness* involved a Georgia state law which conditioned access to the ballot for candidates running outside the primary process on the filing of a petition with the signatures of at least five percent of the registered voters in the previous election. It also exempted parties from petition requirements if they had received twenty percent support in the previous election. Several candidates who could not satisfy the petition requirement challenged the exemption as a violation of equal protection.

The Court upheld the ballot restrictions, even though they admittedly favored the two major parties. The outcome was difficult to reconcile with *Williams*. In this instance, the Court relied upon a view of political association that clearly impinged upon individual voting rights. The stated aims of the ballot requirements were to assure the legitimacy of the organization seeking to place its candidate on the ballot. In the process, the law narrowed the voting options of citizens by limiting the number of candidates. The associational function of running campaigns and elections warranted constitutional protection, even at the expense of unfettered individual voting rights.

The opinion implicitly acknowledged the parties' role as organizers of electoral majorities. It conditioned ballot position rights on the level of support the party received.[17] The state had a legitimate interest in requiring a "significant modicum of support before printing the name of a political organization's candidate on the ballot."[18] This reflected an appreciation for the function of parties in organizing elections. Unfortunately, that recognition was unfocused and superficial, as the Court offered little more than faint, conclusory praise of the parties. It noted the "obvious differences in kind between the needs and potentials of a political party with historically established broad support, on the one hand, and a new or small political organization on the other . . . "[19] Yet it did not elaborate upon or specify what those were. It merely recognized the goals of avoiding confusion, deception, and frustration of the democratic process, leaving unexplained how the major parties accomplished those goals.[20]

In *Lubin v. Parrish*,[21] while reaffirming the propriety of reasonable ballot access restrictions, the Court vacillated back toward the highly individualistic approach of *Williams v. Rhodes*. In *Lubin*, the Court struck down a California statute which had been invoked to bar an indigent who could not afford a $700 filing fee from running for the Los Angeles Board of Supervisors. In doing so, the Court enumerated several policies underlying state control of candidate access to the ballot, including the need for rational voter choices and the "fundamental importance" of reasonably sized ballots.[22] Nonetheless, California's failure to provide alternative means of qualifying for the ballot violated the plaintiff's freedom of association. The Court eschewed the notion that parties had a special role in promoting the state's interest in ballot control. It made no distinctions between individuals and associations, or between major or minor parties. It only required that "ballot access . . . be genuinely open to all, subject to reasonable requirements."[23] The major parties' abilities to shape voter choices gave them no greater rights than the "equally important interests" in political opportunity for individual candidates.[24]

Once again, the dominant consideration was the right of individual voters to political participation:

> The interests involved are not merely those of parties or independent candidates. The voters can assert their preferences only through candidates or parties or both and it is this broad interest that must be weighed in the balance. The right of a party or an individual to a place on a ballot is entitled to protection and is intertwined with the rights of voters.[25]

The *Jenness* recognition of the value of associational activity was wholly absent. Instead, the fundamental objective was to maximize voter choices by removing ballot restrictions that hobbled those choices.

The wavering line in ballot access cases continued in the seminal decision of *Storer v. Brown.*[26] In *Storer,* the Court upheld ballot restrictions based on a lukewarm endorsement of parties. At issue was a California statute that denied ballot access to independent candidates if they had been affiliated with a political party within a year of the primary. The plaintiffs were two candidates running for congressional office as independents. Since they had been registered as Democrats only months earlier, they were refused a spot on the California ballot. The Court upheld the one year minimum independent status as a reasonable state policy aimed at "maintaining the integrity of the various routes to the ballot."[27]

The decision was pro-party in one sense, as the Court articulated a legitimate interest in avoiding "splintered parties and unrestrained factionalism."[28] The people were entitled to "understandable choices" and an election winner "with sufficient support to govern effectively."[29] Parties were a reflection of that support. The basic goals of representative government necessitated giving voters defined, meaningful electoral choices, to ensure that the winner could govern effectively.[30] The Court implicitly accepted the elementary importance of a stable two-party system in achieving these goals.

At the same time, the Court overlooked the obvious organizational and institutional differences between parties and independent candidacies. It found:

> no sufficient state interest in conditioning ballot position for
> an independent candidate on his forming a new political party
> as long as the state is free to assume itself that the candidate
> is a serious contender, truly independent, and with a satisfac-
> tory level of community support.[31]

The Court ignored the nexus between political parties and the goals the Court articulated. People are given rational ballot choices via candidates wearing a party label with an ideological identity, a substantive definition, and backed by a policy platform. Similarly, the election winner is able to govern effectively through party organizations existing at all levels of government. Competent governance is facilitated by being able to draw from party ranks to fill the government with those who share the candidate's general philosophy and political identity. The same cannot be said to exist for independent candidates.

These differences in organizational character were glossed over by the Court. It rightly concluded that ballot position should not be contingent upon one's joining or establishing a political party.[32] But it disregarded the associational significance of the party label, for party candidate and supporter. Association acquires an added dimension when manifested in party designation. The sacrifices, the level of commitment, and the undertaking of the "serious responsibilities of qualified party status" suggest a greater content and depth to the association.[33]

Unlike the independent voter, whose interests focus on a particular candidate for a particular office, the party voter's interest is more broad-based and substantial. It encompasses a roster of candidates, and a general acceptance of a policy agenda for which the party stands. For the independent, association is an incidental byproduct of the vote for a person. One associates only to the extent one expresses the same electoral support for a candidate as do other voters. This is association in the most ephemeral sense. For the party voter, association is a conscious decision to accept the substantive identification that accompanies the label. *The willingness to bear the associational responsibilities attendant to party involvement should also be reflected in distinctions on the "rights" side of the equation.*[34]

The Court's pronouncement in *Anderson v. Celebrezze*[35] further submerged the functional distinctions between independent and party-designated candidates. In 1980, John Anderson mounted an independent bid for the presidency, but only after he had initially (and unsuccessfully) sought the Republican presidential nomination. Anderson did not announce his intention to run as an independent until April, after it became clear that he was unlikely to obtain the Republican nomination. The April declaration was too late to satisfy an Ohio statute that required that independent candidates seeking a spot on the ballot file a petition no later than March. When Anderson filed in Ohio in May, the application was rejected as untimely. Anderson challenged the constitutionality of the early filing deadline for independents.

The Supreme Court agreed with Anderson, concluding that the provision was unconstitutionally burdensome to the associational rights of Anderson's supporters. The Court focused on the political rights of individual voters, offering a rather crabbed logic in support of the doctrine of association. It held that the exclusion of independent candidates from the ballot burdened the right to vote, and by extension, the freedom to associate.[36] The Court portrayed the independent candidate as a rallying point for like-minded citizens. The denial of Anderson's position on the ballot consequently hampered those citizens' freedom to associate. The restriction discriminated:

> against those voters whose political preferences lie outside the existing political parties. (citation omitted) *By limiting the opportunities of independent-minded voters to associate in the electoral arena to enhance their political effectiveness as a group,* such restrictions threaten to reduce diversity and competition in the marketplace of ideas.[37]

This individualistic interpretation of associational rights stood in contrast to the legitimate interest, recognized in *Storer,* in preventing splintered parties and factionalism. It presented political association in an undifferentiated manner, as if all types of political association were equal. Association loosely occurring around an individual candidate was the equivalent of association with a formal political organization. The opinion made no distinctions between the far-ranging, broad-based operations of a party enterprise and the narrower objectives of an independent candidacy. The sole emphasis was on the "interests of voters who chose to associate together to express their support for Anderson's candidacy and the views he espoused."[38]

The Court's characterization of Anderson supporters defied the realities of independent candidacies. It described those voters as "an identifiable political group whose members share a particular viewpoint, associational preference or economic status."[39] In fact, independent voters associate only in the most casual sense. They are an "identifiable political group" only by virtue of their having voted for the particular candidate, in this case Anderson. This makes it difficult to isolate the interest or preference that is the basis of the association. Two Anderson voters may support him for totally different reasons. With an independent candidacy, it is far more difficult to determine whether there is a "particular viewpoint" or identifiable shared interest which comprises an association. With registered party voters, there is an assumption that they share some level of acceptance of the tenets of that party. The casting of a party vote indicates an organizational type of "associational preference," which is absent in a vote for an independent. The act of registering as Democrat or Republican is a public declaration of an organizational affiliation, which represents particular viewpoints.

Membership indicates a formal affiliation with an organized group. It is evidenced by external features, such as dues, party label, and other organizational trappings. Not only do independents not share these traits, but their principal characteristic is their refusal to become members. They are motivated not by an associational preference, but by the desire to avoid association. It is incongruous to speak of party voters and independent voters as having the same associational character.

Justice Rehnquist touched upon those differences in his dissenting opinion in *Anderson*. He considered it perfectly reasonable to give parties preferential treatment, since they have "a continuing existence, representing particular philosophies."[40] He emphasized that with party candidates, the organization remained at the center. But with independent candidacies, the people coalesced around a candidate, not an organization. Any association that exists is personality-based. In contrast, party organization is based on substantive policy agendas, ideology, and policy. Consequently, the state's interest in furnishing voters with reasonable choices and understandable ballots supports restrictions that impinge more on independents than established parties.

Ultimately, *Anderson* rejected the idea that it makes any difference whether voters choose candidates who are independent or party affiliated.[41] It reflected a Court more concerned about the right of easy access to the ballot for third parties and independent candidates than stable party organizations.[42] By actually encouraging candidates to opt for independent status over the party route to the ballot, it undermined the role of parties in representative democracies.[43]

Anderson concluded a haphazard path through ballot access restrictions, from which it is difficult to discern a consistent thread of constitutional principle. On one hand, the individual perspective that characterized voting rights jurisprudence similarly prevails. The individual right to run for office or to vote for the candidate of one's choice is primary. As a general rule, restrictions on ballot access will pass constitutional muster provided they are fair and open to individuals.

At the same time, the Court's consideration of parties is sporadic and erratic. In some instances, it is sympathetic to parties; at other times, they receive no mention whatsoever. In the end, the consequences for the parties are largely unconsidered, the effects unintended and constitutionally irrelevant.[44] Once again the Court reveals a lack of familiarity with the functional attributes of and theoretical justifications for parties.[45]

PARTIES, PRIMARIES AND THE RIGHT OF ASSOCIATION

The Court has also addressed the propriety of a host of state restrictions on access to the voting booth, especially in primary elections. These decisions raise critical issues of party autonomy and associational rights involving the control of the primary nominating process, and voters' participation in those primaries. They demand that the judiciary position voting and associational rights generally on the electoral spectrum, and rank the parties as holders of those rights against individual rights to participate in primaries.

In the final analysis, the Court's resolution of these issues resembles the ballot access cases. It has shown a propensity for explicit recognition of party autonomy, and has expanded associational rights to reflect that. But its inability to comprehend the essential place of party organizations pervades the outcomes. *The result is another perplexing set of cases, with the Court struggling to reconstruct associational rights to better balance individualistic rights of participation with corporate dimensions reflecting political organizational activity.*

Like other areas of constitutional law, the initial balancing of associational rights with the state's interest in regulating elections was typically resolved in favor of individual voting rights. An early example was *Kusper v. Pontikes,* in which the Court struck down an Illinois state statute that precluded anyone who had voted in one party's primary from voting in another party's primary in the following twenty-three months.[46] The statute unconstitutionally infringed upon individual associational rights by locking a person into a preexisting party affiliation for unnecessarily long periods of time.

At the same time, *Kusper* contained the seeds of a party-regarding doctrine of association. The Court noted the right to affiliate with "the political party of one's choice,"[47] and emphasized the basic function of parties in selecting candidates to run for public office. Participation in party primaries was especially important, since it impacted the right to associate "with a particular party . . . to gain a voice in that selection process."[48]

Those seeds sprouted noticeably in *Cousins v. Wigoda*,[49] several years later. *Cousins* marked an expansion of the Court's willingness to legitimize associational rights as they pertained to political parties. The case addressed a controversy between two rival groups over who would be seated as Illinois' delegation to the Democratic National Convention in 1972. One set of delegates, pursuant to Illinois state law, had been selected in the 1972 Illinois primary elections. That mode of selection, however, directly contravened the national Democratic Party rules. A second bloc of delegates, chosen pursuant to national party rules, challenged the seating of the first group. The challenge brought national party autonomy and associational rights into direct conflict with state law.

In siding with the national Democratic party over the state of Illinois, the Court added an element to the individual right of association that heretofore had been missing. It specifically highlighted the corporate dimension of associational rights, extending the constitutionally protected right to the party itself. Hence, interference with party activity constituted an infringement both of the associational rights of the party and simultaneously of those of its adherents.[50]

The decision was a watershed victory for national party organizations over state laws that attempted to restrain them. Though the state had a legitimate interest in the integrity of the electoral process and in assuring effective suffrage, it was subordinate to party unity. Differing state laws threatened to undermine the "effectiveness of the National Party Convention as a concerted enterprise engaged in the vital process of choosing Presidential and Vice Presidential candidates."[51] The parties' role in choosing candidates and narrowing electoral choices was sufficiently important to compel freeing them from contrary state laws.[52] To this point, the freedom of association had been overwhelmingly individualistic in character. The right had been formally extended to parties, but had held little relevance for them. *Cousins* proclaimed a corporate dimension, entitling the parties to "a constitutionally protected autonomy which permits them to govern their candidate selection process" as they wish.[53] It carved out a newly preferred position and heightened status for national political parties, at least with respect to state regulation.[54]

The favored status of party autonomy was reaffirmed in *Democratic Party of U.S. v. LaFollette*,[55] another conflict between party rules and state law. The national Democratic Party rules allowed only those who were formally affiliated with the Party to participate in the selection of National Convention delegates. In contrast, Wisconsin state law permitted nonaffiliated voters to participate in candidate preference primaries. While convention delegates were chosen separately, they were bound to act in accordance with the results of the primary. Consequently, the arrangement indirectly undercut the intent of the national party rule, which was to limit input in choosing the nominee to those officially associated with the party. The matter came to a head, when the national party refused to seat the Wisconsin delegation at the 1980 National Convention.

The Court again sided with the party, concluding that state law cannot constitutionally compel the National Party to seat delegates chosen in violation of the party rules. Building on *Cousins*, it elaborated on the associational rights of the party. They included the party's "freedom to identify the people constituting the association, and the right to limit the association to those people."[56] Limiting participation to affiliated party voters was a legitimate exercise of associational freedom. It reflected the party's choice to define its association by limiting those who could take part in choosing delegates. The Court even struck a chord for the ideological purity of parties, worrying that the inclusion of unaffiliated voters would distort the party's ability to coherently act and decide matters collectively.[57]

Justice Powell's dissent in *LaFollette* offered an interesting contrast, as he voiced the more traditional judicial fondness for the purity of unmediated personal democratic participation. He spoke in idyllic terms, emphasizing the need to eliminate the middlemen between the people and their representatives. He praised the open primary as a legitimate attempt to eliminate "potential pressures from political organizations on voters to affiliate with a particular party."[58] He discounted the ideological component of parties, characterizing them as having a "fluidity and overlap of philosophy and membership."[59] This minimized any threat of allowing relatively independent voters to cast their lot in a party primary. The party's right to exclude voters was outweighed by the state's interest in ensuring that voters were allowed to participate in a primary.[60] Powell saw the majority decision as a dangerous departure from the necessary "accommodation of the interests of the parties with those of the states and their citizens."[61]

Cousins and *LaFollette* evidenced a judicial commitment to the view that "political parties may protect themselves from the interference of those unaffiliated with the party."[62] In *Tashjian v.*

Republican Party of Connecticut,[63] the Court was asked to balance party autonomy and voting rights in a somewhat different context. *Tashjian* arose out of revisions made by the Connecticut Republican Party to its rules in 1984, allowing independents to vote in Republican primaries for federal and statewide offices. The abandonment of closed party rules by the Republicans was clearly motivated by a desire to attract the large numbers of independent voters in Connecticut. However, the new rules conflicted with a long-standing state statute which only allowed registered party members to vote in primary elections to determine the major party nominees. When the state Republican party challenged the statute as a deprivation of its right to freely associate with those of its choosing, the Supreme Court agreed.

Justice Marshall, writing the majority opinion, adopted a broad interpretation of the party's right to define its association. In so doing, however, he downplayed the formal affiliation between party organization and the individuals included in the association. He contemplated a variety of forms of partisan association, from giving time or money to the party, to party-building activities, to merely voting for the party's candidates. "Formal enrollment or public affiliation with the party is merely one element on the continuum of participation in Party affairs," and not necessarily the most important one.[64] Marshall loosely defined the "association" entitled to constitutional protection as the "group of registered voters whom the party may invite to participate in the 'basic function' of selecting the party's candidates."[65] From this definitional vantage point, the restrictions imposed by the state's closed primary rule came at "the crucial juncture at which the appeal to common principles may be translated into concerted action and hence to political power in the community."[66] The state law crimped the party's freedom to define itself in ways that would maximize its chances to obtain power.

Connecticut defended its closed primary system on grounds that it promoted the responsiveness of elected officials and strengthened political parties. Marshall easily disposed of these arguments, dismissing the notion that the state could act to protect "the integrity of the Party against the Party itself."[67] He backpedalled from earlier decisions that acknowledged a legitimate state interest in governmental stability through a two-party system.[68] Instead, he explicitly rejected the state's contention that it had an overriding interest in maintaining a strong two-party system or in facilitating responsible party government. Even if the state was correct with respect to the benefits that redounded from closed primaries, neither it nor the Court could substitute their judgment for that of the parties. The crux of association was the "Party's determination of the boundaries of its own association and of the structure which best allows it to pursue its political goals . . ."[69]

Tashjian permitted the party to define itself by identifying those who were allowed to participate in its activities.[70] In this "party autonomy" sense, the result was pro-party and pro-group politics.[71] But the opinion overlooked the central importance of party organizations as institutional structures of representation. Ultimately, *Tashjian* exposed a predisposition against organized corporate political activity and in favor of unadulterated individual participation and associational rights.[72] It is more readily understood as enlarging the rights of independent voters to vote in primaries than as a conferral of greater rights upon a political organization. The anti-institutional tone of the opinion suggests that the Court's approval of the parties' right to adopt open primaries was driven less by a respect for party autonomy than by a desire for more open and "democratic" voting, which would allow anyone to vote, whether party affiliated or not.

In a withering dissent, Justice Scalia berated the majority's anti-organizational definition of association. Scalia viewed the state primary law only as excluding those individuals who are not, and refuse to become, party members. He derided the conclusion that independents and party members who might vote for the same candidate constituted a political association.

> The Connecticut voter who, while steadfastly refusing to register as a Republican, casts a vote in the Republican primary forms no more meaningful an "association" with the Party than does the individual or the registered Democrat who responds to questions by a Republican Party pollster. If the concept of freedom of association is extended to such casual contacts, it ceases to be of any analytical use.[73]

Scalia argued that the state did indeed have authority to save the party from itself. To assure election laws were properly representative and democratic, the state could reasonably "require that significant elements of the democratic election process be democratic—whether the party wants that or not."[74]

While *Tashjian* was superficially reassuring on its face to party proponents, its minimizing of party structures undercut their

representative character. *Tashjian* offered little evidence that the
Court comprehends the theoretical import of party politics, or
that it will take necessary steps to ensure that the corporate dimensions of political activity receive adequate constitutional protection. The theoretical rationale for the right of association is
that identifiers with a group associate with it for the pursuit or
advancement of political objectives.[75] Group theories presume that
the group exists for empowerment of the individuals who choose
to join it. Rights, therefore, demand an objective and accurate
means of measuring and identifying the group and its members.
One option is to focus exclusively on individual membership.
Another is to acknowledge the organization itself and one's willingness to officially identify with it. One line for delineating
collective rights is the organization itself and the tangible organizational form of the group claiming the right.

This suggests that an organization compromises its constitutional right of association when it acts contrary to its organizational identity (by allowing non-affiliated people to vote in the
party primary). It also inflicts a corollary upon individual associational freedoms. To the extent that an individual behaves in a
way that is obviously incompatible with the organization, his association with it is more equivocal. An open primary, by blurring
the formal lines of associations, invites limits on associational freedoms, on the party accepting independent voters and on the voter
who refuses to formally assume party identification. From this organizational perspective, the outcome in *Tashjian* is questionable.
It extends the party's right of association in the loosest sense, and
at the expense of more meaningful forms of party association. It
frees party members to "associate" with nonparty voters, by let-
ting anyone vote in the party primary. It affirms the right to associate with those who have refused to affiliate with a party, and
who have avoided formal party association.[76] This is a contradictory sort of association.

Moreover, it diminishes formal party affiliation, which should
be the cornerstone of the legal right to association. The institutional benefits of party structures to political representation lie in
party organization. Those who don the party label, as voters, vol-
unteers, activists, financial supporters, or leaders, exhibit the requisite seriousness about pursuing political objectives through
corporate means. They sacrifice some freedom to support whom-
ever they like, or to change party or candidate preferences on a
whim. That commitment is undermined when party affiliation is

treated no differently as independent status. *The open primary approach condoned in Tashjian creates a disincentive to more substantial participation in the party organization, which is the hub of the structural subsystems that generate political representation.*

The philosophy underlying *Tashjian* also seriously impedes the parties' capacity for displaying a strong identity on a programmatic and ideological level.[77] Parties do not exist exclusively for the capture of political power. The ultimate end of the use of that power is to realize policies and ideas that motivate party participation in the first place. People join the party because they accept its message and wish to advance its program. Open primaries negate the ability of party affiliators to define the philosophical and intellectual component of the party. The inclusion of independents in choosing the party torchbearer subverts the political efficacy of party members. It dilutes their influence, obfuscating the party positions and frustrating its ideological appeals.[78] In short, open primaries are anti-organization and anti-party.

In this way, *Tashjian* weakens the representative subsystems of party organizations. It produces plebiscitary majorities, rather than party majorities. The former are ephemeral, shifting, and fluid. They may be the consequence of a temporary surge of passion, shortsighted and emotional. The latter, by contrast, are more permanent and less transitory. Party majorities are "organized, ongoing and institutionalized."[79] They have consistency of leadership, institutional memory, and discipline, all of which are necessary ingredients of representative structures.[80]

Representation theory suggests that the party weakens its claim to constitutional status when it adopts rules that run counter to its organizational existence. When the party includes nonparty people in its essential activities, as it does in adopting an open primary, state regulations are less of an impingement on substantive associational activity.[81] In evaluating the propriety of state regulations of parties, the desire to free parties from legal constraints ought to be balanced against the valid aim of discouraging parties from adopting enervating measures. A theory of representation that is inclusive of party structures would require that association have some content to retain its value as an avenue of representation.[82] It would require some external manifestation beyond merely voting for the same candidate, lest institutional party functions wane.

The Court's distrust of political associations was in full view in *Tashjian*, even as it issued a decision purportedly favoring the

parties. Its disdain for the organizational prerequisites of political
association cut away at the parties'. representative capacity as vehicles of group politics, and as clarifiers and mediators of elections. *Tashjian* put associational rights at the disposal of individuals
and party members, but not in the party organization as an
organization.

This slights the central place of primaries in the parties' fulfillment of their institutional representative character.[83] Intraparty
politics is critical to the accomplishment of the goals of representation. It is essential to the parties' ability to build group coalitions. Competition within the party structure is the opportunity
for input by groups seeking power. It places a premium on organizational activity, such as caucuses, drafting party platforms, and
nominating and supporting candidates.

Likewise, intraparty politics militates against factionalism and
the fragmentation of political issues.[84] Intraparty politics assuages
group tensions by providing political effectiveness for those political interests that otherwise might not be heard. It allays political pressure by giving groups voice on specific issues. At the same
time, it is a decisive point at which political conflict begins to be
distilled into cohesive, competing programs.[85] It is the start of the
process of focusing and narrowing public opinion into alternative
choices for the general election. From the politicking within parties come the competing guides to governance from which the
voters can choose.

Tashjian's belittling of the significance of the organizational
criteria of association impeded the representational goals underlying the right. Group facilitation and clarification of public opinion are not substantially accomplished by open primaries. Strict
party-based primaries serve those objectives far better (although
not nearly as well as a caucus system). Consequently, the right
should not extend to people or to activities that do not further
the values of representative democracy. *Ultimately, it is a meaningful affiliation with the institutional forms of the party that warrants a
recognition of constitutionally protected association.*

PARTY AUTONOMY IN *EU V. SAN FRANCISCO*:
PARTIES ON THE RISE?

In *Eu v. San Francisco Democratic Committee,*[86] the Court issued another decision that prompted observers to conclude that it is
embracing a more sympathetic, expansive view of parties. In *Eu,*

the Court unanimously struck down a California statute that was probably the most stringent curtailment of party activity to be found in any state. That state law forbade political parties from endorsing candidates in primary elections, and in turn prohibited candidates from claiming official party endorsement. It also dictated the organization and composition of the parties' governing bodies, as well as imposing other rules and procedures on the parties themselves. Representatives of both major parties challenged the law.

In overturning the ban on party endorsements, the Court focused on the party's right to select the standard-bearer best reflecting its ideologies and preferences.[87] The ban on endorsements was an ominous barrier to party influence on elections. It prevented parties from stating "whether a candidate adheres to the tenets of the party."[88] As a result, candidates could be nominated under the party label even though they held views antithetical to the party.[89] This prohibition severely inhibited the parties in their efforts to spread their message.[90]

Along with *Tashjian*, *Eu* has been heralded as a positive marker for the future of the parties, enabling them to reassert control over the nominating process.[91] Political scientists have read these cases as ensuring that determinations on who votes in party elections, who runs under the party banner, and who participates on nonelectoral activities remain in the parties' hands. They see it as enabling parties to more clearly advance their programs and policies and to better recruit leaders. In short, it equips parties for "the very functions that make them most useful and necessary in democratic government."[92]

The commentators have it half right. They accurately propound the importance of party-controlled primaries, but their reading of *Tashjian* and *Eu* as substantially promoting this end is unduly optimistic. An elevated role of parties in primaries is critical to enhancing their influence. Party structures within the context of elections are crucial to achieving democratic values of leadership, legitimacy, and public choice. Parties permit groups to coalesce, compromise, and bargain amongst themselves to eventually produce choices that are reflective of the electorate. Party organizations permit common viewpoints to emerge, and aid in the effective presentation of those viewpoints.[93]

Parties have already been hindered in the performance of these tasks by the replacement of a caucus system and nominating conventions with primaries.[94] Primaries do not

facilitate the aggregative tasks of debate, compromise, and consensus as well as caucuses and conventions. They lack the actual physical assembly that is part and parcel of the caucus.
Caucus meetings engender substantive deliberation, discussion,
and exchange, which strengthen "institutionalized and continuing political organizations."[95] Primaries favor individual political campaigns.

Removing primaries from party control further undermines
party functions. Party control of primaries allows them to aggregate voters, define common views, and make elections comprehensible. Contemporary primaries, featuring candidate-centered
campaigns and comprised of media-driven events, subordinate
parties to other groups and special interests. In the process, they
disaggregate coalitions of voters and fragment broader-based programs and ideologies.

The *Eu* decision ignores these issues. Justice Marshall could
have based his decision on the parties' unique ability to inform voters and clarify electoral choices. Instead, he struck
down the statute on grounds that party influence was not significant enough to warrant the restriction. California defended
the endorsements ban as an effort to protect voters from confusion and undue influence. This gave the Court a perfect opportunity to note that parties do precisely the opposite, that
they make elections decipherable. Instead, Marshall found party
endorsements to be essentially meaningless. He concluded that
"voters are [not] unduly influenced by party endorsements," and
their "endorsement . . . carries [no] more weight than one issued by a newspaper or a labor union."[96] Marshall found the
proscription against endorsements unreasonable only because
party endorsements were of such little importance. Instead of
highlighting the unique abilities of parties to shape voter
choices and subsequently govern, Marshall's conclusion did
precisely the opposite by assuming that parties were irrelevant
to voter choices.

Marshall did invoke stronger pro-party language in rejecting
California's attempts to dictate the organizational structures parties must employ. Those statutory provisions impermissibly limited the party's power to "organize itself, conduct its affairs, and
select its leaders."[97] On the heels of *Eu*, parties are legally equipped
to maintain a healthy control over internal affairs involving organizational structure, choice of leaders, and the like. They are subject to regulation only when necessary to ensure that parties fulfill

their "external responsibilities in ensuring the order and fairness of elections."[98]

In its totality, however, Marshall's opinion belies the enthusiastic prognostications of a judicial embrace of the parties. It echoes the persistent theme of these cases. When the Court rules on parties' behalf, it acts more out of a nebulous, imprecise sense of fairness than from a theoretical or functional defense of the parties.[99] Its acceptance of party rights is almost unpremeditated and inadvertent. These decisions reveal little evidence of a Court consciously aware of the uniqueness of party functions. While they generally reflect a corporate dimension, the treatment of and effect on parties is virtually incidental to a broader devotion to individualistic rights of association.[100] These cases cast further doubt upon the Court's capacity to constitutionally protect and facilitate the functions that only the parties can perform.

CONCLUSION

The constitutional unevenness in the realm of voter and candidate access suggests a fertile field in which to sow pro-party arguments. This is especially true in light of the contradictory signals emanating from the most recent judicial comment on ballot access. *Burdick v. Takushi*[101] reflected a modest retreat from the highly individualistic approach to association and an awakening to group considerations in individual voting rights.

In *Burdick*, the Court denied a voter's challenge to a Hawaii state law that prohibited write-in voting. In ratifying the restrictions, the Court made it clear that individual voting rights are not absolute,[102] but can be regulated to ensure fair, honest, and orderly elections. The Court noted the state interests favoring strong, stable parties. The interdiction against write-in voting was warranted by the interest in "avoiding unrestrained factionalism."[103] It sought to reserve the ballot for major struggles rather than intraparty squabbles, and to avert divisive "sore loser" candidacies.[104] The Court also noted the interest in guarding against party raiding, when voters switch parties in an effort to manipulate the other party's primary results.[105] The Court's appreciation of these justifications marked a relatively cordial reception for an election system premised upon parties.

More importantly, the Court described the electoral objectives in a way that accentuated the rudimentary role of parties, though it never explicitly made that connection. It identified a principal function of elections as the winnowing out of all but the chosen candidates. Elections were meant to do more than give vent to "short-range political goals, pique, or personal quarrel[s]."[106] The purely expressive individual act suggested by voting rights detracted from states' ability to run elections fairly and efficiently. Regulations aimed at "channeling expressive activity at the polls"[107] were necessary to realize electoral objectives.

The tensions the Court grappled with in *Burdick* should sound vaguely familiar. They mirror on a smaller scale the countervailing considerations that lie at the heart of the pluralist dilemma. On one hand, the Court rightly noted the paramount goal of enriched individual political participation. But it also realized that individual participation requires orderly electoral institutions to make it meaningful. The Court acknowledged the fundamental right to a voice in elections, but tempered it with the need for "an electoral process structured to maintain the integrity of the democratic system."[108]

The Court was poised intellectually to accept party structures as the answer to meaningful political participation. It recognized that individual participation means little as an isolated expressive act. Rather, political activity acquires meaning when funneled through electoral structures as part of a coalition or majority of voters. But the Court slid over the role of party systems in attaining structured orderly elections that yield comprehensible results. Despite its thoughtful statement of the competing interests, it could not comprehend parties as the structural components that resolve pluralist tensions.

Observers have been emboldened by the Court's handling of disputes involving state regulation of parties. John Moeller finds the Court engaged in a healthy debate about "politics, the Constitution, and the idea of a fair society that is as old as the nation itself."[109] It matters not to Moeller that the Court is pro- or anti-party, but that it is concerned with larger issues regarding the nature of our politics; whether it is individual and egalitarian, pluralist and representative.

But the fundamental premise of this discussion is that our politics must be both. It is at its core individualistic, but in a way that can only be attained by pluralist means. It demands representative structures and organizations that respond to both facets. This is the value of party systems. They are institutionalized actors uniquely constituted to alleviate that contradiction. Parties are the "organizational prerequisites of democratic politics."[110] Only through party organizations are public opinions aggregated and expressed in electoral politics, and expressed preferences translated into representative governance. Consequently, the repeated juristic slighting of party systems demonstrates a dangerous indifference toward the institutional safeguards of representative democracy.

CHAPTER NINE

Party and Patronage: Organizational Glue, Payment for Services, or Graft?

The final piece of evidence of the Court's disregard for parties as institutional forms of representation is found in a line of decisions limiting political patronage.[1] Patronage has long been the scourge of American party politics. Associated with the powerful urban party machines of this century, it has been thought to be a primary tool of corruption and improper influence in politics. Consequently, it typically faces general condemnation and is opposed by everyone from the Progressives to the media to "good government" types of various stripes and colors.

Legal controversies involving the propriety of patronage present a unique challenge to the Court and its willingness to acknowledge parties in American democracy. In light of the grave disapprobation of patronage in most circles, the path of least resistance would be to simply dismiss it as an obsolete remnant of another era without contemporary value. But patronage cases "call forth strong theoretical discussion about the role of political parties in the American democracy."[2] Efforts to justify patronage are uniquely cast in responsible party terms. They are closely coupled with the institutional and organizational aspects of parties. Patronage practices can be condoned only by accepting parties as essential tools of democracy. Consequently, these disputes severely test the Court's ability to take judicial notice of party structures and activity.

The goal of this chapter is not to reach some ultimate conclusion regarding the merits of patronage. When parties were at their zenith late in the nineteenth century, patronage was an invaluable tool for providing the people with personal services and making the parties relevant in real ways. At the same time, abuses of patronage practices undeniably contributed to pervasive corruption both in party organizations and in government institutions. It is beyond the scope of this book to try to resolve whether the benefits of patronage outweighed its drawbacks.

Rather, the objective is to evaluate the Court's capacity to consider patronage in terms that fully account for the interests at stake. Does the Court give credence to pro-party arguments offered to justify patronage practices? Do the cases reflect an appreciation for parties as vehicles of representation and agents of governance? Once again, the decisions in this area confirm the Court's deep distrust of political organizations. Once again, the Court opts for unchannelled personal rights over organizational forms of representative democracy. The party prerogative to dispense patronage is subordinated to the individual right to public employment irrespective of party affiliation.

The patronage decisions also reveal a striking dichotomy in the Court's attitude toward parties. A majority of the Court has accepted, then extended, substantial constraints on the parties' resort to patronage. That segment of the Court has demonstrated little regard for the singular institutional role of parties in American politics. It has shown little concern for the party apparatus, refusing to entertain the possibility that patronage is a legitimate means of strengthening the institutional foundations of parties. But a sizeable minority bloc of the Court would grant substantial deference to the parties to rely on patronage. Justices Powell and Scalia have penned dissenting opinions that are unparalleled in the extent to which they embrace the responsible two-party system to justify far-reaching patronage practices. Those opinions evidence a sympathy for parties and their role in the political system in a language and to a degree rarely found on the Court.

THE JUSTIFICATION FOR PATRONAGE

The defense of patronage practices consists of a twofold justification.[3] First, it is necessary to ensure representative government. It connects the actions of government to the expressed preferences of the electorate. Only through patronage hiring can elected executives be certain of having people of like mind working for them, employees dedicated to implementing those policies endorsed by voters at the polls.[4] The hiring of those who supported the winner or who shared the winner's partisan affiliation ensures efficient implementation of the programs upon which the winner campaigned and was elected. The freedom to replace those who disagree on policy assures loyalty and discipline within government and secures its orderly and efficient operation.[5] Thus, patronage fulfills the governmental interest in effective, efficient administration.[6]

Second, patronage is defended as an essential means of achieving the perpetuation and vitality of political organizations. V.O. Key described the spoils system as "a method of consolidating into a cohesive and disciplined group the persons constituting the machine."[7] It is a means of underwriting party activities that are essential to the business of conducting elections. Voter registration, literature drops, canvassing of neighborhoods, and a host of other campaign activities require people to carry them out. The promise or prospect of appointment to public office has long been put forth as a primary mode of enticing people into party service.[8] By providing tangible rewards and incentives for party service, patronage contributes to a vital and energetic party system.[9]

These arguments are premised upon parties as critical tools of representative democracy. Patronage is defensible only if parties occupy a central place in politics. It is a way of financing the party machinery that is essential to our form of government. It is the incentive for people to join and remain loyal to parties. Consequently, there is "nothing derogatory in saying that a primary function of parties is patronage."[10]

PARTIES AND PATRONAGE IN CONSTITUTIONAL DOCTRINE

The Supreme Court first entertained a constitutional challenge to patronage hiring in the 1976 decision of *Elrod v. Burns*.[11] The case involved efforts by the Cook County Sheriff's office to discharge certain employees based on their political affiliation. Upon taking office, the newly elected sheriff, a Democrat, promptly moved to replace Republicans who occupied a variety of county positions, including deputy sheriffs, the clerk, and a process server. The fired employees sued under the First and Fourteenth Amendments,

claiming violations of their right of association and freedom to
express their political beliefs.

In striking down the patronage dismissals, the Court demonstrated little regard for parties, either as basic components of the
electoral process or as agents of governance within the state.[12] The
most interesting point of entry in *Elrod*, however, is Justice Powell's
dissent. It is unparalleled in its favorable view of parties and its
willingness to factor them into constitutional jurisprudence. Powell
made a forceful pitch for upholding the patronage practices engaged in here, relying on the arguments of responsible party proponents within the political science discipline. He noted the
importance of parties within government as mediating, aggregating electoral structures. Patronage enabled parties to fulfill these
dual functions.

Powell viewed parties as essential to the electorate's ability
to make informed choices in elections. Only through "established
parties [are] the 'people . . . presented with understandable
choices.'"[13] The stability, permanency, and visibility of parties
make party affiliation a meaningful guidepost for voter choices.[14]
At the same time, parties in government are the key to institutional responsibility to the electorate. They permit discipline and
responsibility in government.[15] Preferences expressed through
elections are realized only via coherent, programmatic parties in
government.

Powell argued that these functions warrant a strong governmental interest in fostering invigorated parties, justifying judicial
deference to patronage practices. Strong parties ensure accountability, responsiveness, and responsible administration in government, as they clarify electoral alternatives, make choices
decipherable, and promote coherent governance. Patronage is an
important means of augmenting these functions. On one hand, it
is the organizational glue that ensures distinct and competitive
parties. On the other hand, it aids policy coherence in government by allowing a unified, cohesive administration.

Powell also recognized parties as democratizers of the political process, and saw patronage as a key incentive for greater
participation. Patronage attracts party activists to keep the
organizations operating and thriving, especially at the lower levels
of the political process. Powell saw local party structures as the
critical stage in the process for achieving large-scale public participation. It was at this level that incentives were especially needed:

Election campaigns for lesser offices in particular usually attract little attention from the media, with consequent disinterest and absence of intelligent participation on the part of the public. Unless the candidates for these offices are able to dispense the traditional patronage that has accrued to the offices, they also are unlikely to attract donations of time or money from voluntary groups. . . . *Long experience teaches that at this local level traditional patronage practices contribute significantly to the democratic process.*[16]

Powell contended that the issues in local races are not enough to draw people into the fray. Nor are people inspired by democratic impulse, altruism, or public service. Rather, they are enticed into politics by the potential for rewards. They contribute based on the expectation that they will benefit if their candidate wins and is able to distribute those benefits that accompany the office.[17]

In contrast to Powell's strong pro-party rhetoric, the plurality summarily dispensed with the responsible party arguments. A single cryptic paragraph was devoted to the assertion that political parties were central to the democratic process, and that their vitality necessitated patronage. The cursory rejoinder to Powell ignored the possible value of patronage to democratization, facilitation of group politics, or enhancement of political participation. Instead, it stated in blanket fashion that:

We are not persuaded that the elimination of patronage practices . . . will bring about the demise of party politics. Political parties existed in the absence of active patronage practice prior to the administration of Andrew Jackson, and they have survived substantial reduction in their patronage power through the establishment of merit systems.[18]

The Court's conclusory rebuttal suggests a superficial analysis characterized by a less than rigorous weighing of the pro-party arguments.[19] It led Powell to comment that "one cannot avoid the impression, however, that even a threatened demise of parties would not trouble the plurality."[20] The Court's low regard for parties was confirmed in a foreboding footnote, in which it concluded that "partisan politics bears the imprimatur only of tradition, not the Constitution."[21] The Court rebuffed the idea that the government has an interest in bolstering parties. Nor would it acknowledge parties as institutional mechanisms for carrying out elections or the task of governing. The Court warned that "care must be taken not to confuse the interests of partisan organizations with government interests. Only the latter will suffice."[22] It rejected the connection between the governmental interest in a healthy democratic process and the activities of parties in achieving that goal.[23] It snubbed the party-in-government argument out of hand, ignoring the political science literature indicating that parties continue to be the tools by which governmental action is carried out.[24] The cavalier manner in which the Court partitioned governmental interests off from those of partisan organizations was highly debatable. The stronger party organizations are within government, the more closely intertwined the interests of party and government become.

Associational rights provided the footing for the Court's decision. But its vision of associational rights again exhibited a preference for individual political activity over collective expression.[25] The Court made it clear that association was, first and foremost, an individual right aimed at protecting "the unfettered judgment of each citizen on matters" of politics.[26] The Court would not impose impediments on individual rights (such as the fear of job-related reprisal due to party affiliation) to foster corporate dimensions of the same right (the strengthening of the organizational cohesiveness of political parties). Parties were free to exist and to continue their activities, provided they did not impinge upon the rights of any citizen to believe as she wished and to act accordingly.[27] In the First Amendment scheme of things, individual belief and association stood well above party associational rights, at least in the context of dispensation of public employment.

The fractured *Elrod* Court did not settle the question of patronage.[28] An opportunity to clarify the limits of patronage arose four years later in *Branti v. Finkel*, a decision involving the public defender's office in Rockland City, New York.[29] The new Chief Public Defender, a Democrat, sought to replace six assistant PDs (all of whom were Republicans) with fellow Democrats. Those faced with the loss of their jobs sued, alleging an infringement of their right to associate with the party of their choice.

In holding the patronage dismissals to be unconstitutional, a divided Court gave a marginal degree of credit to parties and the role of patronage in the perpetuation of the parties. The Court conceded that party affiliation was a legitimate requirement for those cases in which an employee's private political beliefs might interfere with the performance of his duties. The Court went beyond *Elrod*, acknowledging the state's interest in maintaining governmental efficiency.[30] Restraints on association were justified when "party affiliation is an appropriate requirement for the effective performance of the public office involved."[31] Since party allegiance was deemed irrelevant to the performance of a public defender's duties, the plaintiffs were entitled to keep their jobs.

Justice Powell again lodged a vigorous dissent. He identified a litany of functions the parties perform, including raising money, recruiting candidates, providing information and other assistance to voters, and linking voters and governmental bureaucracy.[32] Patronage appointments were instrumental in building stable parties.[33] Patronage stimulated voter interest in lower level campaigns and generated participation in party activities.[34] Powell elaborated on the contribution of patronage to effective governance once the election was over. It assured that elected officials could rely upon like-minded appointees to wholeheartedly pursue their policies. In this manner, it facilitated "the implementation of policies endorsed by the electorate."[35]

Powell saw the patronage issue as more than an empty theoretical debate. The inability to offer patronage to supporters had caused a "failure to sustain party discipline."[36] That breakdown in party discipline was injurious to the parties' capacity to function as tools of governance. Legislators with little allegiance to their party were free to deviate at will from the party's efforts to enact its programs. Weak party discipline, fuelled by restraints on patronage, undercut public choice and accountability. Said Powell:

> Voters with little information about individuals seeking office traditionally have relied upon party affiliation as a guide to choosing among candidates. With the decline of party stability, voters are less able to blame or credit a party for the performance of its elected officials. Our national party system is predicated upon the assumption that political parties sponsor, and are responsible for, the performance of the persons they nominate for office.[37]

By dissolving the organizational glue of patronage, the Court was irreparably harming the unique capacity of the parties to inject reason and accountability into the system. To Powell, the decision was nothing short of a "denigrat[ion of] the role of our national political parties."[38]

Powell's opinion is remarkable for its enthusiastic application of the classic responsible party view to constitutional jurisprudence. His endorsement of parties and his willingness to grant them constitutional consideration are a marked departure from the lukewarm attitude generally exhibited toward parties. No pro-party political scientist could have put it better than this:

> Broad based parties supply an essential coherence and flexibility to the American political scene. They serve as coalitions of different interests that combine to seek national goals. The decline of party strength inevitably will enhance the influence of special interest groups whose only concern all too often is how a political candidate votes on a single issue. The quality of political debate, and indeed the capacity of government to function in the national interest, suffer when candidates and officeholders are forced to be more responsive to the narrow concerns of unrepresentative special interest groups than to overarching issues of domestic and foreign policy. The Court ignores the substantial governmental interests served by reasonable patronage. In my view, its decision will seriously hamper the functioning of stable political parties.[39]

By the time the patronage issue was revisited in *Rutan v. Republican Party of Illinois,*[40] Justice Powell had retired. Despite his absence, the decision involved a lively debate over parties and patronage, as Justice Scalia assumed the pro-party mantle. *Rutan* involved the propriety of a 1980 executive order issued by Illinois' Republican governor which imposed a hiring freeze on all state employees. The order prohibited the creation of any new positions or the hiring to fill currently vacant ones without the explicit approval of the governor. Democrats argued that the order was nothing more than a patronage tool for the Governor to use to reward his friends and supporters with available state jobs.

The Court upheld the plaintiffs' challenge to the executive order. It rejected the justifications proffered in *Elrod,* concluding that patronage was unnecessary to preserve the democratic process. Patronage had the opposite effect, impairing the elective process by discouraging free political expression by public employees.[41] Rationalizing that the parties had survived despite limits on patronage, the majority again disregarded the institutional role of parties in democracy.

Justice Scalia's dissent, in contrast, rivalled Powell's opinions for its forceful advocacy of the party position. Scalia lambasted the majority for its "inadequate appreciation of the systemic effects of patronage in promoting political stability" or "its potential to facilitate the integration of previously powerless groups."[42] Scalia noted the need for patronage to lure people into politics.

Ideological conviction alone would not "motivate sufficient numbers to keep the party going through the off years."[43] Without the
carrot of patronage to draw activists into campaign work, the inevitable result was to bypass parties in favor of increased reliance
on money and special interests.

Scalia also chastised the Court for its refusal to "acknowledge the link between patronage and party discipline, and between
party discipline and success."[44] Weakened party organizations led
to a system in which individual officeholders seek accommodation with the competing special interest groups. Scalia mimicked
the Court's assertion that "parties have already survived the substantial decline in patronage employment practices in this century." Noting the pervasiveness of divided government and the
overwhelming rate of incumbency reelection, Scalia rhetorically
asked:

> Parties have assuredly survived—but as what? As the forces
> upon which many of the essential compromises of American
> political life are hammered out? Or merely as convenient ve-
> hicles for the conducting of national Presidential elections?[45]

Finally, Scalia echoed Powell's observation in *Elrod* regarding the historical value of patronage as a tool of social and political integration for disadvantaged groups. Party politics has long
been characterized by the support given to the dominant party
machine by racial and ethnic minorities who benefit from the
rewards that the party machine confers. The elimination of patronage plugged a real point of access for those without other
avenues to power.[46]

THE INSTITUTIONAL BASIS
FOR THE RIGHT OF ASSOCIATION

The Supreme Court opinions on patronage have a greater significance than whether a particular government personnel decision
is an infringement on one's right of association.[47] The critical point
is the Court's refusal to give serious consideration to the party
organization justifications for patronage. Patronage issues have
ramifications for the institutional representative capacity of parties. Patronage is a defensible, even reasonable, practice when
parties are understood as critical components of representative
democracy. Patronage practices implicate party subsystems in realizing the values of authority and accountability. They also bear

on the collective dimensions of representation, enhancing the capability of the legislature to engage in activity that is responsive to the public.

A theory of representation cognizant of party structures warrants at least a forthright evaluation of these issues. But the majority did not even pay them lip service. In the final analysis, the Court's wielding of the doctrine of association raises problematic questions as to its application to parties. While the Court has conceded that the right applies to parties,[48] the patronage cases reflected a fixation on its individualistic forms.

This denies the ability of the institutions of parties to associate effectively, both in campaigns and in governance. The freedom of association is rooted in group politics. It is fundamental because it allows people to combine with others to make their voices heard. It is worthy of constitutional protection because the hope of advancing one's political ideas rests on finding others who share those ideas. To eliminate the right to associate is to leave one politically powerless.

A meaningful right of association, however, has collective dimensions. A constitutional recognition of the individual right that wholly ignores its corporate manifestation (in the form of a party, for example) may only have the practical effect of eviscerating purposeful association. It is incongruous to hold individual associational rights as sacred while withholding legal recognition from the fruits of such association (i.e., when association along party lines is successful in installing a party as the majority). The associational rights of parties (and groups) are logical extensions of the individual freedom to associate. Parties are the collective embodiment of individuals associating. But they are also more than the sum of those individuals who comprise them. *Both the paradigms of representation and positive pluralism rely on the institutional activities of parties to enlarge and augment individual political effectiveness.* People gain power by associating with party organizations that recruit and support candidates, register voters, and develop programs. Representation is realized via institutional structures that vigorously pursue a raft of electoral enterprises.

That institutional mode continues after the election with party organizations within government. Association not only rests on parties as shapers and organizers of electoral behavior, but also continues thereafter with the winning of power and with party governance. The right yields tangible results when translated into a presence within the official institutions of government. One

realizes political power when one's party is in control of government, crafting legislation, affecting public policy, and procuring
benefits for constituents. An awareness of both aspects of party
involvement is necessary to accomplish their representative potential, as mediating and aggregating vehicles for individuals and
groups.

Once again, the delineation of meaningful political rights
was hampered by the Court's failure to appreciate the representative, democratizing, and mediating functions performed by party
systems. The proper balance between individual rights and group-
based concerns will elude the Court until it incorporates the functional dimensions of party activity. This requires a comprehension
of the foundational importance of institutionalized, organized
political activity in the realization of representative government.
Individual associational rights have little practical significance when
the formal organizational structures into which people coalesce
and express themselves are legally submerged or ignored.

CHAPTER TEN

A "New and Improved" Theory of Representation: Institutionalized "Conflicts of Interest"

THE CONDITION OF REPRESENTATION IN AMERICAN POLITICS

The challenges presented by representation theory are grounded in the nature of representation itself. The path to effective representative government is through a labyrinth of theories, modes, and practices. The ideal of representative democracy fuses multiple concepts of representation, a variety of modes and practices that generate representation, and a host of political players acting in a representative capacity. It demands a recognition of a variety of understandings of representation; from the formalism of voting, to a legislature that is descriptive of society, to representative relationships, to the activity of government, which must correspond to the needs and wishes of the represented. It acknowledges the preferences of individual citizens while simultaneously promoting shared interests. It operates on multiple levels, as individuals and collectivities participate officially in the *selection* of leaders and informally in the *petitioning* of those leaders. Finally, it transpires only through intermediate structures of representation, namely political parties and associations of a variety of stripes and colors. Ultimately, the nature of representation requires systematic institutional arrangements to reconcile the intricacies and complexities of representational concepts and actors.

The greatest obstacle to this understanding of representation lies in *the liberal tradition in America*.[1] The liberal emphasis on individualism remains the fundamental feature of our popular belief system, occupying a core position in our cultural and social institutions, and dominating our political thought and practice.[2] It is manifested in a predisposition toward pure, unhindered individualistic forms of political participation, and is the dominant theme in constitutional jurisprudence on issues of voting, elections, and representation. The Court's theory of representation is grounded in a strong preference for unchanneled personal political activity. Politics is most desirable when practiced by individuals unrestrained by political organizations.

The corollary of this individualistic conceptualization of politics is a fundamental distrust of political organizations. The Court's guiding principle in campaign finance disputes, patronage, and voter and ballot access cases is an abridged version of representation aimed at promoting greater participation and fairness for individuals, often at the expense of political organizations. More recently, this judicial preoccupation with individualistic representation has been tempered by an infusion of an element of group consciousness. Group-regarding jurisprudence surfaced with race-conscious rules of redistricting designed to enhance the representation of minorities. It was then extended to general partisan gerrymandering activities, as the Court explicitly announced a group right to "fair and effective representation."

The Court's recognition of group rights, however, was driven by political considerations rather than a theoretical understanding of institutionalized group structures as representative in character. The Court found itself dispensing "group representation" rights to isolated groups out of political pressure or necessity, but with no basis for defining those rights or the premise upon which they could be assigned. It was reduced to making descriptive assignments based on political, rather than legal, considerations. The result was a potential morass, with the Court making political calculations beyond its capabilities and outside its authority.

The missing theoretical tool is found in the pluralist, group-constituted character of the American political landscape. Group theories suggest that individual political efficacy hinges on the collectivities that exist to represent one's interests. Only through the struggles and conflicts between group forces and influences are the divergent goals of representative democracy realized. Individuals are empowered by vigorous group competition, which simultaneously generates policies in the public interest. The pluralist character of our political terrain compels formal mechanisms for identifying shared interests and responding to them.

The defects of pluralism in practice cast this justification into doubt, as the assumptions underlying group activity proved suspect. The failings of pluralism included the gradual erosion of party systems, imperfections in group competition, wide disparities in group resources and influence, and the private nature of group influence, coupled with the democratic shortcomings of political groups. These factors contributed to the fragmentation of public policy and the disintegration of government administration into interest-group liberalism. In the end, a system built exclusively around groups was unlikely to realize the main goal of pluralist theory, the enhancement of individual political equality and effectiveness.

For a Supreme Court searching for a framework for incorporating group considerations, the imperfections of pluralism revealed the central challenge of representation: how to reconcile the fundamental objective of individual equality with the need to remedy organizational inequality. It demanded institutional arrangements that would simultaneously enrich the individualistic assumptions of representation while addressing the shortcomings of pluralist and partisan representative structures; structures that enhance the representative quality of groups without sacrificing fundamental standards of individual equality.

The approval of race-conscious remedial measures in redistricting and reapportionment suggested one response: the conferral of formal legal rights directly upon certain groups. The goal was to elevate the representative status of disadvantaged groups to create a fairer, more level group playing field. In campaign finance, the Court embraced the neopluralist approach, as groups were ranked and accorded different rights. It marked an effort to balance and equalize the political influence of groups by monitoring and managing the resources they could bring to bear on the system, and distinguishing between groups based on character, structure, and representative capabilities.

But solutions premised upon formal group representation confront serious challenges in theory and in practice. The focus on the rights of separate, discrete groups suggests a proclivity to divide and segment the polity, undermining the delicate tension between the paradoxical goals of representation. Group representation's factionalizing tendencies make it more difficult to simultaneously satisfy particular group interests and the common good. Empirically, the categorizing and ordering of groups for purposes of dispensing special representative privilege presents insurmountable challenges. The gauging of political resources to permit the rationing of influence is equally problematic. Finally, group representation abandons the complex reality of representation in favor of a one-dimensional substitute consisting mostly of descriptive elements. In sum, it is difficult to construct a theory of group representation that logically and consistently advances the goal of political equality of individuals.

By comparison, a party systems model offers a more comprehensive response to the myriad of representational demands. Party structures are instrumental at both levels of the dual system of representation; they assist in the selection of rulers via elections, and they petition government in the realm of policy-making. They act as agents of governance and help achieve policy outputs that represent the people's preferences. In these multiple roles, party systems serve the essential democratic values of accountability and public control in a nonpareil way.

Parties also alleviate the contradictory demands of pluralism by facilitating both individual and group activity. They empower individuals by aggregating, channelling, and giving expression to individual participation. They also serve as vehicles of group influence, building their electoral success upon coalitions of groups. On one hand, they foster diversity and amplify the multiplicity of voices. But they also unify and coalesce, cultivating a civic consciousness and enlightened perspective among party members. *In short, the unique institutional and structural attributes of party organizations enable them to satisfy the multiple demands of representation. These distinctive functional capabilities compel a party-informed constitutional jurisprudence.*

Party structures, however, are the missing component in the Court's theory of representation. The Court has displayed a basic misunderstanding of parties as integral tools of representative democratic politics. In ballot and voter access issues, it has submerged the obvious differences between independent candidates and party organizations. It has actually subordinated parties to other political associations in carving out a group right to representation in gerrymandering disputes. In campaign finance decisions, the parties are excluded from the discussion altogether. In severely circumscribing party patronage, the Court has refused to entertain the possibility that those practices might contribute to the institutional foundations of parties. *Ultimately, the Court's decisions on electoral politics show a dangerous indifference toward the institutional safeguards of representative democracy that reside in the form of political parties.*

WHY DOES IT MATTER?

The judicial disregard for parties has significant consequences for the American polity. The fading of parties from the political balance mirrors the decline of mediating organizations on a broader scale. Without the tempering effect of intermediate entities such as churches, civic organizations, public service associations, and political parties, the individualistic, rights-based side of liberalism threatens the efficacy of a group-constituted society.[3] The liberal-pluralist dichotomy is a fundamental aspect of the political character of this country. It compels the existence of institutional means of muffling its inherent contradictions. It requires intermediate structures with the capacity to serve our liberal heritage, while promoting the unified voice that is the glue of our pluralist society.[4]

In this light, the responses to the dilemma of representation suggest markedly divergent consequences. Societal trends create the distinct impression that the perspectives of the various groupings of people are narrowing instead of broadening, that they are becoming more polarized and less harmonious, more singular and self-interested and less community-minded and public-directed. The neopluralist distribution of group rights will not counteract, and may even intensify, the threat of group polarization and atomism. The essential role of intermediate party systems, in contrast, is to soften and mute those differences, and to foster the requisite spirit of tolerance.

The nature of representation presents imposing challenges to successful representative government. The neglect of party subsystems makes that complex reality more difficult to attain. It compromises basic democratic goals of accountability and control. The preference for unfettered personal politics slights those entities capable of aggregating and molding political behavior for the achievement of those values. The submergence of parties has left the public without effective means of directing their representatives to act or of removing them when they fail. It has widened the disconnect between the governed and their governors.

The result is a palpable public disillusionment with politics. The deterioration of the equipment for transforming diffused individual activity into meaningful political input has begotten an environment of alienation, distrust and dissatisfaction. One's perception of political participation and its consequences (or lack of consequences) is an important determinant of one's regard (or disregard) for government. While citizens have enjoyed an inexorable expansion of individual political rights and opportunities, they have been deprived of a corresponding increase in political efficacy. People perceive their influence as marginal, as special interests dominate and the government becomes less responsive to individual needs and preferences. The result is large numbers of citizens who see little value in the basic democratic exercise of casting a ballot, and who forego the most elementary form of political activity.

The irony is that this disillusionment breeds a greater desire for direct and unmediated involvement. The layperson's natural inclination is to blame the political institutions and actors for this state of affairs. Parties provide convenient scapegoats for a restless electorate and for incumbents intent on keeping their office. Officeholders with little need for the parties are all too eager to impose additional restraints on them to appease the public hue and cry for change.

Nor are political parties the only actors to bear unfairly the brunt of public cynicism. PACs and pressure groups have acquired a reputation in the current climate bordering on criminality. Without the institutional structures to moderate and control group influence, the inherently representative character of group activity is overlooked. Group politics, as legitimate means of representing individuals, have fallen into disrepute. But when additional restraints on parties and groups in the name of untrammeled personal participation fail to generate a more responsive government, the result is a cycle of escalating skepticism and alienation.

THE PARTY POTENTIALITIES: ISSUES AND OPPORTUNITIES

The cynicism that pervades public attitudes is not only the major consequence of the judicial neglect of parties; it is also the primary obstacle to redressing that neglect. Public skepticism is evident in the low esteem in which parties are held. Public attitudes toward parties are highly unfavorable. The prevalent public distaste for political organizations generally, and parties specifically, means that any effort to alter judicial attitudes toward parties must do so within the context of those negative perceptions.

What is the significance of this observation? First, it is appropriate for the Court to take public opinion into account. The Court is ultimately one arm of a representative form of government. It is, at the most basic level, a representative institution. We no longer operate from the naive assumption that the Court is untainted by politics, nor do we desire it to be. The Court is responsive to public attitudes and opinions, and is representative of them. The Court's legitimacy is derivative of its representative character, and it is incumbent upon the Court to function generally within the bounds of public opinion.

But the Court behaves as a representative institution in a manner much different from that of the legislature or executive. The Court ought not to merely reflect the existing state of public opinion on whatever matter is before it. Rather, it is the Court's task to ensure that representative government is functioning in a manner consistent with those criteria and characteristics that the people agreed to in ratifying the Constitution. The Court is acting representatively when it decides current issues congruously with the values and ideas at the heart of the form of government to which the people have consented. This requires that the Court carefully craft and enunciate constitutional theories and philosophies that permit traditional constitutional values to be applied to contemporary circumstances. It is this more subtle representative role that gives the Court the appearance of sometimes leading, and sometimes following, public opinion.

The parties' low standing with the public is relevant to the Court's consideration of issues pertaining to the parties' constitutional status. The Court as an institution is cognizant of how its decisions are likely to be received, and strong negative reactions act as practical restraints on judicial behavior. In this way, the people's disdain for parties may furnish outer limits or bounds on how far the Court is willing to go or what it can do.

The constraining influence of public dissatisfaction with parties depends on the particular party function under consideration. For example, party organizations have retained a vitality and cohesiveness within government that they have failed to sustain among the voters themselves. It is within the electorate itself that parties' influence and salience are waning the most. Party functions that operate at the grass roots level, then, are more seriously affected by public contempt than party functions in government. The argument that parties ought to be instrumental tools in redistricting methods loses some of its force when many voters participate without reference to parties. The patronage argument, which rests in part on parties as agents of democratization, is weakened when parties are failing in that respect. Hence, it is not for the Court to artificially boost the parties' representative character where it does not actually exist.

But public sentiments ought not to affect the Court's explication of constitutional principles, the purpose of which is to treat parties according to constitutional values which the people have sanctioned. Those values that the Court is responsible for representing include notions of democratic responsiveness, equality, consent, public choice, accountability, and authority. If political parties are imperative to realizing these constitutional values, as is contended here, then the Court should incorporate them into its analysis, notwithstanding low public regard, the absence of parties from the constitutional text, or their own often anemic performance.[5]

Reflections on the constitutional status of parties are more than idle ruminations. Party structures are not beyond rehabilitation, nor are the consequences of their neglect irreparable. On the contrary, a number of battlefields loom which will present new opportunities to consider the importance of party organizations. In several of those areas, the Court is on the cusp, seemingly poised to avail itself of a party-centered response to the challenge of representation.

One such area is the *group right to fair and effective representation.* That right was established in *Bandemer* in 1986, but has since remained dormant, perhaps waiting for fertile testing ground in future rounds of elections. The right clearly encompassed political parties, although its scope was much broader. *Bandemer* marked an explicit acknowledgment by the Court of the relevance of group politics to focusing representation. But it avoided any discussion of the substance of that right. Consequently, its future remains uncharted (some may even contend it has no future, in view of the length of the dormancy).

Redistricting and reapportionment issues continue to provide opportunities for the Court to reassess the roles of the cast of political actors in achieving representation. *Shaw v. Reno* and *Miller v. Johnson* revealed a Court searching for a mode of analysis that would deal with a broader range of collective interests in electoral systems. Those cases suggested the ripening of the Court's group-conscious instincts, as it sought to moderate race-based remedies in favor of accommodating a greater array of group identities. They showed the Court moving beyond descriptive representational goals to incorporate additional criteria in its theory of representation.

Nor is the judicial whittling away at *patronage practices* necessarily a *fait accompli*. Defenders of patronage as the glue of strong party organizations have found an articulate and vocal minority on the Court. The personnel changes on the Court since *Elrod* could turn that minority into a majority. Were another dispute over the parameters of patronage to find its way to the High Court, it might result in an explicit judicial acceptance of a party-centered system of representative structures.

The Court's recent struggles in *ballot access* cases also reveal a fruitful area for enriching constitutional concepts of representation. In *Burdick*, the Court saw the need to structure electoral processes to clarify and give significance to the exercise of the ballot, supplementing individual voting activity with the "channeling [of] expressive activity at the polls." The Court remains in need of a constitutional principle that will rectify the unevenness of the line of ballot and voter access cases. The timing is ripe for a recognition of party structures as the answer to these dual objectives.

The tensions in the ballot access cases likewise point to emerging issues relating to the status of additional parties in what has been predominantly a two-party system. Multi-party systems are on the rise on the state level, and have important implications for a theory of representation that is properly cognizant of parties. The Court is not alone in its struggle over where to place minor and new parties on the political spectrum. Analyzing the status of parties from a functional perspective suggests that minor and new parties are perfectly legitimate means of satisfying important democratic functions which the two-party system sometimes fails to address.[6]

The current climate is likely to produce constitutional battles over the proper role of all kinds of parties. A party-based theory of representation would give the Court a framework for confronting such issues. The emphasis on organizational structures certainly has room for multi-party systems. It would enable the Court to draw distinctions between major parties, minor parties, and independent candidacies in a less arbitrary and more consistent fashion than that which has characterized the ballot access area.

Finally, the war will continue over the limits of *states' author-ity to regulate the parties.* On one hand, the Court has expanded party freedoms by extending associational rights to the parties. Parties have greater autonomy in endorsing candidates and con-trolling internal party procedures. They have broader latitude to define themselves and their membership, and to determine who can participate in party activities. Greater associational freedoms are also evidenced in the Court's sanctioning of modest ballot restrictions that favor party affiliation.[7]

But the Court has been inhibited by the absence of a theo-retical framework for formulating those associational rights. Even when deferring to parties, it has ignored their institutional con-tributions. The Court treats parties as just another politically ac-tive interest group, overlooking their unique attributes. While the Court may not be consciously anti-party, the cases reflect the ab-sence of a theory for treating parties as tools of representation. The current climate will produce additional challenges to party rights. In an environment that is anti-incumbent, anti-political es-tablishment, and anti-political party, parties remain easy targets for security-seeking incumbents who wish to create the illusion of positive political reform.

REDEFINING REPRESENTATION:
INSTITUTIONALIZED "CONFLICTS OF INTERESTS"

This, then, is the challenge facing the Court in its search for a theory of representation: to reconcile the variety of demands emanating from the web of representation theory while squaring theories of group activity with the criticisms of pluralism applied, and doing so within the confines of a hostile political environ-ment, in which parties are treated almost as illegitimate organiza-tions. The key to meeting these challenges hinges on the Court's ability to think of representation in a new light. The Court's stab at group theory has been to grant special rights status to certain groups, usually along racial or ethnic lines. There are two prob-lems with this approach. First, representation of groups based on ethnicity misses the underlying goal of government, which is to represent and reflect the policies and political interests in society. Race and ethnicity are not synonymous with political interests, and may not be accurate measures of them. But it is the interests that are of ultimate significance for purposes of representation, not race. Second, the formulation of a right to representation only makes the representational paradigm more difficult to realize. Reducing representation to rights, rather than thinking of it in terms of contending interests or preferences, rigidifies the contradictions of representation theory. It only renders the problems of representation more intractable.[8]

These weaknesses could be remedied if the Court were to apply a traditional legal concept in a nontraditional way. The difficulties disappear when representation is conceptualized as a "conflict of interests." Conflicts of interest typically have a negative connotation in the legal context. The lawyer with a conflict of interest is compromised in his ability to wholeheartedly represent his client. The judge with a conflict of interest is hampered in her capacity to fairly and objectively hear the matter before her. From these perspectives, conflicts of interests are pitfalls to be avoided.

But in the context of representation rightly understood, a conflict of interests is a desirable state of affairs. It simply recognizes that the effectiveness of political representation directly corresponds to the number of interests and influences brought to bear on representatives and on representative institutions. The greater the range of interests represented, the higher the caliber of representation. Conflicts of interest do not disqualify a representative or hinder him in the performance of his duties, but enable him to represent. The goal should be to heighten the conflict of interests by including as many interests as possible. Only the legislator or representative assembly that maximizes its conflicts of interest is likely to approach the complex representative paradigm. The representative endowed with a healthy conflict of interests will appreciate the set of representational modes at his disposal, the vast array of interests to which he must respond, and the various forms (individual and collective) in which those interests present themselves.

The conception of representation as existing in a state of interest conflict captures the pluralist vision of policy outcomes as the product of conflicts between competing interests. Legitimate democratic choices are made out of conflict and competition. The greater the conflict and the higher the number of interests involved, the sounder the policy is likely to be. Moreover, this notion returns the focus of representation to its proper place. The emphasis is not on peoples or races or ethnic types, but on representing political interests. Representation is not achieved by bestowing rights, but by attaining a state of competing, contending interests.

Envisioning representation as a conflict of interests (or more accurately as a set of conflicts of interests) underscores the indispensibility of the substructures of representation in the form of parties and groups. Without them, the conflict is dampened and diffused. Through representative parties and groups, a greater number of interests speak, and with a stronger and clearer voice. As more interests are brought into the representative forum, the conflict is increased. At the same time, that conflict must yield representative action. Party institutions provide means for acting upon those interest conflicts. The representative who absorbs conflicts but who is cut loose from the moorings of the party system is inadequately equipped to act on them. She is relegated to giving the appearance of representing, without actually doing so. The same is true on a corporate scale, where a government without party structures cannot act upon a set of conflicts or translate them into coherent policy outputs.

It is within party structures that the interests conflict and compete, and are resolved by the representatives. Party structures permit the ranking and prioritizing of interests. They allow the representative to pick and choose and decide in settling interest conflicts in a democratically legitimate fashion, as opposed to yielding to isolated special interests. Similarly, defined structures in government in the form of majority and opposition parties provide governance out of what would otherwise be a paralyzing set of conflicts of interests.

The theory of representation, therefore, demands that democratic structures first create a conflict of interests and then operate to turn it into representative action. The premise of this discussion is that the challenges of representation can only be met through the acknowledgment of subsystems and structures as conceptions of representation. It requires a consistent attitudinal embrace of political entities that serve as organizational and institutional prerequisites of representative democracy, namely, political parties and associations.

The Court has confronted questions of political representation in a variety of contexts. Its tendency is to consider them in isolation, without taking into account the implications of a decision for other areas. It has lacked an integrated theory of representation that would provide a common theme for redistricting issues, ballot access questions, campaign finance regulation, or patronage disputes. The challenge is to arrive at an integrated understanding of representative institutions and arrangements that is consistently applied regardless of the context.

To reconcile these cases requires a uniform focus on the institutional and organizational criteria of representation. The point is not to expect a pro-party outcome in every setting. But whether the dispute is over gerrymandering, campaign finance, patronage, ballot or voter access, or party rights of association, it should be resolved with an eye toward the institutional criteria of representation and the indispensable functions performed through party/group structures. It dictates that the Court's analysis be infused with a cognizance of the functional value of parties and groups in creating conflicts of interest and in shaping the activity arising out of those conflicts into representation.

The case for elevating parties constitutionally arises not out of some sentimental fondness but from a realization of and appreciation for the functions they perform. The organizational and institutional activities of parties are instrumental to our democracy's functioning. A consistent adjustment in judicial attitudes would better equip parties to satisfy their primary theoretical justifications. For example, it would go far toward correcting the legal imbalance between parties and interest groups. This would help counteract the personal, candidate-centered elections that now dominate, and in the process enable parties to better shape and mold opinions to give elections greater meaning.

A focus on parties might also provide a legitimate and realistic avenue to controlling groups in a way not possible through the neopluralist approach. It would heighten the incentives for groups to work through parties, thereby enhancing the parties' abilities to act as group facilitators. It would dampen the divisive splintering of the public interest, which stems from the primacy of interest group influence. It would avoid the setting of group against group, which grows out of the neopluralist strategy of group rights.

The institutionalization of conflicts of interests brings us back full circle in the quest for true political representation in a pluralist democratic setting. Representation is ultimately about ensuring that the subjects have control over what their government does. The complexities of representation confirm that this is certainly not self-executing, nor is it realized through haphazard, random, or informal means. On the contrary, "representative government requires that there be machinery for the expression of the wishes of the represented, and that the government respond to those wishes."[9] Party structures provide this, in a public and systematic way. The dual components of interest expression and policy realization demand formal organizational means of channeling political activity. Individuals can and will act discretely, as will individual legislators. But political representation is realized only as actors behave in concert as citizens and as members of a representative body, in participation and in governance. Without the institutional devices to do this, the ideal of representation is an elusive goal.

APPENDIX A
THE ATTITUDINAL ENVIRONMENT

A SURVEY OF EXPERTS AND PRACTITIONERS ON THE ROLES OF INDIVIDUAL, ASSOCIATIONAL, AND PARTY PARTICIPATION IN POLITICAL REPRESENTATION

The research for this project included canvassing a variety of political actors who are practically involved with issues of political representation, political parties and interest groups, and the legal dimensions thereof. The survey was targeted at a cross-section of experts and practitioners whose work is directly relevant to the issues and dilemmas touched upon in this study. They included: (1) law professors, political scientists, and other academics with a special interest in questions of political representation; (2) legal practitioners, especially those representing political actors or litigating disputes in the electoral arena; (3) political party leadership and activists; and (4) lobbyists and interest group representatives.

The objectives of the survey were multi-fold, but interrelated. First, it was intended to enlarge and enrich the perspective of the dissertation with the pragmatic insights of practitioners. Their views and opinions, coming at the issues from the inside, are especially important for a deeper understanding of the attributes and dimensions of the problems of political representation. Second, it was hoped that they would offer opinions and reactions specifically with respect to the conclusions reached based on the textual analysis of the Supreme Court decisions. Again, agreement or disagreement of those involved on the real-life level ought to serve either to support and augment my judgments or suggest the need for further critical thinking and examination of the issues. Finally, the survey was intended to reflect the likelihood of legitimate reform of representative structures, by testing the beliefs held by those from whom reform is most likely to come. In short, the survey ought to check (in an admittedly modest fashion) the judgments and conclusions arrived at in this dissertation with the attitudinal environment, as reflected by the selected participants.

105 surveys were mailed, and all but one was delivered. Of the 104 delivered surveys, 24 provided written responses, for a return rate of 23 percent. However, five of those declined to furnish substantive responses to the questionnaire. I therefore received 19 substantive responses, for a return of 18 percent. The bulk of the responses came from self-identified legal practitioners and party activists (question 9). Of those who provided substantive answers, nine identified themselves as legal practitioners, eight as party leaders or activists, three as political scientists, two as law professors, two as interest group leaders, and three miscellaneous. (These exceeded the total number of responses because a number of the respondents placed themselves within more than one category.) The identities of the respondents certainly are relevant to their perspectives. For example, party leaders are likely to have a much different perspective on the dilemmas explored herein than interest group representatives. The special interest of those responding must be kept in mind when considering the results. (I did not break down the responses according to the specialization of the respondents because of the small sample size.)

The survey consisted of a total of ten questions, most of them with numerous subparts. It was divided into four general areas: (1) Political representation; (2) Individuals and groups; (3) Political parties and interest groups; and (4) Background information on the respondents. The results of the survey are discussed in Appendix C. Care must be taken not to draw too firm conclusions from a sample of this size. Nevertheless, several general conclusions can be drawn from the responses, which provide an interesting supplement to the themes running through the text of this work.

TENTATIVE CONCLUSIONS

A. The Nature and Effectiveness of Political Representation

Chapter One included a thorough review of the literature pertaining to political representation. It concluded that the model of effective political representation necessitated a complex interweaving of a host of representational modes and concepts. Unfortunately, representative ideals are too often reduced to well-intended but simplistic formulas. The first section of the questionnaire sought to flesh out the experts' understanding of what constitutes real political representation.

In questions one and two, the experts were asked to rate the importance of five different concepts of representation (question 1), and to judge how well U.S. electoral structures accomplish each of them (question 2). The responses generally supported the conclusion that we are lacking both a broadly held definition of political representation and agreement on how to attain it. In some areas, there was a strong consensus, while in others there exists a lack of even marginal agreement about what actually constitutes effective representation.

The clearest level of agreement pertained to the acceptance of *formal* electoral structures as assuring political representation (1a). Ninety percent of those responding judged formal representation (through elections, voting and equally weighted votes) to be important or very important, with almost four-fifths (79 percent) of those viewing it as very important. Hence, there is a dominant allegiance to modes of formal representation. In this respect, the views of the experts largely mirror the formalistic approach which has prevailed on the Court since the early 1960s with the implementation of one person one vote. Moreover, the respondents expressed satisfaction with the extent to which our representational system meets this criterion. They were generally of the opinion that our system serves that function well or very well (2a). Over three-fourths (78 percent) responded positively to the question of whether U.S. electoral structures accomplished formal representation. The responses to these questions reflect a strong preference for formalism, and a desire to reduce our politics to process.

Reactions to other modes of representation were far more mixed and muddy. Forty percent of those responding thought the *deliberative* character of representative bodies to be very important (1b). At the same time, they were skeptical of the system's ability to accomplish that (2b). The respondents generally had little sympathy for the notion, proferred by Lani Guinier and others, that representation requires that actual government *outcomes* reflect individual citizen preferences (1c). Over 60 percent judged this to be of little or modest importance.

More surprising were the responses to the desirability of *descriptive* representation (1d); that is, that the legislature actually reflect the physical characteristics of the relevant groups found in society. The respondents were less than enthusiastic, with 50 percent responding negatively compared to only 22 percent who considered this to be an important dimension of representation. In this case, the opinions of the practitioners seem to run contrary to the Court's predilection for promoting descriptive avenues of representation, as reflected in redistricting and Voting Rights cases.

Finally, the respondents generally accepted the importance of representative schemes that focus on *national* interests rather than local or regional ones (1e). Sixty-eight percent agreed that this should be the focus of legislative action. They were more dubious, however, as to the system's proficiency at furthering the national interest. Sixty-three percent felt that U.S. electoral systems accomplished this poorly (2e).

B. Individuals and Groups as Political Actors

Chapter Four reviewed in some detail the group theory of politics and the group-constituted pluralist vision of democracy that it spawned. Questions 3–6 of the survey questionnaire explored the respective importance and roles of individuals and groups in representative government. The purpose was to examine the extent to which the principles of group theory and pluralism are embedded in the views of those responding.

The results of this section suggest that the American liberal values of individualism, which dominate the constitutional jurisprudence, are held just as strongly by the survey respondents. These questions reveal three general themes. First, the overwhelming preference in the responses to questions 1–2 for formal means of equalizing individual input assume the central importance of the individual in issues of representation. Similarly, this set of responses confirm that the individual remains the primary political unit of analysis. Hence, 42 percent of the respondents considered individual participation as *very important* to ensuring that citizen preferences were heard by representative structures (compared to 21 percent for groups and 26 percent for parties) (question 3). In addition, half of those responding felt that individuals exert too little influence on U.S. policymaking, while only 11 percent thought they had too much influence (4a). The progressive emphasis on individual participation as the democratic ideal remains strong.

This is accompanied, however, by an equally healthy respect for the parties. An even higher number of the respondents, 55 percent, believe that political parties' influence on policymaking was too little, while only 5 percent thought it to be too much (4c). This is especially significant for several reasons. First, the experts' desire to elevate the influence of parties diverges from the public perception of parties as superfluous and unnecessary. Second, the general opinion that the parties wield little influence on policymaking runs counter to the opinions of political scientists, who maintain that party affiliation and organization in government remain determinative in Congress, where policy is made.

Despite a general wish for greater party influence, several questions exposed a lack of faith in parties' capacity to perform certain functions attributed to them. When asked to rate the importance of parties' endorsements of candidates, 55 percent of the respondents believed they had no effect on or benefit for individual political effectiveness (question 5d). Similarly, 50 percent responded that party activity generally has no effect in realizing individual political effectiveness (question 5f). This suggests a misunderstanding of the parties' theoretical role, even among the purported experts.

In contrast to their regard for individuals and parties, the respondents expressed real apprehension over the level of group involvement in policymaking. Two-thirds (67 percent) agree that groups have too much influence over policymaking (4b). Thus, the experts appear to share the public's discomfort with the extent of group influence in interest group liberalism. Question 6 further explored those reservations by examining the criticisms that have been leveled at group politics. The results raise serious misgivings about the propriety of groups acting as primary and formal units of political representation. One respondent, however, refused to accept the demarcation of political actors along individual and collective lines. This anonymous interest group representative editorialized that "[g]roups and parties are made up of individuals and represent their interests," and therefore he did not see significant political distinctions between individuals, groups, and parties.

Sixty-eight percent agreed with the proposition that a system of group representation may cause additional division, separatism, and tension between groups in society (6a). Sixty percent were similarly apprehensive about whether groups could be trusted to adequately serve the interests of their members. Finally, 65 percent considered groups to be too self-interested and single-issue oriented to justify granting them formal representative status (6d).

Several of the more serious theoretical objections to group representation are confirmed by these attitudes of the practitioners.

C. The Party-Group Relationship in Pluralist Democracy

Chapter Six concluded with the party response as an alternative to group representation as a means of alleviating the pluralist dilemma. At the heart of that argument is the capacity of parties to act as vehicles for increasing effectiveness of political participation by individuals and groups. Questions 7 and 8 of the survey look more closely at this aspect of party theory, by examining the relationship between parties and groups in attaining effective representation.

Those results provided little by way of consensus regarding the parties' capacity to function according to the party-based ideal set out in Chapter Three. For example, there was no clearly preferred answer to the question of whether parties are effective in providing groups with a public voice and forum to air their concerns (7a). The respondents as a group were equally uncertain about the parties' ability to function as moderators of group conflict (7c). One respondent, a self-described party leader/activist no less, provided an editorial disclaimer, emphatically denying that such was the parties' purpose.

If anything, the results suggest some doubt as to whether parties do in fact act according to the model. Over half (52 percent) disagreed or strongly disagreed with the contention that parties do an adequate job of moderating and integrating group interests into a coherent party program and plan for governing (7b). Only 31 percent expressed agreement with that statement. At the same time, the answers reflect a general assumption that the parties remain necessary tools of democratic government. Fifty-seven percent refused to accept the notion that there are other political organizations that might emerge to satisfy the democratic functions that parties perform (7e). In short, the ambivalence over the democratic value of parties so prevalent in the public is shared among our field of experts, although perhaps to a lesser degree.

Finally, the survey inquired about possible legal reforms that might be pursued as means of rejuvenating the parties. These included proposals involving (1) restrictions on partisan gerrymandering, (2) campaign financing reform, (3) greater freedom of parties to resort to patronage, (4) restructuring of nominating procedures, and (5) enhanced party autonomy. Several of these proposals received broad support. Sixty-three percent thought that reforms that elevate the role of party influence in campaign financing would have a major positive impact on their performance (8b). Fifty-seven percent also agreed that giving the parties greater control over nominating candidates would have a major constructive impact on the parties (8d). Both of these conclusions are firmly in line with political science orthodoxy.

At least one respondent expressed strong dissatisfaction with the current state of things. Michael Greve, Executive Director of the Center for Individual Rights, wondered (perhaps facetiously) whether we should "reverse every Congressional reform of the past three decades."

D. A Concluding Word

For those who see parties as integral components of a sound representational structure, these results are moderately encouraging. While the conclusions are admittedly skewed by the perspectives of those responding, they nevertheless reflect a general regard for parties that is lacking in the judicial treatment of them. Moreover, they fit rather neatly within the theoretical construct that is responsible for the pluralist dilemma.

Those responding desire greater influence and effectiveness for individual participants. They also see parties as preferable to interest groups in achieving that. They desire greater substantive influence for parties, even though they have some reservations about parties' abilities to serve as effective tools of group politics. Finally, they are willing to entertain changes in the laws that impact the electoral and representational structures as ways of improving the parties' standing.

APPENDIX B
SURVEY QUESTIONNAIRE AND
STATISTICAL TALLIES

INDIVIDUAL, ASSOCIATIONAL AND PARTY
PARTICIPATION IN POLITICAL REPRESENTATION

A. Political Representation

1. Political representation encompasses numerous concepts and ideas. On a scale of 1 to 5, rate the *importance* of the following principles of representation in achieving a political system which is truly representative (1 = little or no importance, 5 = very important).

   a. Every citizen should be formally represented through elections, and through the right to cast a ballot and have an equally weighted vote. (Formal)
   [N=19]   1: 10.5%   2: 0   3: 0   4: 10.5   5: 79%

   b. Every citizen should have an equal opportunity for his/her preferences to be heard and considered by the legislature. (Deliberative)
   [N=18]   1: 16.67%   2: 11   3: 16.67   4: 16.67   5: 39

   c. Every citizen should have an equal opportunity to see his/her preferences enacted in actual government outcomes. (Output)
   [N=18]   1: 44.4%   2: 16.67   3: 27.7   4: 0   5: 11

   d. The legislature, in its makeup, should reflect or mirror the relevant groups existing in society. (Descriptive)
   [N=18]   1: 33.3%   2: 16.67   3: 27.7   4: 11   5: 11

   e. Legislative action should be primarily focused on accomplishing what is in the interest of the nation or the whole. (National)
   [N=19]   1: 5.2%   2: 10.5   3: 15.8   4: 26   5: 42

2.   How successfully do the U.S. electoral structures *accomplish* these principles of representation? (1 = poorly or not at all, 5 = very well)

    a.   Formal (elections and voting)
        [N=18]   1: 5.5%   2: 0   3: 16.67   4: 39   5: 39

    b.   Deliberative (preferences heard)
        [N=18]   1: 0   2: 22%   3: 27.7   4: 50   5: 0

    c.   Output (preferences enacted)
        [N=17]   1: 11.7%   2: 35   3: 47   4: 5.8   5: 0

    d.   Descriptive (mirroring of relevant groups)
        [N=18]   1: 11%   2: 44.4   3: 39   4: 5.5   5: 0

    e.   National (interests of the entire nation)
        [N=19]   1: 21%   2: 42   3: 15.8   4: 15.8   5: 5.2

B. Individuals and Groups

3.   Citizens engage in political activity in different ways; directly through individual participation and indirectly through group or associational participation, including involvement with political parties. On a scale of 1 to 5, rate the *importance* of individuals, groups, and/or parties in ensuring that citizen preferences are heard by our representative structures (1 = of little or no importance, 5 = very important).

    a.   Individual participation
        [N=19]   1: 15.8%   2: 15.8   3: 21   4: 5.2   5: 42

    b.   Group participation
        [N=19]   1: 5.2%   2: 10.5   3: 26   4: 36.8   5: 21

    c.   Party participation
        [N=19]   1: 5.2%   2: 15.8   3: 36.8   4: 15.8   5: 26

4.   State whether you think the following political participants have too much, too little, or about the right *level of influence* on U.S. policymaking.

    a.   Individuals:
        [N=18]   Too much: 11%   Too little: 50
        About right: 38.8

    b.   Groups/Associations:
        [N=18]   Too much: 67%   Too little: 5.5
        About right: 27.7

c.   Political parties:
     [N=18]   Too much: 5.5%   Too little: 55.5
     About right: 38.8

5.   Political participation by groups and organizations is justi-
     fied as a means for individual citizens to be more effective
     in influencing government. On a scale from 1 to 5, rate
     whether the following group activities have the *overall effect*
     of fostering or frustrating the goal of individual political ef-
     fectiveness (1 = serious impediment, 3 = no effect, 5 = very
     effective).

     a.   Lobbying
          [N=18]   1: 11%   2: 22   3: 16.67   4: 38.8   5: 11

     b.   Financial campaign support
          [N=18]   1: 11%   2: 22   3: 16.67   4: 38.8   5: 11

     c.   Other campaign support
          [N=18]   1: 0   2: 5.5%   3: 38.8   4: 44.4   5: 11

     d.   Candidate endorsement
          [N=18]   1: 0   2: 11%   3: 55.5   4: 22   5: 11

     e.   Bloc voting
          [N=16]   1: 0   2: 12.5%   3: 31   4: 43.7   5: 12.5

     f.   Party activity
          [N=18]   1: 5.5%   2: 5.5   3: 50   4: 33.3   5: 5.5

6.   One way to remedy group inequalities (and therefore fur-
     ther individual equality of the members of those groups) is
     through a system of formal group representation. This idea
     has generated controversy, as well as a number of objections.
     On a scale of 1 to 5, state whether you agree or disagree
     with the following *issues* of group representation (1 = strongly
     agree, 5 = strongly disagree, N = no opinion).

     a.   Group representation may cause division, separatism
          and tension between groups in society.
          [N=19]   1: 15.7%   2: 52.6   3: 5.2   4: 15.7
          5: 5.2   N: 5.2

     b.   Groups are usually not sufficiently democratic in their
          character to warrant giving them formal representation.
          [N=18]   1: 16.7%   2: 16.7   3: 27.7   4: 16.7
          5: 5.5   N: 16.7

c   Groups often cannot be relied upon to serve the inter-
        ests of their members (i.e. they are not adequately
        representative).
        [N=18]   1: 22%   2: 38.8   3: 16.7   4: 16.7
        5: 5.5   N: 0

d.   Groups tend to be too self-interested and single-issue
        oriented to justify formal representative status.
        [N=18]   1: 38.8%   2: 16.7   3: 22   4: 11
        5: 5.5   N: 5.5

C. Political Parties and Groups

7.   Parties are, in theory, vehicles for increasing the effective-
        ness of political participation by individuals and groups. On
        a scale of 1 to 5, state whether you agree or disagree
        with the following *characterizations of parties and groups*
        (1 = strongly agree, 5 = strongly disagree, N = no opinion).

a.   Contemporary parties in America are generally effec-
        tive in providing a variety of groups with a voice and
        forum to publicly address their concerns.
        [N=19]   1: 5.2%   2: 31.5   3: 21   4: 26.3
        5: 15.7   N: 0

b.   Contemporary parties do a good job of mediating and
        integrating a variety of group interests and concerns
        into a coherent party program and plan for governing.
        [N=19]   1: 0   2: 31.5%   3: 15.7   4: 26.3
        5: 26.3   N: 0

c.   Contemporary parties are effective in moderating and
        dampening the potential tension and conflict between
        groups.
        [N=19]   1: 0   2: 42%   3: 36.8   4: 15.7
        5: 5.2   N: 0

d.   Groups and associations are likely to have better suc-
        cess influencing public policy by working independently
        of the parties rather than through them.
        [N=18]   1: 22%   2: 11   3: 22   4: 33.3
        5: 5.5   N: 5.5

e.   Other emerging political organizations (in particular
        multi-issue oriented think tanks, public interest firms,
        and ideologically based associations) have the potential

to perform the democratic functions traditionally carried out by parties.
[N=19]   1: 5.2%   2: 5.2   3: 26.3   4: 42
5: 15.7   N: 5.2

8.   Legal and constitutional restraints on political parties have
been blamed in part for their decline. On a scale of 1 to 3,
rate the likely impact of more *preferential legal treatment of
parties* in the following areas on their abilities to better perform their traditional functions (1 = little or no impact, 2 =
moderate impact, 3 = major impact).

    a.   Impose stricter legal standards on partisan gerry-
mandering.
[N=19]   1: 21%   2: 52.6   3: 26.3

    b.   Restructure campaign finance regulations to enhance
the role of political parties in financing campaigns and
elections.
[N=19]   1: 15.7%   2: 21   3: 63

    c.   Rearm the parties with greater patronage privileges in
office.
[N=19]   1: 21%   2: 42   3: 36.8

    d.   Give the parties greater control over nominating
candidates.
[N=19]   1: 15.7%   2: 26.3   3: 57.8

    e.   Broaden the parties' constitutional right of association
to free them of restrictive state regulations and give
them greater autonomy with which to operate.
[N=18]   1: 27.7%   2: 33.3   3: 38.8

D. Background Information

Thank you for responding to my questions. You are assured of
anonymity unless you indicate otherwise below. The following information is requested for purposes of analysis only. Please circle
the appropriate answers.

9.   Would you describe yourself as a:

    a.   Legal practitioner. (9)

    b.   Political party leader/activist. (8)

    c.   Interest/political group or association executive/leader. (2)

    d.   Law school professor. (2)

    e.   Political scientist. (3)

    f.   Other: _____. (3)

10. If you added extended comments to any of your responses, do you wish:

    a.   Not to be quoted at all

    b.   Quoted anonymously

    c.   Quoted with attribution (if yes, please sign below)

_____

Date: _____

Conducted by David K. Ryden, Ph.D. Candidate, Department of Politics, The Catholic University of America, Washington, D.C. 20064. Please direct any inquiries to Mr. Ryden at the CUA Politics Department, phone no. 202-319-5128; fax no. 202-319-6289.

APPENDIX C
GROUP TYPOLOGIES AND THE
CHALLENGES OF IMPLEMENTATION

Doubts about the divisive tendencies of group representation are difficult to alleviate scientifically, as they do not lend themselves to easy quantitative examination. The practical problems of constructing a scheme of group representation are more amenable to empirical or behavioral analysis.

The sociological and political science literature on group categorizations pose formidable practical questions to group/interest representation.[1] First, do fixed groups or interests actually exist? Second, are they quantifiable and verifiable? Third, which ones are deserving of preservation in a system of formal representation? Attempts to catalogue interests or groups illustrate the perplexing nature of these questions. Groups of people can be catalogued for political purposes along any number of lines, each with significant ramifications for establishing representation. There are countless determinants of collectively held interests that could serve as a basis for determining claims to representative status. These include: 1) the *motivations* underlying group participation; 2) the *benefits* sought or conferred by the group; 3) the *functions* performed by the organization; 4) *organizational* structure or formality; 5) the *subject area* of concern to the group; 6) the *political resources* at the group's disposal; 7) the physical, or sociological *characteristics* shared by group members; 8) group *size*; 9) the *nature and scope of group activities*; and 10) the group's *representative character.*

POSSIBLE GROUP TYPOLOGIES[2]

Motivation	Benefits sought/conferred
Political Resources	Substantive Interests
Member traits	Organization/Formality
Representativeness	Scope/Nature of Activities
Functions	Size

Attempts to construct a scheme of group representation around any of these components soon lead to complications. For example, consider the basis for the decisions in campaign finance, the typing of groups pursuant to political resources. Debunkers of pluralism decried the unequal distribution of resources which caused disparity in group influence. Hence the goal of equalizing political resources as a basis for meting out representative status. Creating a typology to accomplish this is no easy task. It is not enough simply to equalize monetary resources. Electoral and organizational resources may be equally important to political effectiveness. "The wealth of one group thus may be matched by the human resources or voting power of another."[3] Broadly based political power requires the equalization of all political resources.

Certain political resources, such as membership size and financial assets, are easily quantifiable. Others are more nebulous and difficult to quantify. For example, what intangible assets does the group have? How does one rate its prestige, status, or organizational strengths? Does it benefit from cohesion, strong leadership, and established organizational structure? Does it have expertise in politics? Does it have access to media outlets, and the expertise to exploit them?

Even if membership and bank account are easily measurable, their importance in assigning representation is less clear. Is a group that is rich in these resources less in need of formal representation? Or does it reflect representativeness, making it more deserving of formal status? Political resources are not inherent but result from a group's willingness and ability to engage in the necessities of politics.[4] A group that exhibits political savvy, organization, or motivation ought not to be penalized for its effectiveness.[5] Similarly a sizeable financial base may reveal the wealth of its members or it may reflect a group adept at raising funds.[6]

TYPOLOGY BY POLITICAL RESOURCES[7]

Financial assets	Media access
Size of membership	Expertise
Experience	Organizational strength
Motivation	Intangibles

In sum, classifying and handicapping groups according to political resources quickly becomes complicated. It becomes more

so when one considers how resources should be prioritized, especially when they overlap and merge together.[8] Selecting and defining the proper benchmarks of measuring political equality in
resources among groups is extremely problematic.

A typology founded on organization and form is equally challenging. Organization suggests a "routinized pattern of interaction . . . for the furtherance of group goals."[9] It is reflected in
structures and procedures that furnish a framework for group activity. A threshold question is whether a collectively held interest
is legitimated solely by virtue of the organizational trappings that
spring up around it. More defined levels of organization suggest
greater intensity of the group preference or interest. If so, the
existence of the organization enhances the claim to formal representation. But at the same time, organization facilitates political
effectiveness, presumably easing a group's need for formal recognition.

How does one assess the pertinence of organizational traits
to representational issues? Different elements of organization have
different consequences for the validity of group claims to representation.[10] For example, what are the members' roles, responsibilities, and relations with other members and the group
leadership? How is the leadership constituted? What is the
decisionmaking process of the organization? Is it authoritarian or
democratic? Do the procedures of the organization evidence a
capacity for entering into coalitions with other groups? How formal is the organization? Does it suggest greater stability and permanency? The answers to these questions have repercussions for
conferring representation. The more democratic the decisionmaking procedures, the more representative the group and deserving of formal status. Similarly, structures evidencing stability,
duration, or coalitional capacity arguably strengthen a group's
claim to representative status.

TYPOLOGY BY ORGANIZATION/FORMALITY

Leadership	Member roles and relations
Stability/duration	Decisionmaking procedures
Structures	Coalition building capacity

Other typologies require similarly perplexing distinctions.
Consider interest-based categorizations. A disturbing element of
pluralism has been the imbalance in group influence in favor

of higher socioeconomic groups. While public interest firms and citizen action groups have emerged and thrived in recent decades, group inequities are still rampant. If representation is conferred on the basis of substantive interest, should not the equalization of interests be a primary goal? And if so, how is it to be accomplished? Consider this partial listing of interest areas:[11]

SUBJECT AREA/INTEREST TYPOLOGY

Business	Foreign Lobbying	Public interests
Labor	Agriculture	Civil liberties
Education	Environmental	Profession orgs.

How does one determine which interests are in need of group representation in policy debate? Which interests lack a voice? Which ones are merely weaker than others? Do we differentiate between "business" in its variety of forms, between Fortune 500 companies and small business, between profit and nonprofit corporations? "Labor" and "agriculture" each has multiple distinctive groups within it, which suggests different treatment. Even the worthiness of the causes of public interest organizations are not self-evident. Efforts to organize to effect political change in the public interest have yielded a variety of forms, from improvement associations like the Sierra Club or League of Women Voters, to citizen action and participation groups, aimed at endowing their members with a sense of power, to community groups for social action.[12] But some causes may be more worthy than others, and hence deserving of favorable treatment? Furthermore, their representative character is implicated by their organizational structure, strategies, resources, and so on. In short, the designation of interests and the assignment of representation compel a morass of choices and distinctions that are exceedingly problematic.

The same problems plague typologies cast around group functions or objectives. Groups perform a number of functions.[13] Some are primarily expressive, designed to create a heightened sense of identity among their members. Others serve informational objectives and needs of members. These groups seem less "representative" (and arguably less in need of political representation). Other groups pursue specific political objectives, seeking tangible economic benefits for members, advancing ideological perspectives, or pursue legislative efforts on issues of concern.

TYPOLOGY BY FUNCTION

Symbolic/Expressive
Economic/Tangible benefits
Ideological pursuits
Informational purposes
Legislative agendas

Similarly, the motives underlying group activity are relevant to the allocation of representation. Some groups are driven by the self-interest or personal desires of the membership or the group as a whole. Others are altruistically motivated, working to garner benefits for those outside the group or for the entire community. The number of people who stand to benefit by the group's activities, and the extent to which it advances the public interest, strengthen its claim to representation.

TYPOLOGY BY MOTIVE[14]

Self-oriented/personal benefits
Pursuit of group benefits
Benefit for others outside group
Benefit general community

Finally, overlaid upon this web of categories and considerations are sociologically designated classifications, such as race, ethnicity, gender, religion, and age. Identity politics along racial, ethnic and gender axes have received the bulk of the attention to date. It is unlikely that a scheme of representation could be structured without accommodating racial and ethnic designations. This entails subtle distinctions between groups, and determinations of when group traits beget political interests sufficiently monolithic to warrant representative status.

TYPOLOGY BY CHARACTERISTICS

Race
Ethnicity
Religion
Gender
Age

This cursory glance at the demands of typing and ranking groups hints at the complexity of the task. Many categorizations require nothing less than substantive value judgments regarding group traits and whether they warrant a grant of formal representation. These are particularly difficult judgments for the state to make. Unelected judicial officers lack the legal standards and democratic accountability to make them. The existing structures of representation and accountability constraining legislators make it difficult for them to make such decisions.

Other typologies (resources, characteristics, organization) are more amenable to application of neutral principles, at least at first glance. But problems of quantification are still overwhelming. How does one measure prestige, leadership, or organizational strength as a political resource? How are they to be ranked or prioritized? What racial or ethnic identities are significant in generating political interests? Is it enough to speak of African Americans, Hispanic Americans, Puerto Rican Americans, and Native Americans, or do political interests diverge within these groups?[15] For purposes of organization, how does one measure a group's "representativeness," or democratic character?

Each typology presents a myriad of complex determinations which exceed the rational capabilities of our governmental institutions. Furthermore, to consolidate or incorporate multiple typologies would magnify those complexities exponentially. Moreover, the determination of group status occurs in a dynamic environment, not a static one. Groups and interests are fluid and changing, emerging or fading away with each policy debate. Institutional arrangements would compel constant adjustment of the assignments and weighting of group representation.

In short, a model of group representation faithful to the democratic ideal of individual equality looks to be empirically unattainable. The justification for group representation is its attainment of individual political equality through the equalization of politically relevant groups. It presupposes that systematic inequalities in individual influence can be neutralized by taking note of group status.[16] The theoretical and empirical implications of this create insoluble practical obstacles. It is not enough to merely identify the groups entitled to representation. It also implies a need to gauge the amount of representation to be dispensed. Not only must the relevant groups be identified, but they must be weighted so that their political input is equal. The aim of individual equality requires that collective representation be structured so that each person's group-based input is equal to that of others.[17]

This is possible only if we operate from the flawed premise that all individuals within a group are in precisely the same posture.[18] This oversimplifies group structures and ignores the complexities of multiple affiliations and disparities in intensity of group association. Regardless of how the group is defined, its members are positioned differently. Consequently, according official representative status will give some in the group too much and others not enough. Group status "cannot be determined independently of the degree of disadvantage of the individuals who are and are not members of the group."[19] This is empirically impossible to execute. Group rights are:

> grossly unjust as applied to specific individuals within those groups. Application would almost certainly be both over-inclusive and underinclusive, granting significant benefits to many who did not need or deserve them and discriminating against many who badly merited greater solicitude.[20]

Ultimately, the question revolves around the nature of political equality. Proponents of group representation desire an equality which is group-oriented and bloc-regarding.[21] The empirical riddle is of little concern if groups are the primary units of analysis. But if individuals are the most relevant units, it matters a great deal. Group equality in a pluralist system is not primary, but derivative. Its goal is to foster individual equality. Thus the goal of group equality as an end becomes difficult to justify, and the empirical obstacles fatal.

The empirical conundrum is amplified by multiple affiliations which vary in nature and intensity. How one's several associational contacts might be interwoven through a group structure of representation to produce individual equality is bewildering. Nor are the difficulties avoided by limiting the scope of group-based representational arrangements to dispossessed groups blocked out of existing structures. Group claims to compensatory remedies based on a history of discrimination have assumed that one's inclusion in the group is sufficient evidence of a socially determined disadvantage. The goal of individual equality still demands that we take into account specific individual disadvantages.[22]

Selective group representation also strays from the theoretical justification for its advancement, which is a fair distribution of interest representation.[23] The pluralist dilemma is not limited to oppressed groups, but includes the range of disparity existing between group participants. It is not just entry, but also equality of influence which is the basis for group representation. It only raises a different set of problems. How do we determine which groups are oppressed?[24] The system has always been armed with filters which allow certain groups into policy debate, while barring or restricting others. Politics is the triumph of certain groups at the expense of others. The exclusion of groups is made on any number of grounds, the propriety of which is not always clear. Few disagree with the impropriety of disfavoring groups on the basis of race or sex. On moral grounds alone, there ought to be consensus against such exclusions and for representative structures that assure their inclusion. But other groups may be barred for seemingly legitimate reasons. An extreme policy position, an eccentric ideological slant, or an obscure interest seems to justify exclusion. But should it? Limiting the scope to suppressed groups still requires a determination of what constitutes valid grounds for suppressing groups.

And what is the basis for courts and legislatures to make these distinctions? Is there a moral framework for determining who is admitted or banned from the public square? The temptation is to determine who is allowed to be heard by rating the moral worth of their underlying claims or distinguishing characteristics. But does the state have either the authority or the ability to decide which group claims are stronger or more legitimate?

These decisions have generally been left to the operation of the free markets of politics, except where the basis for group exclusion is so blatantly unjustified as to warrant government intervention. Denial of the vote to a class of people, or peculiar electoral arrangements combined with racially polarized voting, evidenced racism as a basis for excluding certain groups, namely blacks. But rarely are the grounds for exclusion so obviously unacceptable. Additionally, lack of influence might be self-inflicted rather than the result of oppression. Inability to affect policy might be due to organizational flaws or shortcomings, poor leadership, inactive membership, or poor marshalling or use of resources. The absence of a political presence may be the consequence of the group's failure or refusal to engage in practical politics, or to do it well.[25]

It may even be a conscious group strategy. Groups may find it advantageous to bypass political channels, and opt instead for legal avenues to achieve their objectives. They may choose to wage their battles for legitimacy in courts instead of in legislatures or the realm of public opinion. But legal remedies should be a last resort, for groups with no recourse for whom the institutional barriers to political effectiveness are insurmountable. Strategies that skirt democratic avenues to group legitimacy, and seek it initially through judicial notice, are questionable. Groups with political resources and multiple points of access to the political arena ought not to seek formal legal representative status until other, extralegal means have been exhausted.

In sum, discerning the real sources of political ineffectiveness and deciding whether they warrant a remedial form of group representation requires a depth and subtlety of analysis beyond the expertise of legislatures or courts (or political scientists, for that matter). It assumes that equality of group influence can be reduced to scientific determinations. Proponents of group representation forget that certain basic questions are essentially political questions not susceptible to scientific or objective analysis. Basic criteria of fairness and representation depend largely on the attitudes and actions of citizens. As such, the "basis of people's right to choose 'their own' representatives . . . can be decided only in the political (and constitution-making) arena, not at the analysts' desks."[26]

The pluralist operation of group forces in an open political market, while concededly imperfect, nevertheless provides countless outlets for the expression and representation of political identity. A legal construct of group-based rights to representation, in contrast, ossifies and hardens those political identities, making effective representation more difficult to achieve. Unlike the "scientific" distillation of group rights, subsystems of representation permit these fundamental questions to be resolved politically. These systems are premised on the unique ability of parties to reconcile the contradictory goals of individual political autonomy and the need for group influence.

NOTES

INTRODUCTION

1. *Buckley v. Valeo*, 424 U.S. 1 (1974).

2. 369 U.S. 186 (1962).

3. 377 U.S. 533 (1964).

CHAPTER ONE

1. Hannah Pitkin, *The Concept of Representation* (Berkeley: University of California Press, 1967), 3–4. Indeed, the author will argue that the lack of clarity and careful thinking about the meanings and forms of representation has poisoned efforts at the highest level, the U.S. Supreme Court, to examine and improve representative institutions.

2. The framework for this discussion of concepts of representation relies heavily on the work of Hannah Fenichel Pitkin in *The Concept of Representation* (Berkeley: University of California Press, 1967); see also *Representation*, ed. Hannah Fenichel Pitkin (New York: Atherton Press, 1969).

3. Pitkin, *The Concept of Representation*, 42.

4. *Ibid.*, 43.

5. "Accountability to the governed is what defines representation, whether it is achieved by elections or by other means." Pitkin, 56.

6. Pitkin, 57, quoting John Dewey in *Responsibility*, Carl Friedrich, ed., (Nomos III) (New York: Liberal Arts Press, 1960), 73.

7. For a critical look at both formalistic accounts of representation, see Pitkin, 49.

8. This is what A.H. Birch refers to as "microcosmic representation." A.H. Birch, *Representation* (New York: Praeger Publishers, 1971).

9. What Pitkin terms "descriptive representation" finds its purest expression in strict proportional representation, the goal of which is to "secure

a representative assembly reflecting mathematically the various divisions
in the electorate." *Ibid.*, citing Carl J. Friedrich, *Constitutional Government
and Democracy* (Boston: Ginn & Co., 1950), 304–305. For a discussion of
variants on the theme of "descriptive representation," see Arend Lijphart,
"Comparative Perspectives on Fair Representation: The Plurality-Majority
Rule, Geographic Districting, and Alternative Electoral Arrangements,"
Representation and Redistricting Issues, ed. Bernard Grofman (Toronto: Lexington Books, 1982), 143.

10. Descriptive representation was the foundation for earlier notions of
random sample selection of legislatures, which now strike us as extremely
obsolete:

> The principle of sampling in democratic theory is that a
> smaller group, selected impartially or at random from a larger
> group, tends to have the character of the larger group. Ac-
> cordingly a part, if properly chosen, may be as truly repre-
> sentative of the whole and substituted for it. . . . Throughout
> modern "representative" democracy, this principle of the valid
> substitution of the part for the whole is central.

Pitkin, 74, (citing Marie Collins Swabey, *Theory of the Democratic State* (Cambridge: Harvard University Press, 1937), 25.

11. Pitkin, 99–100; see also Birch, *Representation,* 17–18.

12. Pitkin, 99–100, 104.

13. *Ibid.*, 100–101.

14. *Ibid.*, 102.

15. *Ibid.*, 108 (citing James Hogan, *Election and Representation* (Cork University Press, 1945), 144.

16. *Ibid.*, 116.

17. Pitkin, 116, (citing Avery Leiserson, "Problems of Representation,"
Journal of Politics XI (August 1949), 570.

18. *Ibid.*, 119.

19. See Pitkin's discussion generally at 121–126, 131–134.

20. The delegate or mandate position was manifested in the early nine-
teenth-century doctrine of instructions, in which the legislator's actions
were to be guided by, and taken pursuant to, the will of the majority of
those he represented. The representative was considered "the mouthpiece
and organ of his constituents, effectively bound to enact the preferences
of the majority of his constituents." Alfred de Grazia, *Public and Republic:
Political Representation in America* (New York: Alfred A. Knopf, 1951)
123–24.

21. *Ibid.*, 166.

22. *Ibid.*, 166.

23. *Ibid.*, 166.

24. Harold F. Gosnell, *Democracy: The Threshold of Freedom* (New York: The Ronald Press Company, 1948), 132.

25. Gosnell, *Democracy*, 216.

26. Pitkin, 219–220.

27. According to Heinz Eulau, it is the means by which the government "commits the community." Heinz Eulau and Kenneth Prewitt, *Labyrinths of Democracy: Adaptations. Linkages, Representation, and Policies in Urban Politics* (New York: The Bobbs-Merrill Co., 1973), 25.

28. Eulau and Prewitt, *Labyrinths of Democracy*, 425.

29. Pitkin, 221–222 (emphasis added).

30. Pitkin renders a harsh judgement of those who assert that representation is nothing more than the reflection of the opinions of every opinion-holding group in the public. She laments that this thinking has no room for any kind of representing as acting for, or on behalf of, others, which means that in the political realm it has no room for the creative activities of a representative legislature, the forging of consensus, the formulation of policy, the activity we roughly designate by "governing." *The Concept of Representation*, 83.

31. Eulau and Prewitt, 401.

32. Pitkin, 112.

33. See the discussion by Eulau and Prewitt regarding the importance of empirical inquiry and its relation to our conceptualization of representation. *Labyrinths of Democracy*, 403.

34. *Ibid.*, 438.

35. *Ibid.*

36. *Ibid.*, 443.

37. For an early statement of the relevancy of group theory within institutions of government, see Arthur Bentley, *The Process of Government* (Cambridge: Belknap Press of Harvard University Press, 1967); see also Eulau and Prewitt's study of city councils in urban politics, especially the analysis of social relations which affect group dynamics and shape the political behavior of the members of the council. *Labyrinths of Democracy*, 90–96.

38. Pitkin, 145.

39. Edmund Burke, "Speech to the Electors," *Burke's Politics*, eds. Ross J.S. Hoffman and Paul Levack (New York: Alfred A. Knopf, 1949), 116. Representation of the whole is not to be mistaken with Burke's ideas of "virtual representation." He also observed a different sort of representation of collective interests, in which a sympathy of feeling and desires existed between the actors and those in whose name they acted. Unlike representation of the entire nation, Burke was speaking of "particular disenfranchised groups or localities. Even if unable to send a member to Parliament, they were still represented by some member from some other constituency. Thus some disenfranchised groups are virtually represented and others are not." Pitkin, 173–74.

40. de Grazia, *Public and Republic*, 89.

41. Birch, *Representation*, 37–40.

42. Pitkin, 188.

43. Though this view of representation on its face appears outmoded, similar assumptions of deliberative character are implicit in certain contemporary trends. The case for formal interest or group representation is based upon an unspoken reliance on this view. Those who wish to have one of their own in the legislature cannot harbor the unrealistic goal of acquiring a majority, or even of being a very significant presence in constructing coalitions within the legislature. On the contrary, their primary objective is to have a voice in the legislation, with a greater sense of being represented. But its translation into hard policy outcomes in their favor rests on there being a significant element of deliberation in the legislature.

   The issue is far more complicated than this cursory mention suggests. There are a variety of reasons to put one's own in office. More ethereal ends such as enhanced legitimacy as a group or feelings of corporate validation or affirmation might be generated by having a representative the group can call its own. But if a group expects its electoral gains to translate into tangible, substantive policy gains in the legislature, it must to a greater or lesser extent adopt the idea of the legislature as a deliberative body, one which can be moved and persuaded to see the rightness and interest in a position advocated by only one or a small number of voices.

44. Edmund Burke, "Speech on the State of the Representation," *Burke's Politics*, (New York: Alfred A. Knopf, 1949), 230.

45. de Grazia calls this "enlightened individualist" representation, that situation in which individuals are a law unto themselves, without regard for group effects or socially communicated patterns of conduct. *Public and Republic*, 174.

46. Samuel H. Beer, "The Representation of Interests," *American Political Science Review* LI (September 1957), 629–631.

47. Pitkin, 215. Pitkin resolves the debate simply by noting the dual role of the representative, as agent of his constituency and as governor of the country. "His duty is to pursue both local and national interest, the one because he is representative, the other because his job as a representative is governing the nation." *Ibid.*, 218.

48. de Grazia, *Public and Republic*, viii.

49. Arthur N. Holcombe, *Politics in Action: The Problems of Representative Government* (Menasha, Wisconsin: George Banta Publishing Co., 1943), 23.

50. de Grazia, 251–252.

51. Eulau and Prewitt, 612–613.

52. *Ibid.*, 613.

53. *Ibid.*, 309.

54. *Ibid.*, 225.

55. *Ibid.*, 307.

56. *Ibid.*, 21.

57. *Ibid.*, 365.

58. *Ibid.*, 309; Jane J. Mansbridge, "A Deliberative Theory of Interests and Representation," *The Politics of Interests: Interest Groups Transferred*, ed. Mark P. Petracca (Boulder: Westview Press, 1992), 37–47.

59. Pitkin, 219.

60. Charles Beitz contends that the implications of political equality and representation vary with the issues under examination, and argues for a theory of representation sufficiently detailed and complex so as to apply to all situations. Charles R. Beitz, "Equal Opportunity in Political Representation," *Equal Opportunity*, ed. Norman E. Bowie (Boulder: Westview Press, 1988), 155–156.

61. Pitkin, 227–228.

CHAPTER TWO

1. John Wahlke describes the collective import of decisions on electoral politics as nothing less than whose ideas prevail, and who is actually entitled to political representation. "Logic and Politics in Electoral Engineering," *Representation and Redistricting Issues*, eds. Bernard Grofman et al (Toronto: Lexington Books, 1982), 163.

2. Douglas W. Rae, *The Political Consequences of Electoral Laws* (New Haven: Yale University Press, 1967), 3.

3. John Moeller, "The Federal Courts' Involvement in the Reform of Political Parties," *Western Political Quarterly* 40 (Dec. 1987): 717, 718.

4. Stephen Gottlieb, "Rebuilding the Right of Association: The Right to Hold a Convention as a Test Case," *Hofstra Law Review* 11 (1982): 191, 203.

5. Mary Ann Glendon, *Rights Talk: The Impoverishment of Political Discourse* (New York: The Free Press, 1991), 110.

6. Glendon, 110.

7. This account of voting rights reform begins with the modern era and the 1960s reapportionment revolution. For a thorough discussion of the full history of voting rights before the Supreme Court, see Ward E. Y. Elliott, *The Rise of Guardian Democracy: The Supreme Court's Role in Voting Rights Disputes, 1845–1969* (Cambridge: Harvard University Press, 1974).

8. *Baker v. Carr*, 369 U.S. 186 (1962). Elliott provides a concise and insightful backdrop for *Baker*, describing the spirit and substance of the debate over voting rights in the years preceding the decision. *The Rise of Guardian Democracy*, 13–20.

9. See *Colgrove v. Green*, 66 S.Ct. 1198 (1946) (Frankfurter, J.). In *Colgrove*, the Court had refused to entertain a claim that the apportionment of Illinois Congressional districts violated various provisions of the Constitution. Because the task of supervising the election machinery was specifically assigned to Congress by Article I, Sec. 4 of the Constitution, the Court held that the constitutionality of the challenged apportionment plan was a political question directly implicating another branch of the federal government, and therefore nonjusticiable.

10. *Wesberry v. Sanders*, 376 U.S. 1 (1964); *Wright v. Rockefeller*, 376 U.S. 52 (1964).

11. *Reynolds v. Sims*, 377 U.S. 533 (1964); *WMCA v. Lomenzo*, 377 U.S. 633 (1964); *Maryland Committee for Fair Representation v. Tawes*, 377 U.S. 656 (1964); *Davis v. Mann*, 377 U.S. 678 (1964); *Lucas v. Colorado General Assembly*, 377 U.S. 713 (1964).

12. *Wesberry*, 376 U.S. 1 (1964).

13. 376 U.S. 1, 18.

14. *Reynolds v. Sims*, 377 U.S. 533, 565.

15. 377 U.S. 533, 565 (emphasis added).

16. *Lucas v. Colorado General Assembly*, 377 U.S. 714, 744 (1964) (Stewart, J., dissenting) (emphasis added).

17. 377 U.S. 714, 744 (emphasis added).

18. *Ibid.*, 751.

19. 377 U.S. 533, 578.

20. *Ibid.*

21. *Kirkpatrick v. Preisler*, 394 U.S. 526, 530–31 (1969).

22. In *Kirkpatrick*, the Court rejected a plan with an average deviation of 1.6 percent and a maximum deviation of under 6 percent. *Ibid.* These figures refer to the amounts the actual district populations deviate from that figure which represents perfect equality of population between districts.

23. In *Karcher v. Daggett*, the state of New Jersey was forced to reapportion its congressional districts when it lost a seat in Congress following the 1980 decennial census. The Court struck down the proposed plan, rejecting state policies articulated above, and invalidating a plan with a deviation average of just 0.19 percent and a maximum deviation of 0.7 percent. 462 U.S. 725 (1983)(Brennan, J.).

24. In *Reynolds*, Warren issued a memorable phrase seemingly incongruent with his expressed desire to maintain a flexible standard that would accommodate legitimate state policies. Opining that "legislators represent people, not trees or acres," and that they are "elected by voters, not farms or cities or economic interests," Warren overlooked the aim of geographic districting, the grouping together of farmers, urban dwellers, people of similar socio-economic standing, and other groups with common interests and concerns. The objective of territorial districts was to give people with common interests effective representation through a meaningful vote. *Reynolds v. Sims*, 377 U.S. 533, 562.

25. *Kirkpatrick* involved a 1967 Missouri reapportionment plan that created congressional districts ranging in population from approximately 420,000 to 445,000. Brennan and the Court found that range to be too large to satisfy federal constitutional demands. *Kirkpatrick*, 394 U.S. 526, 533 (1969) (emphasis added).

26. A host of critics have assailed strict adherence to mathematical equality as actually contributing to the blatant resort to partisan gerrymandering practices. Robert G. Dixon, "Fair Criteria and Procedures for Establishing Legislative Districts," *Representation and Redistricting Issues* 14; Congressional Quarterly, *State Politics and Redistricting*, 1–22 (1982); Richard Engstrom, "The Supreme Court and Equipopulous Gerrymandering: A Remaining Obstacle in the Quest for Fair and Effective Representation," *Arizona State Law Journal*, 277, 278 (1976); Gordon E. Baker, "One Man One Vote and 'Political Fairness'," *Emory Law Journal* 23, 701, 710 (1974).

27. Daniel Hays Lowenstein, "*Bandemer's* Gap: Gerrymandering and Equal Protection," *Political Gerrymandering and the Courts*, Ed. Bernard Grofman (New York: Agathon Press, 1991), 73 (emphasis added).

28. The Court's tendency to segregate groups from individuals has been harshly criticized. Lowenstein, "*Bandemer's* Gap," 73; see Note: "The Constitutional Imperative of Proportional Representation," *Yale Law Journal* 94, 163 (1985). Proponents of a group-regarding conceptualization of representation argue that the political effectiveness of individuals and groups in elections are inextricably intertwined. They are complementary aspects of effective political participation. A failure to properly account for both in electoral arrangements yields an incomplete understanding of political representation. Kousser put it this way (within the context of racial vote dilution):

> Disenfranchisement and vote dilution are not pure concepts. . . . To discourage from voting a significant proportion of members of a group that others treat as distinct reduces the value of the vote for every individual member of that group, and vice versa. For members of such groups, individual and group rights, disenfranchisement and dilution, are integrally related.

J. Morgan Kousser, "The Voting Rights Act and the Two Reconstructions," *Controversies in Minority Voting*, 135, 174–75 (1992); cf. Abigail Thernstrom, *Whose Votes Count? Affirmative Action and Minority Voting Rights* (Cambridge: Harvard University Press, 1987), 7 (asserting that there are no group rights to representation in the American constitutional tradition).

29. *Reynolds v. Sims*, 377 U.S. 533, 563 (1964).

30. Stephen E. Gottlieb, "Election Reform and Democratic Objectives—Match or Mismatch?" *Yale Law Review* 9, 219, 209 (1991).

31. As early as 1965, one observer noted that the Court had effectively limited:

> its consideration of the inequalities of voting power and effective representation in apportionment plans to the relative number of constituents in each electoral district. The Court appears to have given little weight to . . . factors which obviously would affect the ability of a citizen-voter to pick a representative of his choice and to have some influence on which bills pass.

John F. Banzhaf III, "Multi-member Districts—Do They Violate the 'One Man One Vote' Principle?" *Yale Law Journal* 75, 1309, 1310–1311 (1965).

32. Lani Guinier, "Comment: Voting Rights and Democratic Theory: Where Do We Go From Here?" *Controversies in Minority Voting*, 283, 286 (1992).

33. An early critic of a purely numbers-based approach to apportionment foresaw the difficulties it presented for recognition of group behavior:

> The equal-population numerology... is a dangerous flirtation with mass neurosis. Man loses standing as a citizen ... when he is reduced to naked, abstract number. He has a faceless equality with other numbered citizens. They become equally devoid of group ties and human responsibilities until they become the mass. The "mass" in fact cannot be said to exist until citizenship has been destroyed through individuals being torn loose from their social relations and reduced to separate items, helplessly confronting the central state.

Alfred de Grazia, *Apportionment and Representative Government* (Washington, D.C.: American Enterprise Institute, 1963), 130–31.

34. Comment: *"United Jewish Organization v. Carey* and the Need to Recognize Aggregate Voting Rights," *Yale Law Journal* 87, 571, 588–89 (1978).

35. The conflict between expanding voting rights and issues of group representation was on display in another line of cases, albeit in more subtle form. In the late 1960s, the Court extended one person one vote principles to elections, usually involving municipal or local issues, which arguably only affected certain distinct and identifiable blocs of voters. In each case, the Court refused to limit the right to vote, even though the elections created group distinctions based on the economic issue at stake. See *Avery v. Midland County*, 390 U.S. 474 (1967); *Kramer v. Union Free School District*, 395 U.S. 621 (1969) (striking down local school board election that limited the vote to owners of taxable realty and those with children enrolling in public schools); *Hadley v. Junior College District*, 397 U.S. 50 (1969) (extending *Reynolds* to the election of trustees of a community college).

The Court then reversed course, refusing to extend *Reynolds* to several subsequent cases. In *Salyer Land Co. v. Tulane Lake Basin Water Storage District*, 410 U.S. 719 (1972), the Court approved of a voting scheme for electing a water storage district's directors, proportioning the vote along the lines of the assessed valuations of landowners' property. See also *Ball v. James*, 451 U.S. 355 (1980).

36. As Daniel Lowenstein has described it:

> The rights protected against discrimination were conceptualized as voting rights, and can be described as representational rights only in the sense that the right to vote and have one's vote counted and weighted equally with the votes of others is a part of the system of representation.

Daniel Hays Lowenstein, *"Bandemer's* Gap: Gerrymandering and Equal Protection," *Political Gerrymandering and the Courts*, ed. Grofman, 73.

37. See generally Andrew Stark, "Corporate Electoral Activity, Constitutional Discourse, and Conceptions of the Individual," *American Political Science Review* 86 (1992): 626, 633; Peter Schuck, "Partisan Gerrymandering: A Political Problem Without Judicial Solution" *Political Gerrymandering and the Courts,* ed. Grofman, 244.

38. Note: "Group Representation and Race-Conscious Apportionment: The Roles of States and the Federal Courts," *Harvard Law Review* 91, 1847, 1852 (1978).

39. Wright, "Politics and the Constitution: Is Money Speech?" *Yale Law Journal* 85, 1001, 1015–16 (1976).

40. In the pluralist vision, groups:

> rise and decline, coalesce and fragment, confront counter-vailing groups and aid complementary groups. . . . [t]hey thereby achieve a form of "functional representation," based upon intersecting economic and social groupings, which cuts across our usual conception of political representation based upon "one person—one vote."

Wright, "Politics and the Constitution", 1015–1016.

41. Bruce Cain, "Perspectives on *Davis v. Bandemer:* Views of the Practitioner, Theorist, and Reformer," *Political Gerrymandering and the Courts,* 130.

42. Donald W. Jackson, *Even the Children of Strangers: Equality Under the United States Constitution* (Lawrence, Kans.: University Press of Kansas, 1992), 224.

43. See the survey results set forth in Appendix A, p. 195.

44. Strict application of the one person, one vote standard has been blamed for precluding various electoral arrangements built around unique geographic or regional interests or concerns. Bruce Cain, "Voting Rights and Democratic Theory," 276, discussing *Board of Estimates of New York v. Morris,* 489 U.S. 688 (1989).

45. Note: "The Constitutional Imperative of Proportional Representation," *Yale Law Journal* 94, 163, 177.

46. Note, "Group Reapportionment and Race-conscious Apportionment: The Roles of States and the Federal Courts," *Harvard Law Review* 91, 1847 (1978).

47. Bruce E. Cain, "Voting Rights and Democratic Theory: Toward a Color-Blind Society?" *Controversies in Minority Voting: The Voting Rights Act in Perspective,* eds. Grofmand and Davidson, 264.

48. No system of apportionment can be neutral, due to the inherently political nature of the task. As one astute observer noted:

> the process of apportionment, like the other stages of repre-
> sentation, is a point of entry for preferred social values. Any
> existing system of apportionment, whether legal, illegal, or
> extra-legal, institutionalizes the values of some groups in the
> jurisdiction.

Alfred de Grazia, *Apportionment and Representative Government* (Washington, D.C.: American Enterprise Institute, 1963), 20.

49. To the extent political scientists concur with this criticism, they need only look to their professional predecessors for scapegoats. The American Political Science Association played a substantial role in pushing for the reforms that eventually culminated in *Baker* and *Reynolds*. An APSA committee helped pave the way with its recommendations of equal numbers of people in each electoral district. It further proposed that local governmental units be disregarded in districting, opining that local political units were no longer accompanied by distinctive interests of their own, and hence need not be accounted for in representative arrangements. For a summary of the role of the political science community generally in leading the reforms that transpired in the 1960s, see Ward E.Y. Elliott, *The Rise of Guardian Democracy*, 13–14.

50. This consequence was anticipated by Justice Byron White in his dissenting opinion in *Wells v. Rockefeller*. Justice White argued that the threat of mathematical equality:

> downgrades a restraint on a far greater potential threat to
> equality of representation, the gerrymander. Legislatures in-
> tent on minimizing the representation of selected political or
> racial groups are invited to ignore political boundaries and
> compact districts so long as they adhere to population equal-
> ity among districts.

394 U.S. 542, 544 (1969).

51. Bernard Grofman, "Criteria for Districting: A Social Science Perspective," *UCLA Law Review* 33, 77, 112–113 (1985)(citations omitted).

CHAPTER THREE

1. Timothy O'Rourke, "The 1982 Amendments and the Voting Rights Paradox," *Controversies in Minority Voting: The Voting Rights Act in Perspective*, eds. Bernard Grofman and Chandler Davidson (Washington, D.C.: The Brookings Institution, 1992), 85–113.

2. *Gomillion v. Lightfoot*, 364 U.S. 339 (1960).

3. *Fortson v. Dorsey*, 379 U.S. 433 (1965).

4. 379 U.S. 433, 439. See also *Burns v. Richardson*, 384 U.S. 73 (1966).

5. *Whitcomb v. Chavis*, 403 U.S. 124, 144 (1971). While rejecting a claim that a multi-member district in Marion County, Indiana unfairly diluted the minority vote, the Court required plaintiffs to show that they had less opportunity "to participate in the political process and to elect legislators of their choice." *Ibid.*, 149.

6. *Gaffney v. Cummings*, 412 U.S. 755 (1973).

7. Those criteria included (1) a history of official racial discrimination, (2) election campaigns that resorted to racial appeals, (3) a lack of elected minority officials in the past, (4) slating organizations that were controlled by whites, and (5) the election of officials who were inadequately responsive to the minority group interests. *Ibid.*, 769.

8. The 1982 amendments to the Voting Rights Act were in response to *City of Mobile v. Bolden*, 446 U.S. 55 (1980), a controversial Supreme Court decision which marked a serious setback to racial voting rights claims. In *Mobile*, the Court upheld an at-large arrangement for electing Mobile, Alabama's three city commissioners. Though the city was 35 percent black, no black candidate had ever been elected to the city council. For the first time, and in logic that diverged from its earlier reapportionment cases, the Court indicated that the Equal Protection Clause required a showing of a discriminatory intent behind the plan, in addition to a discriminatory impact. The Court seriously limited those circumstances from which a discriminatory purpose could be inferred, instead requiring specific proof of an intent to discriminate. The result was to drastically undercut the "totality of the circumstances" test set forth in *White v. Regester*.

For a more detailed analysis of the *Mobile* decision, see Bernard Grofman, Lisa Handley, and Richard Niemi, *Minority Representation and the Quest for Voting Equality* (New York: Cambridge University Press, 1992), 34–38. Chandler Davidson also gives a concise but insightful summary of the political forces that culminated in the passage of the 1982 amendments. "The Voting Rights Act: A Brief History," *Controversies in Minority Voting*, eds. Bernard Grofman and Chandler Davidson (Washington, D.C.: The Brookings Institution, 1992), 37–42.

9. The "totality of the circumstances" test relied heavily on *White v. Regester*, but included several additional factors. The relevant factors included:

1. Evidence of a history of official discrimination;

2. Racially polarized voting in elections;

3. The use of various voting procedures that lend themselves to discrimination against minority groups;

4. Preclusion of minority group participation in the candidate slating process;

5. Evidence of discrimination against the minority group in other areas, such as education, employment, and health, which may hinder their participation in the political process;

6. Political campaigns characterized by overt racial appeals; and

7. The extent to which members of the minority group have been elected to office.

United States Senate, Senate Report no. 97–417 (1982).

10. *Davis v. Bandemer*, 478 U.S. 30 (1986).

11. *Ibid.*, 50–51.

12. Laughlin McDonald, "The 1982 Amendments of Section 2 and Minority Representation," *Controversies in Minority Voting: The Voting Rights Act in Perspective*, eds. Bernard Grofmand and Chandler Davidson (Washington, D.C.: The Brookings Institution, 1992), 70.

13. Bernard Grofman, Lisa Handley, and Richard G. Niemi, *Minority Representation and the Quest for Voting Equality* (New York: Cambridge University Press, 1992), 131.

14. Some observers have predicted dire consequences, as the group-oriented theory of race-based remedies is extended to other groups. Andrew Kull, for example, contemplates an "irreversible tendency toward the convenient and destructive practice of allocating social resources by racial and ethnic groups." Andrew Kull, *The Color-Blind Constitution* (Cambridge, Mass.: Harvard University Press, 1992), 221.

15. Bernard Grofman, "Toward a Coherent Theory of Gerrymandering," *Political Gerrymandering and the Courts*, ed. Bernard Grofman, (New York: Agathon Press 1990), 53 (citing Robert G. Dixon, Jr., "The Courts, The People and One Man One Vote," *Reapportionment in the 1970s*, ed. Nelson Polsby (Berkeley: University of California Press, 1971), 7–45.

16. See Justice Stevens's dissent in *Shaw v. Reno*, 125 L. Ed. 2d 511, 549 (1993), in which he countenances affirmative use of linedrawing to favor underrepresented groups, be they political parties, economic, religious, or ethnic groups. For an opposing view, see Judge Patrick Higgenbothaum's dissent in *LULAC v. Midland Independent School District*, 812 F. 2d 1494 (5th Cir. 1987), in which he expressed concern about the courts moving into the area of political group distinctions, as opposed to racial groups.

17. 412 U.S. 735 (1973).

18. *Ibid.*, 738.

19. *Ibid.*, 754.

20. *Ibid.*

21. For a rejection of that view, see Justice O'Connor's subsequent statement in *Davis v. Bandemer*, 478 U.S. 109, 154. In a concurring opinion, O'Connor blamed *Gaffney*-type use of partisan data for employing the same techniques as the more typical discriminatory partisan gerrymandering, with equally deleterious effects on individual voters and their ability to choose their representatives.

22. 412 U.S. 735, 748 (citing *Reynolds v. Sims*, 377 U.S. 533, 565–566).

23. One could even conclude from *Gaffney* that collective representation via party affiliation was as important as formal individual representation. The Connecticut plan sought political balance by creating as many safe seats for each party as possible. That tactic greatly reduces the opportunity for minority party voters located in those "safe" districts to realistically choose the representative of their choice. The substantive policy views of those voters are less likely to be represented vigorously when their legislator is from the opposite party. If so, their representation is largely contingent on party representation. Those of the minority party within the district are relegated to depending, for representation on policy matters, upon officeholders who belong to their party but are from other legislative districts. *Gaffney*, however, allowed impediments on the ability to choose one's individual representative to secure better representation by one's party as a whole. It permitted shortcomings in *individual* choice to be compensated for by enhancement of *collective* representation.

24. *Ibid.*, 131. The Court's willingness to allow states room for affirmative use of data or party affiliation in redistricting was lauded by political scientists as a step in the right direction toward fairer districting procedures. See Robert G. Dixon, Jr., "Fair Criteria and Procedures for Establishing Legislative Districts," *Representation and Redistricting Issues*, eds. Bernard Grofman et al. (Toronto: Lexington Books, 1982), 11; Richard Niemi and John Deegan, Jr., "A Theory of Political Districting," *American Political Science Review* 72 (1978): 1304 (responsive representative bodies are possible only by incorporating "the partisan division of the vote into the criteria for fair districting").

25. *United Jewish Organization v. Carey*, 430 U.S. 144 (1977) (White, J.).

26. *UJO v. Carey*, 430 U.S. 161.

27. *Ibid.*, 165.

28. *Ibid.*

29. As Justice Powell explained in a later case:

> *United Jewish Organization v. Carey* properly is viewed as a case
> in which the remedy...measures to improve the previously

disadvantaged group's ability to participate, without excluding individuals belonging to any other group from enjoyment
of the relevant opportunity—meaningful participation in the
electoral process.

Regents of University of California v. Bakke, 438 U.S. 265, 304–305 (1978).
Carey was to be read as permitting affirmative remedial action for minorities, provided it did not preclude meaningful political participation
by other groups. Provided the other group was perceived as being comprised generally of whites, rather than specifically of Hasidic Jews, the
Court was safe in its conclusion.

30. At least one justice had difficulty with this tendency to talk of whites
and nonwhites as monolithic entities. In his dissent, Justice Burger com-
plained that:

> The assumption that "whites" and "nonwhites" in the county
> form homogeneous entities for voting purposes is entirely
> without foundation. The "whites" category consists of a veri-
> table galaxy of national origins, ethnic backgrounds, and reli-
> gious denominations. It simply cannot be assumed that the
> legislative interests of all "whites" are even substantially iden-
> tical. In similar fashion, those described as "nonwhites" in-
> clude in addition to Negroes, a substantial portion of Puerto
> Ricans (citation omitted). The Puerto Rican population, for
> whose protection the Voting Rights Act was "triggered" in
> Kings County, see n. 2, supra, has expressly disavowed any
> identity of interests with the Negroes, and, in fact, objected
> to the 1974 redistricting scheme because it did not establish
> a Puerto Rican controlled district within the city.

430 U.S. 161, 185.

31. Only Justice Brennan hinted at this reality in his concurring opinion. "The impression of unfairness is magnified when a coherent group
like the Hasidim disproportionately bears the adverse consequences of a
race-assignment policy." *Ibid.*, 175. In fairness to the Court, it appears
that the Hasidim did not directly assert a group voting claim. Justice
Brennan readily acknowledged that the plan denied them the opportunity to vote as a group, but this was irrelevant, since "they do not press
any legal claim to a group voice as Hasidim." *Ibid.*, 178.

32. Kull, *The Color-Blind Constitution* (1992), 216–219.

33. *Karcher v. Daggett*, 462 U.S. 725 (1983).

34. 462 U.S. 725 (1983), (Stevens, J., concurring in the judgment).

35. *Ibid.*, 753.

36. *Ibid.*, 751. Stevens conceded the possible implications of his expansive view of this group right, noting the "large number of potentially

affected political groups." *Ibid.*, 761, n. 27. His solution was to make the right a function of group strength, as manifested by voting power.

> From the standpoint of the groups of voters that are affected by the line-drawing process, it is also important to recognize that it is the group's interest in gaining or maintaining political power that is at stake. The mere fact that a number of citizens share a common ethnic, racial or religious background does not create the need for protection against gerrymandering. *It is only when their common interests are strong enough to be manifested in political action that the need arises.* For the political strength of a group is not a function of its ethnic, racial or religious composition; rather *it is a function of numbers—specifically the number of persons who will vote in the same way.*

Ibid., 749–750 (citing *Mobile v. Bolden*, 446 U.S. 55, 88 (1980) (Stevens, J., concurring in the judgment) (emphasis added).

37. 462 U.S.725, 776.

38. *Ibid.*, (White, J., dissenting from the judgment). For a forceful articulation of this argument, see political scientist Bernard Grofman's statement in "Criteria for Districting: A Social Science Perspective," *UCLA Law Review* 33, 77, 112–113 (1985).

39. 462 U.S. 725, 787.

40. *Ibid.*

41. *Ibid.*

42. This emerging bloc of justices stood in contrast to the more representative view on the Court reflected in Justice Stewart's opinion in *Mobile v. Bolden*, 446 U.S. 55, 75–76. The Court in *Bolden* imposed a discriminatory intent requirement in racial vote dilution cases, prompting passage of the 1982 amendments to the Voting Rights Act. Those loosened the legal standard to require only discriminatory effect to establish an unconstitutional burden on the voting rights of racial groups.
Stewart categorically rejected the idea that a political group might have a right to have its candidates elected:

> It is, of course, true that the right of a person to vote on an equal basis with other voters draws much of its significance from the political associations that its exercise reflects, *but it is an altogether different matter to conclude that political groups themselves have an independent constitutional claim to representation.*

446 U.S. 55, 78 (emphasis added).

43. *Davis v. Bandemer*, 478 U.S. 109 (1986).

44. The Indiana General Assembly consisted of a 100 member House of Representatives and a 50 member Senate. The House members served

two year terms, while Senators served for four years. Each Senator exclusively represented a single district, while the House members were elected from a mixture of single- and multi-member districts. Reapportionment was required by state statute every ten years, based on the U.S. census.

45. Other parties joining in the lawsuit presented a classic illustration of the old adage that politics makes strange bedfellows. The national Republican party, recognizing that it was more often than not the victim of political gerrymandering by Democratically controlled state legislatures, joined with the Indiana Democrats in propounding the justiciability of partisan gerrymandering claims. Likewise, the national Democratic party sought to preserve its upper hand by supporting the Indiana Republicans in keeping the courts out of this area.

46. *Baker v. Carr*, 369 U.S. 186 (1962).

47. 478 U.S. 109, 125.

48. A review of the procedures employed in preparing the Indiana plans left little doubt that Republicans had drawn the map for the purpose of strengthening themselves politically and weakening the Democrats. The Republican State Committee hired a computer firm to assist in the task. The sole data used in drawing the new districts were precinct population, race, precinct political breakdown, and statewide voting trends. The Democrats were also virtually shut out of the process. No Democrats were given information used or generated by the computer program. The Democrats had no input or access to the districting procedures. The Conference Committee Chairman's response to this was that the Democrats could offer a minority map, "but I will advise you in advance that it will not be accepted." *Ibid.*, 131. Furthermore, the Republicans held no hearings, and the plans were not revealed until two days before the end of the Assembly's final session.

49. *Ibid*, 132–133.

50. *Ibid.* (emphasis added).

51. *Ibid.*, 132–133 (emphasis added). Factors to be considered in weighing effective influence on the political process at the district level include the opportunity to participate in party deliberations regarding slating and nominations of candidates, and the opportunity to register and vote.

52. Issuance of the *Bandemer* decision on the same day as *Thornburg v. Gingles* led some to assert that the Court was attempting to extend racial groups' right to fair representation to other politically cohesive groups, to remove the "legal firebreak between racial and political groups." See Bruce E. Cain, "Perspectives on *Davis v. Bandemer:* Views of Practitioner, Theorist and Reformer," *Political Gerrymandering and the Courts*, ed. Bernard Grofman (New York: Agathon Press, 1990), 135. This conclusion

hardly seems justified by the distinct language and tone of the two decisions. *Thornburg* went much further than *Bandemer*, interpreting the mandate of the amended Voting Rights Act to ensure the right of ethnic and
racial minorities to elect representatives of their choice. While the Court
in *Thornburg* defined a concise three-pronged test for identifying racial
groups as victims of gerrymandering, the claim extended in *Bandemer* to
other politically cohesive groups was far more tentative, evidencing the
Court's ambivalence in this area.

53. For a statement in general agreement with this assessment, see Bruce
E. Cain, "Perspectives on *Davis v. Bandemer*: Views of the Practitioner,
Theorist and Reformer," *Political Gerrymandering and the Courts*, ed. Ber-
nard Grofman (New York: Agathon Press, 1990), 117–142. cf., Daniel
Lowenstein, "*Bandemer*'s Gap: Gerrymandering and Equal Protection,"
Political Gerrymandering and the Courts, ed. Grofman, 70.

54. The four justices were White, Brennan, Marshall, and Blackmun.

55. 478 U.S. 109, 167. Powell received little comfort from mathematical
equality of the vote. It failed to protect voting rights of groups of people
who affiliated with a party or organization to acquire representation by
combining their voting strength. *Ibid.*, 171.

56. *Ibid.*, 124. O'Connor bemoaned that the creation of such a group
right was never intended by the Framers. Moreover, she contended that
"the one person, one vote principle [of *Reynolds*] safeguards [only] the
individual's right to vote, not the interests of political groups." *Ibid.*,
149.

57. *Ibid.*

58. The expert survey provides a surprising indication of the extent to
which the judicial preference for formal modes of representation has
become well established as a legal standard among the practitioners as
well. The discussion of the results of the survey of legal and political
practitioners, set forth in Appendix A, p. 195, suggests that formal routes
to representation are as revered by legal and political practitioners as
they are by the Court.

59. Peter Schuck, "Partisan Gerrymandering: A Political Problem Without Judicial Solution," *Political Gerrymandering and the Courts*, ed. Grofman,
244–245. As an example, Schuck asserted that "to treat blacks, for example, as if they were political monoliths is to ignore both the evidence
of significant diversity among their members in precisely these respects."
Ibid., 245.

60. 478 U.S. 109, 132.

61. Lowenstein, "*Bandemer*'s Gap," 82–83.

62. Lowenstein, 76.

63. 125 L. Ed. 2d 511 (1993).

64. 132 L. Ed. 2d 762 (1995).

65. Justice O'Connor, who wrote the majority opinion, described the district in question as winding in "snakelike fashion through tobacco country, financial centers, and manufacturing areas until it gobbles enough enclaves of black neighborhoods. . . . Of the ten counties through which district twelve passes, five are cut into three different districts; even towns are divided." 125 L. Ed. 2d 511 (1993).

66. A partisan gerrymandering claim was also asserted, but its dismissal was summarily affirmed by the Supreme Court. *Pope v. Blue*, 121 L. Ed. 2d 3 (1992).

67. 125 L. Ed. 2d 511, 525.

68. *Miller v. Johnson*, 132 L. Ed. 2d 762, 763.

69. See Thomas Mann's foreword to *Controversies in Minority Voting: The Voting Rights Act in Perspective*, ed. Bernard Grofman and Chandler Davidson (Washington, D.C.: American Enterprise Institute, 1980), xiv. Abigail Thernstrom, a vociferous critic of race-based redistricting, has warned of the threat to political integration from "categorizing individuals for political purposes along lines of race and sanctioning group membership as a qualification for office." *Whose Vote Counts? Affirmative Action and Minority Voting Rights* (Cambridge: Harvard University Press, 1987) (quoted by O'Rourke, supra at 108). For a defense of the Voting Rights Act by one of its staunchest supporters, see Frank Parker, *Black Votes Count: Political Empowerment in Mississippi After 1965* (Durham: University of North Carolina Press, 1990).

For an earlier judicial expression of these concerns, see Brennan's concurrence in *United States Jewish Organizations v. Carey*, 430 U.S. 144 (1977). He worried that:

> An explicit policy of assignment by race may serve to stimulate our society's latent race consciousness, suggesting the utility and propriety of basing decisions on a factor that ideally bears no relationship to an individual's worth or needs. (citation omitted). Furthermore, even preferential treatment may act to stigmatize its recipient groups, for although intended to correct systemic or institutional inequities, such a policy may imply to some the recipients' inferiority and especial need for protection.

Ibid., 173–174.

70. 125 L. Ed. 2d 511, 529.

71. *Ibid.*, 529. O'Connor condemned racial classifications for reinforcing:

> the belief . . . that individuals should be judged by the color
> of their skin. Racial classifications with respect to voting carry
> particular dangers. Racial gerrymandering, even for remedial
> purposes, may balkanize us into competing racial factions; it
> threatens to carry us further from the goal of a political sys-
> tem in which race no longer matters.

Ibid., 535. One senses a frustration with this debate even from proponents of race-based vote dilution protections. See Bernard Grofman, Lisa
Handley and Richard Niemi, *Minority Representation and the Quest for Voting Equality*, 134–135. The authors welcome the idealistic sentiment of
representatives being able to represent constituents of different color. But
they reject it as an empirical reality, decrying the level of racial polarization in voting which leaves no alternative but to aggressively pursue litigation to increase minority representation. They also accept in theory
the importance of coalitional politics between minorities, which will yield
tangible political results. Yet they doubt the ultimate utility of multiracial
coalitions.

The apparent predicament lies in the need to tap polarized racial
voting, by structuring electoral arrangements to ensure minority representation. But the fact that such arrangements are necessitated by racial
polarization strongly suggests that those strategies serve to ossify and in-
stitutionalize those racial polarizations, making it more difficult to move
beyond them. Racial divisions compel special minority group protections,
which in turn entrench those divisions. The result is a cycle in which
there is no foreseeable end to (or easing of) the racial distinctions.

72. *Miller v. Johnson*, 132 L. Ed. 2d 762, 776–777.

73. 125 L. Ed. 2d 511, 549.

74. 132 L. Ed. 2d 762, 780.

75. 125 L. Ed. 2d 529.

76. 132 L. Ed. 2d 782.

77. *Ibid.*, 774.

78. 125 L. Ed. 2d 528–529. The dissenters agreed:

> But while district irregularities may provide strong indicia of
> a potential gerrymander, they do no more than that. In par-
> ticular, they have no bearing on whether the plan ultimately
> is found to violate the Constitution.

Ibid., 545; *Miller*, 135 L. Ed. 2d 777.

79. Richard Morrill, "A Geographer's Perspective," *Political Gerrymandering
and the Courts*, ed. Bernard Grofman (New York: Agathon Press, 1990), 217.

80. Morrill, "A Geographer's Perspective," 216. A legislator cannot represent his constituents properly—nor can voters from a fragmented district exercise the ballot intelligently—when a voting district is simply an artificial unit divorced from the various communities and interests within.

81. A.H. Birch, *Representation* (New York: Praeger Publishers, 1971), 89.

82. Morrill refers to this combination of parties and territorial considerations as the dual system of representation around which districting practices are built. Morrill, "A Geographer's Perspective," 217.

CHAPTER FOUR

1. Arthur Bentley, *The Process of Government* (Cambridge: Belknap Press of Harvard University Press, 1967), 205.

2. Bentley, 222.

3. *Ibid.*, 208.

4. *Ibid.*, 177.

5. *Ibid.*, xix.

6. *Ibid.*, 269.

7. *Ibid.*, 272. Even judge-made law, theoretically beyond the reach of pressure group activity, was shaped by group forces. Beginning with their own affiliations, judges were influenced by, and responsive to, a myriad of group influences and pressures: the litigating parties, interested government offices or agencies, discussion groups, interested media and academics, and public opinion. Even Supreme Court decisions, rendered in high-minded legal jargon and premised upon finely spun points of law, were fundamentally resolutions of the underlying group interests. Next to the multiform interest groups present in a highly complex society, "the finest legal logic [wa]s but a trivial fly-by-night, and the very essence of unreliability." *Ibid.*, 394.

8. *Ibid.*, xxiv. Theodore Lowi's *The End of Liberalism*, 2d ed. (New York: W.W. Norton & Co., 1979) and other critiques of pluralist democracy call into direct question Bentley's assertion that "joint participation is always present." Marginalized minorities would certainly take issue with his claim that "even the lowest caste or slave helps to form government, and is an interest group within it." Bentley, 271.

9. *Ibid.*, 415.

10. *Ibid.*, 417.

11. *Ibid.*, 417.

12. *Ibid.*, 431.

13. David B. Truman, *The Governmental Process: Public Interests and Public Opinion* (New York: Alfred A. Knopf, 1951).

14. Truman, *The Governmental Process*, 21.

15. *Ibid.*, 43–44.

16. *Ibid.*, 112–113.

17. *Ibid.*, 64.

18. *Ibid.*, 129.

19. *Ibid.*, 138. Implicit in Truman's account was the assumption that more democracy and participation within the group would inevitably lead to unity and cohesion within the group. Time has proven this assumption to be highly suspect. Contemporary conventional wisdom suggests that those groups that are influential, well-directed and highly motivated may well benefit from an authoritarian leadership, which may or may not pursue action and an agenda consistent with the preferences of the rank-and-file membership.

20. *Ibid.*, 325.

21. *Ibid.*, 368. Truman shared Bentley's view of the courts as group-oriented in their behavior. *Ibid.*, 479. "The significance of a court system in any society is its usefulness as a means of arriving at a viable regulation of human relationships," namely to mediate conflicting group interests. *Ibid.*, 478. Yet Truman was more equivocal than Bentley in his assessment of the judicial process as a function of group politics. Because of the more formalized judicial structures to control group access, group influence on the judiciary was unseen and difficult to discern, and often highly unpredictable. *Ibid.*

22. Truman offered a prescient warning as to the potentially deleterious consequences when the routes of access are blocked, either through rigidly established patterns of access, or as a result of diffused lines of access. *Ibid.*, 523. The latter description is one that arguably describes our contemporary political climate. Ironically, the diffusion of communication between government and subject is attributable to the progressive trends away from groups and toward the individual. Trends in favor of purely participatory democracy on the individual level (primaries, initiative and referenda, electronic balloting proposals, etc.) and away from party organizations and machinery have undercut the ability to interpret public preferences or to relate them to governance. The resultant delay and inaction is responsible for considerable public disenchantment with government.

23. Earl Latham, *The Group Basis of Politics: A Study in Basing-Point Legislation* (New York: Octagon Books, Inc., 1965), 1.

24. Group theory stood in stark contrast to other explanations of political power, especially elitist theories. While Bentley was explicating a group theory, his contemporary, Robert Michel, was offering a strikingly different interpretation of political power. See generally *Political Parties: A Sociological Study of the Oligarchical Tendencies of Modern Democracies* (New York: The Free Press, 1962). Michels castigated, rather than lauded, the place of groups and organizations in democracy. He viewed organizations as characterized by a perverted democracy in which leaders dominated their members. According to Michels' "iron law of oligarchy," neither associations, political parties, nor nation-states themselves could be run without membership relinquishing effective power to the few at the top, who were running the institution.

25. Kay Lehman Schlozman and John T. Tierney, *Organized Interests and American Democracy* (New York: Harper & Row, 1986), 7.

26. Latham, *The Group Basis of Politics*, 49.

27. V.O. Key, *Politics, Parties, and Pressure Groups*, 5th ed. (New York: Thomas Y. Crowell Company, 1964); Robert A. Dahl, *Who Governs?: Democracy and Power in an American City* (New Haven: Yale University Press, 1961); Nelson W. Polsby, *Community Power & Political Theory: A Further Look at Problems of Evidence and Inference*, 2nd ed. (New Haven: Yale University Press, 1980).

28. V.O. Key, *Politics, Parties and Pressure Groups*, 17.

29. This applies to the motivations underlying individual voting behavior, as well. For a classic social science study which noted the important influence of social group experiences on individual voting patterns, see Paul F. Lazarsfeld, Bernard Berelson, and Hazel Gaudet, *The People's Choice: How the Voter Makes Up His Mind in A Presidential Campaign* (New York: Columbia University Press, 1948), 137–149.

30. Key, 20; Darryl Baskin, "American Pluralism: Theory, Practice, and Ideology," *Journal of Politics*, 32 (February 1970): 71–95.

31. Robert A. Dahl, *A Preface to Democratic Theory* (Chicago: The University of Chicago Press, 1956), 131.

32. Dahl's pluralism was certainly not that of James Madison. He offered a thorough critique of Madison's *Federalist Papers*, No. 10, in *A Preface to Democracy*. For an interesting summary of Dahl's criticisms and a rebuttal in Madison's defense, see Garry Wills' *Explaining America: The Federalist* (New York: Doubleday & Company, 1981), xiv–xxi.

33. Dahl, *Who Governs?*, 325; Baskin, "American Pluralism," 76–77.

34. Polsby, *Community Power & Political Theory*, 115.

35. V.O. Key, 20.

36. *Ibid.*, 40.

37. *Ibid.*

38. Carol S. Greenwald, *Group Power: Lobbying and Public Policy* (New York: Praeger Publishers, 1977), 21.

39. Baskin, "American Pluralism," 73.

40. Dahl, 93.

41. *Ibid.*

42. *Ibid.*, 228.

43. Key, 20.

44. *Ibid.*, 130.

45. *Ibid.*, 18–19 (emphasis added). Pluralists have been criticized for reducing the sum of politics to the group forces at work. Kay Lehman Schlozman and John T. Tierney, *Organized Interests and American Democracy* (New York: Harper & Row, 1986), 8–9. Schlozman and Tierney accuse the 1950s voices of group politics of adopting too simplistic a model of politics, by attributing outcomes to the pure aggregate of group struggles and activity. But Dahl, Key, and others emphasized organized interests as only one of many factors shaping eventual government outcomes. The emphasis on the supplemental role of groups and the primacy of parties reflects a more balanced pluralist regard for groups than that for which they are given credit.

46. Giovanni Sartori, *Parties and Party Systems: A Framework for Analysis* (Cambridge: Cambridge University Press, 1976), 18.

47. Sartori, *Parties and Party Systems*, 94.

48. Dahl, 92–93.

49. *Ibid.*, 91.

50. *Ibid.*, 114.

51. *Ibid.*

52. *Ibid.*, 99.

53. *Ibid.*, 100–101. For a discussion of what democracy within groups should look like, see Carol Greenwald's summary of the competing forms of organizational democracy, *Group Power: Lobbying and Public Policy*.

54. Key, 100.

55. *Ibid.*, 102.

56. *Ibid.* This assumption bears the brunt of one of the most scathing criticisms of modern pluralism by Theodore Lowi. In *The End of Liberalism*, Lowi contends that government has abandoned its function of guarding the public realm to make sure it does not become captive to private interests. Instead, the modern administrative state is one in which government has delegated power to the interested private parties. Government, rather than being a check against unrestrained, self-interested private power, has become an accomplice to the private wielding of power outside the elements by which the public maintains democratic control. Lowi, *The End of Liberalism*, 36–44.

57. Arthur N. Holcombe, *Politics in Action: The Problems of Representative Government* (Menasha, Wisconsin: George Banta Publishing Co., 1943), 11–12.

58. Sartori, *Parties and Party Systems*, 17.

59. Michael T. Hayes, "The New Group Universe," *Interest Group Politics*, eds. Allan J. Cigler and Burdett A. Loomis, 2nd ed. (Washington, D.C.: Congressional Quarterly Press, 1986), 135.

60. William Kornhauser, *The Politics of Mass Society* (New York: The Free Press, 1959), 78.

61. Kornhauser, *The Politics of Mass Society*, 80.

62. Key, 150.

63. Harmon Zeigler, *Pluralism, Corporatism, and Confucianism: Political Association and Conflict Regulation in the United States, Europe, and Taiwan* (Philadelphia: Temple University Press, 1988).

64. Baskin, 83.

65. For an example, see William Connolly's "The Challenge to Pluralist Theory," in *The Bias of Pluralism*, ed. William E. Connolly (New York: Atherton Press, 1969), 13–19.

66. E.E. Schattschneider, *The Semi-Sovereign People* (New York: Holt, Rinehart, and Winston, 1960), 30.

67. *Ibid.*, 30.

68. *Ibid.*, 138.

69. *Ibid.*, 2.

70. *Ibid.*, 7.

71. Schattschneider put it this way: "The whole discussion of the role of government in modern society is at root a question of the scale of conflict.

Democratic government is the greatest single instrument for the socialization of conflict in the American community." Ibid., 12 (author's original emphasis).

72. *Ibid.,* 13.

73. For a more recent statement of this flawed assumption, see Michael T. Hayes, "The New Group Universe," *Interest Group Politics,* eds. Allan J. Cigler and Burdett A. Loomis, 2nd ed. (Washington, D.C.: Congressional Quarterly Press, 1986), 141. Even noted pluralists picked up on Schattschneider's observations regarding the inequalities in the group system. Robert Dahl, one of pluralism's most articulate advocates, nevertheless recognized the imbalance between groups, attributing it to unequal distribution of resources. Inequities between groups had the potential to distort pluralism as a positive account of policymaking, since unequally distributed resources permitted the unequal exercise of influence when it came to defining the agenda, or resolving issues once they made the public agenda. Robert A. Dahl, *Dilemmas of Pluralist Democracy: Autonomy vs. Control* (New Haven: Yale University Press, 1982), 46–47. V.O. Key likewise noted the conservative nature of group systems, as the highly organized sought to maintain the status quo and avoid disruption of the systems of governance. Key saw groups less as instigators of change than as powerful brakes on political change. Key, *Politics, Parties, and Pressure Groups,* 68–70.

74. Schattschneider, 35. Recent studies confirm that the problem not only still exists, but has grown worse. Schlozman and Tierney offer empirical data which suggests that the Washington pressure scene is even more slanted in favor of business than it was in the 1950s. *Organized Interests and American Democracy,* 67–75.

75. Schattschneider, 35. Schattschneider had no desire to remove special interests from the realm of politics. Instead, he sought a synthesis of pressure politics and party politics to better socialize conflict. Pressure groups were necessary to the socialization of conflict. Conflict was initiated by motivated, self-interested groups. But those groups were unable to see the justice of competing claims or the larger public good. Hence the need for parties and other institutions to enlarge and publicize the conflict. *Ibid.,* 38–39.

76. *Ibid.,* 65–66.

77. *Ibid.,* 70.

78. *Ibid.,* 71–74. This accounted for Schattschneider's explanation of the tepid state of the parties. Their receding power and increasing irrelevance were attributable to their failure to define the alternatives in a way suitable to large numbers of the nation. This interpretation has a comfortable fit even today in explaining the relative ease with which someone like Ross Perot could build a sizable following in the 1992 presidential

election. Few would disagree that it was largely due to the inability of the parties to present a persuasive substantive case to the public of how they would govern.

79. *Ibid.*, 102.

80. *Ibid.*, 138.

81. Economist Mancur Olson followed on Schattschneider's heels by seriously questioning whether organized interests would emerge as easily as group theorists suggested. Mancur Olson, *The Logic of Collective Action* (Cambridge: Harvard University Press, 1965). Relying on economic principles involving collective goods as a motivator of individual participation in group activity, Olson concluded that, at least with respect to those groups that sought collective benefits (i.e., benefits flowing to everyone in the group), "rational, self-interested individuals will not act to achieve their common or group interests." *The Logic of Collective Action*, 9. Collective benefits cannot be withheld from anyone who fits the definition of group member. Hence the free rider who realizes the organizational benefits without helping bear its costs. This view of rational, self-interested individuals undermined the pluralist assumption that the formation of organizations to represent collective interests is a given.

Olson's conclusions owed an intellectual debt to Anthony Downs, who proffered an explanation based upon economic principles of why abstention from voting by individuals was rational. Anthony Downs, *An Economic Theory of Democracy* (New York: Harper & Row, 1957). Downs's scenario rested on self-interested political actors on all levels. He understood voters as basing their voting on the benefits they anticipated receiving from that party. Downs, 49. Parties, motivated by their desire to win office, formulate policy to win elections. Once in power, government (which Downs described as the governing party) sets its policies in order to maximize its vote in the next election. *Ibid.*, 31.

Downs described an American two-party system in which the parties looked much like each other. This tendency toward similarity and policy/ideology overlap put a burden on the voter to discover the parties' real differences before voting. Ultimately, voters could be expected to do this only when the anticipated benefits of voting outweigh the informational costs of informing themselves. Since this is often not the case, the decision to abstain from the election is a rational one. *Ibid.*, 274.

James Q. Wilson also offered an analysis constructed around the costs and benefits implicated by a particular issue, as a framework for predicting when a group would or would not organize for political activity. James Q. Wilson, *Political Organizations* (New York: Basic Books, 1973), Chapter 15. Wilson contended that the structure of conflict and the path an issue would take would be determined in large part by whether the costs imposed and benefits conferred would be widely or narrowly distributed. An issue that entailed the narrow concentration of costs upon one group and the narrow distribution of benefits on another group would likely induce highly intense, narrow group activity by each of those groups. In contrast, widely distributed costs and benefits were likely to result in minimal interest group activity.

82. Grant McConnell, *Private Power and American Democracy* (New York: Alfred A. Knopf, 1966).

83. McConnell, *Private Power and American Democracy*, 3–8.

84. *Ibid.*, 162.

85. *Ibid.*, 164. McConnell's identification of the sources of private power, and his account of its rise, are perceptive, indeed fascinating. He traced the ascendancy of private power to two derivations, one the deeply ingrained American philosophical preference for small social and political units, the second this country's longstanding aversion to power, as manifested in the Progressive movement and the reforms it spawned. One primary tenet of American orthodoxy was "the belief in small units of social and political organization as the citadels of the values associated with democracy." *Ibid.*, 91. From the founding era and before, small groups and associations were thought to be rooted in liberty, self-government, and autonomy, and served as safeguards against a potentially intrusive, overreaching state. From New England town meetings to those of the Quakers, from churches to rural co-ops, unions, and trade associations, small organizations assured stability, served the public interest, and guaranteed liberty.

This furnished the ideological framework for private power. The Progressive movement of the early twentieth century, however, served as the catalyst, providing a specific set of circumstances which allowed groups to flourish as wielders of political power. The irony of the Progressive movement was its propagation of that which it sought to exterminate. McConnell traced the origins of Progressivism to the American fear of power, more specifically the pressure being exerted at the turn of the century by the lobbies of big business, railroads, and the like. In short, the energy of Progressivism was driven by a fear of the emerging special interests and their corrupting influence.

The Progressive legacy was how they chose to attack that problem. Progressives concluded that political parties were the means by which private power flourished, and therefore needed reform. *Ibid.*, 32–43. "The general progressive conclusion, then, was that parties were a medium of special interest power; to strike at the special interests themselves involved some kind of change in the party system." *Ibid.*, 42. Through Progressive eyes, the excessive influence of business, railroads, and bankers corrupted party organizations, city machines, and legislatures. The irony of anti-party reforms such as initiative and referenda, and direct primaries, was two-fold. First, it emasculated those institutions that were best able to serve as a countervailing force to private interests, and capable of harnessing and controlling them.

Second, the Progressive attack on parties was coupled with a belief in government by experts, which consequently led to the rapid proliferation of the administrative sphere of government. The Progressives, unfortunately, failed to follow through on the theoretical implications of this combination. Government by expert relied on the necessity of administration. Yet individual citizens could seemingly speak in that realm only through interest groups and associations. Moreover, the expansion into increasingly technical and complex areas was made with little congressional guidance by way of standards and criteria for agency conduct. The inevitable result was heavy reliance by agencies on those organizations and groups with a special interest in the particular matter. *Ibid.*, 47–50. Thus did Progressive ideology contribute to the control of important regulatory agencies by those very groups that they were to regulate. McConnell concluded that the "conditions created by the antiparty 'reforms' were at least as favorable to the growth of new pressure-group machines as any previously existing," *Ibid.*, 49, offering as proof extensive accounts of the twentieth century rise to power of private associations in the areas of business, labor, and agriculture.

86. *Ibid.*, 164.

87. *Ibid.*, 145–46.

88. *Ibid.*, 120.

89. Robert Michels, *Political Parties: A Sociological Study of the Oligarchical Tendencies of Modern Democracies* (New York: The Free Press, 1962).

90. McConnell, 122.

91. *Ibid.*, 134.

92. *Ibid.*, 154. Democratic ideals required that the membership be free to express dissent, or alternatively, to leave the organization and join a rival without losing the benefits of membership. Not only did McConnell find organizations extremely intolerant of dissent, but also highly involuntary in membership. The severity of penalties for not belonging, coupled with the absence of rival organizations, rendered many associations to be involuntary as a practical matter. *Ibid.*, 350.

93. *Ibid.*, 146–150. McConnell's critique of pressure groups has taken on the status of orthodoxy among experts practicing in the field of law and politics. The survey of contemporary legal and political practitioners suggests they share McConnell's skeptical views of the democratic nature of politically motivated groups. The survey results reveal substantial doubt as to whether groups are sufficiently democratic to warrant their taking on official representative status. See Appendix A, pp. 197–98.

94. *Ibid.*, 164.

95. *Ibid.*, 297.

96. *Ibid.*, 164.

97. Theodore J. Lowi, *The End of Liberalism: The Second Republic of the United States*, 2nd ed. (New York: W.W. Norton & Company, 1979).

98. Lowi, *The End of Liberalism*, 32–34.

99. *Ibid.*, 44.

100. See also Schlozman and Tierney, *Organized Interests and American Democracy*, 389.

101. Lowi, 57–58.

102. *Ibid.*, 51.

103. Hamilton, Madison, and Jay, *The Federalist Papers*, No. 10.

104. Lowi, 58. See also Schlozman and Tierney, *Organized Interests and American Democracy*, 400.

105. Like Schattschneider, Lowi roundly castigated liberalism for its inability to resolve political conflict in a way that expands, rather than limits, the scope and number of interested players involved:

> The contribution of politicians to society is their skill in re-
> solving conflict. However, direct confrontations are sought only
> by so-called ideologues and outsiders. Typical American poli-
> ticians displace and defer and delegate conflict where pos-
> sible; they face conflict squarely only when they must.
> Interest-group liberalism offered a justification for keeping
> major combatants apart and for delegating their conflict as
> far down the line as possible. It provided a theoretical basis
> for giving to each according to his claim, the price for which
> is a reduction of concern for what others are claiming. In
> other words, *it transformed access and logrolling from necessary
> evil to greater good.*

Lowi, 55 (the author's emphasis).

106. Lowi, 59–61.

107. *Ibid.*, 62–63.

108. Dahl, *Dilemma of Pluralist Democracy: Autonomy vs. Control*, 43–44.

109. Dahl, *Dilemmas of Pluralist Democracy*, 44.

110. W. Russell Neuman, *The Paradox of Mass Politics: Knowledge and Opinion in the American Electorate* (Cambridge: Harvard University Press, 1986), 126.

111. Neuman, *The Paradox of Mass Politics*, 127.

112. *The Disuniting of America* (New York: W.W. Norton & Co., 1992).

113. Schlesinger, *The Disuniting of America*, 117.

114. *Ibid.*, 117.

115. *Ibid.*, 134 (quoting from Herbert Croly, *The Promise of American Life*, (citation omitted)).

116. Hayes, "The New Group Universe," 142.

117. Dahl, *Dilemmas of Pluralist Democracy*, 82.

118. Dahl, *A Preface to Democratic Theory*, 137–143. Dahl anticipated the constitutional implications of group theory. He saw the importance of constitutional guidelines in determining those groups which shall be accorded formal advantages or handicaps in the political arena. "They are crucial to the status and power of the particular groups who gain or suffer by their operation." Dahl asserted that the Framers understood that the constitutional regime they crafted would inevitably benefit some groups and penalize others. *Ibid.*, 137–143.

119. *Ibid.*

CHAPTER FIVE

1. A statement of the group theory basis of group representation can be found in Iris Marion Young's *Justice and the Politics of Difference*, (Princeton: Princeton University Press, 1990), 9.

2. Young, *Justice and the Politics of Difference*, 92.

3. *Ibid.*, 163.

4. *Ibid.*, at 168.

5. Young, "Polity and Group Difference: A Critique of the Ideal of Universal Citizenship," 99 *Ethics* (1989): 250, 261.

6. Young, *Justice and The Politics of Difference*, 119.

7. *Ibid.*, 183–184.

8. *Ibid.*, 95.

9. *Ibid.*, 167.

10. Young, "Polity and Group Difference": 250, 258.

11. *Justice and The Politics of Difference*, 184. Owen Fiss offers a similar scenario, envisioning a system in which individuals identified by their membership in a group have legal status determined in part by the

well-being and status of their groups. See Fiss, "Forward: The Forms of Justice," *Harvard Law Review* 93: 1 (1982); "Groups and the Equal Protection Clause," *Philosophy and Public Affairs* 5 (1976): 107. See also Larry May, *The Morality of Groups: Collective Responsibility, Group-Based Harm, and Group Rights*, (South Bend: University of Notre Dame Press, 1987).

12. *The Politics of Difference*, 184.

13. *Ibid.*, 157–158.

14. *Ibid.*, 48–64.

15. Young, "Polity and Group Difference": 261.

16. *The Politics of Difference*, 186.

17. *Ibid.*, 185–186.

18. For a similar view, see Cass Sunstein, "Beyond the Republican Revival," *Yale Law Journal* 97: 1539, 1588 (1988); also "Preferences and Politics," *Philosophy and Public Affairs* 3 (1991): 20, 32–34. Sunstein argues that the republican ideal of deliberation is enhanced when there are mechanisms to ensure that multiple groups have access. By ensuring the inclusion of diverse voices, group representation increases "the likelihood that political outcomes will incorporate some understanding of the perspective of all those affected." *Ibid.*

19. See Lani Guinier, "The Triumph of Tokenism: The Voting Rights Act and the Theory of Black Electoral Success," *Michigan Law Review* 89: 1077, (March 1991).

20. Lani Guinier, "No Two Seats: The Elusive Quest for Political Equality," *Virginia Law Review* 77: 1423, 1422 (November 1991). While Guinier casts her discussion in terms of interest representation, she considers it to be primarily a way of advancing group claims. She is at home with the group theorists and neopluralists who advocate the need for enhanced group rights in the political sphere. The group is "an appropriate unit for political participation because the 'right to elect' is valueless at the level of the single individual." Rather, the emphasis on group rights properly recognizes and takes into account the "autonomy and value of group identification and collective participation." Guinier, "No Two Seats," 1460, n. 175.

21. Guinier, "No Two Seats," 1416.

22. For support for Guinier's view, see Charles R. Beitz, "Equal Opportunity in Political Representation," *Equal Opportunity*, ed. Norman E. Bowie (Boulder: Westview Press, 1988), 162.

23. Guinier, "No Two Seats," 1479.

24. *Ibid.*, 1433.

25. See Appendix A, pp. 195–96.

26. Guinier, "No Two Seats," 1457.

27. *Ibid.*, 1479. Guinier makes no mention of the second mode of the dual system of representation, the extralegal, informal activities of groups bringing influence to bear directly on legislators. One can only assume that she would consider those minority groups to be so lacking in political power or resources that it is unrealistic to think that they can wield any effective influence outside formal channels.

28. Guinier, "The Triumph of Tokenism," 1093.

29. *Ibid.*, 1080, n. 9. While the legal community involved in voting rights and representation litigation may share Guinier's distaste for purely descriptive modes of representation, it is at this point that they diverge. For an indication of how Guinier's proposals of interest representation might be received by the larger legal community, see the results of the expert survey conducted to supplement this discussion. The canvassing of legal and political practitioners revealed little sympathy for an outcome-based definition of political representation. Appendix A, p. 195.

30. *Ibid.*, 1035–1036. Guinier does not abandon the importance of a group's ability to elect those of its kind. "Authentic representation" is important in validating particular group consciousness and identity, and in recognizing the distinctive political voice of the group. It promotes a diverse representative body, one in which fuller deliberation can occur because of the richness and diversity of perspectives physically present. A governing body that reflects in its representative character the diversity of those it represents is legitimized as a democratic institution. *Ibid.*, 1128. Guinier would overlay interest representation upon a system designed to maximize authentic representation of disadvantaged groups.

31. *Ibid.* "A crucial characteristic of effective minority representation in collective decisionmaking is the formal ability to express the intensity of constituent preferences and to bargain or deliberate accordingly." Guinier, "No Two Seats," 1444.

32. Guinier, "The Triumph of Tokenism," 1136, n. 28; "No Two Seats," 1458.

33. Guinier, "No Two Seats," 1483.

34. *Ibid.*, 1481. To the question of "which groups" or "which interests" are deserving of recognition, Guinier offers seemingly contradictory answers. Interest representation is a claim on behalf of "statutorily protected minorities who have endured, and continue to endure, consistent disadvantages throughout the political process despite apparent gains." *Ibid.*, 1461, n. 181. It encompasses those groups that can make a strong, historically supported, and congressionally mandated case for their political

influences being degraded over time. *Ibid.*, 1488–1489. This response is vulnerable to charges of circularity. It does not answer how excluded groups gain entry through legislative groups, which Guinier characterizes as racist.

Elsewhere, Guinier offers a more general, open-ended definition of the relevant interests. Proportional interest representation should incorporate the self-identified interests of any politically cohesive group of voters. Interests are not necessarily correlative of a group identity, but are "fluid and dynamic articulations of group preferences." Lani Guinier, "Voting Rights and Democratic Theory—Where Do We Go From Here?" *Controversies in Minority Voting: The Voting Rights Act in Perspective*, eds. Bernard Grofman and Chandler Davidson (Washington, D.C.: The Brookings Institution, 1992), 289, n. 12. This suggests the availability and application of interest representation to a much broader range of groups.

35. Robert C. Grady, *Restoring Real Representation*, (Chicago: University of Illinois Press, 1993).

36. Grady, *Restoring Real Representation*, 163.

37. *Ibid.*, 32.

38. *Ibid.*, 5, 28.

39. *Ibid.*, 147.

40. *Ibid.*, 142.

41. *Ibid.*, 161.

42. *Ibid.*, 147.

43. *Ibid.*, 148. In the end, Grady seems so overwhelmed by the daunting nature of the task that one wonders how seriously he takes his own ideas:

> The complexity of identifying, legitimating, and assigning roles to diverse types of functional jurisdictions, coupled with the overlapping activities of those and elective institutions, compounds the sorts of problems that are thought to be resolved in theories of popular representation.

Ibid., 140.

44. See generally Brooks Jackson, *Honest Graft: Big Money and the American Political Process*, (New York: Alfred A. Knopf, 1988); Herbert E. Alexander, *Financing Politics: Money, Elections, & Political Reform*, 4th ed. (Washington, D.C.: Congressional Quarterly, 1992); ed. Michael J. Malbin, *Parties, Interest Groups, and Campaign Finance Laws*, (Washington, D.C.: American Enterprise Institute, 1980).

45. Robert A. Dahl, *After The Revolution: Authority in a Good Society*, (New Haven: Yale University Press, 1970), 115.

46. 424 U.S. 1 (1976).

47. Stephen Gottlieb, "Government Allocation of First Amendment Resources," *University of Pittsburgh Law Review* 41: 205, 208 (1979).

48. Other provisions in the amendments added strict disclosure requirements, established the creation of a six-member Federal Election Commission, and incorporated public funding provisions for the major party conventions and presidential general election campaigns. See Michael J. Malbin, ed. *Parties, Interest Groups, and Campaign Finance Laws*, (Washington, D.C.: American Enterprise Institute, 1980), 3–4, for a summary of the statute.

49. *Buckley*, 424 U.S. 1, 25.

50. For a discussion of the ways in which contribution limits present serious obstacles to committees in their ability to perform associational or organizational tasks, see Paul M. Weyrich, "The New Right: PACs and Coalitional Politics," *Parties, Interest Groups, and Campaign Finance Laws*, ed. Michael Malbin (Washington, D.C.: American Enterprise Institute, 1980), 74–75.

51. Congress, unfortunately, responded to *Buckley* by taking the Court's lead and further dampening role of parties and associations in campaign financing. *Buckley* produced a set of 1976 amendments to FECA which further limited what individuals and PACs could contribute to political parties and other political committees.

52. *Buckley*, 424 U.S. 1, 48–49.

53. Gottlieb, "Rebuilding the Right of Association," 204.

54. 101 S. Ct. 2712 (1981).

55. 101 S. Ct. 2712, 2722.

56. Stephen E. Gottlieb, "Rebuilding the Right of Association: The Right to Hold a Convention as a Test Case," *Hofstra Law Review* 11: 191, 207 (1982). David Jessup found the same "bias against organizational representation in politics" in the finance reform efforts of the late 1970s. Jessup, "Can Political Influence be Democratized?" *Parties, Interest Groups and Campaign Finance Laws*, 46. He observes that "organizational influence is often the target of the liberal reform movement, that newer, more individualized forms of influence gain in its place . . . " *Ibid.*, 51.

57. That individualistic approach to associational rights was confirmed in *Citizens Against Rent Control v. City of Berkeley*, 102 S. Ct. 474 (1981). A Berkeley city ordinance limited contributions to committees opposing or supporting ballot measures. The city sought to enforce the ordinance against an unincorporated association that opposed a ballot measure to

impose rent controls. Though the Court struck down the provision, the associational rights at stake were those of "individuals to support concerted action by a committee advocating a position on a ballot measure." 102 S. Ct. 474, 483. *Berkeley* shielded the exercise of associational activities, but signalled no "change in the Court's failure to appreciate the ways in which an association functions as anything more than the sum of its members' efforts." Gottlieb, "Rebuilding the Right of Association," 206.

58. For a detailed account of the rise of political action committees and their role in the financing of political campaigns, see Edwin M. Epstein, "Business, and Labor under the Federal Election Campaign Act of 1971," *Parties, Interest Groups, and Campaign Finance Laws,* ed. Michael Malbin (Washington, D.C.: American Enterprise Institute, 1980), 107–151; see also the commentary of Fred Wertheimer in the same publication, 200–204.

59. For statements reflecting those views, see the commentaries by Richard Conlon and Fred Wertheimer in *Political Parties, Interest Groups, and Campaign Finance Laws,* ed. Michael Malbin, (Washington, D.C.: American Enterprise Institute, 1980), 185–206; Edwin M. Epstein, "Business and Labor under the Federal Election Campaign Act of 1971," *Political Parties, Interest Groups, and Campaign Finance Laws,* ed. Michael Malbin (Washington, D.C.: American Enterprise Institute, 1980), 139–140 and citations contained therein; cf. Edwin Epstein, "Business and Labor under the Federal Election Campaign Act of 1971," 107 (citing the comments of former U.S. Congressman Bill Frenzel).

60. 459 U.S. 197 (1982).

61. *FEC v. National Right to Work Committee,* 459 U.S. 197, 207.

62. *Ibid.,* 210 (quoting *California Medical Association v. FEC,* 453 U.S. at 201).

63. Reform-minded political scientists applauded the efforts to achieve greater parity between corporate and noncorporate players. See David Jessup, "Can Political Influence be Democratized? A Labor Perspective," *Parties, Interest Groups, and Campaign Finance Laws,* ed. Michael J. Malbin (Washington, D.C.: American Enterprise Institute, 1980), 26–55. As one academic stated, the "shift of influence from money-based interest groups to people-based interest groups seems likely to be entirely salutary, and most appropriate in a democracy." Jessup, "Can Political Influence be Democratized?" 42, n. 34 (quoting Professor Joel L. Fleashman, Director of the Institute of Policy Sciences and Public Affairs, Duke University, testifying before the Senate Subcommittee on Privileges and Elections, September 20, 1973).

64. 105 S. Ct. 1459 (1985).

65. Presidential Election Campaign Fund Act, 26 U.S.C. sec. 9001 et seq.

66. 105 S. Ct. 1459, 1467 (citation omitted).

67. *Ibid.*, 1468.

68. *Ibid.*, 1469.

69. *Ibid.*, 1470.

70. *Ibid.*

71. *Ibid.*, 1481.

72. 478 U.S. 238 (1986).

73. 478 U.S. 238, 264.

74. *Ibid.*, 259.

75. *Ibid.*, 257.

76. *Ibid.*

77. 478 U.S. 238, 258.

78. *Ibid.*, 257.

79. *Ibid.*, 258.

80. *Ibid.*, 259.

81. Dissenter Justice Rehnquist rued the majority's "effort to carve out a constitutional niche for [g]roups such as MCFL," contending that the Court was becoming embroiled in subtle distinctions better left to the legislature. 478 U.S. 238, 271.

82. 494 U.S. 652 (1990).

83. *Austin,* 494 U.S. 652, 662, 672.

84. *Ibid.*, 695.

85. *Ibid.*, 706.

86. *Ibid.*, 680.

87. *Ibid.*, 679. See Michael Malbin's argument that efforts to restrict the amounts of money that groups can spend may only polarize group politics and favor groups that can organizationally take advantage of the situation. Malbin, "Of Mountains and Molehills," 184.

88. 494 U.S. 652, 679.

89. *Ibid.*, 685.

90. *Ibid.*, 692.

91. See Larry May, *The Morality of Groups*, for a more positive perspective on legal distinctions based on groups' economic and political resources.

92. See Herbert Alexander's discussion of broadly based political power as the solution to equalizing inequities in monetary resources. "Political Finance Regulation in International Perspective," 333. Electoral and organizational constituencies are equally important avenues to representative government. Hence, "the wealth of one group thus may be matched by the human resources or voting power of another." *Ibid.*

CHAPTER SIX

1. Arnold Kaufman, "Participatory Democracy: Ten Years Later," *The Bias of Pluralism*, ed. William E. Connally (New York: Atherton Press, 1969), 201; Cynthia Ward, "The Limits of 'Liberal Republicanism': Why Group-Based Remedies and Republican Citizenship Don't Mix," *Columbia Law Review* 91: 581, 585 (1991).

2. Xandra Kayden, "The Nationalizing of the Party System," *Political Parties, Interest Groups, and Campaign Finance Laws*, ed. Michael Malbin (Washington, D.C.: American Enterprise Institute, 1980), 281. Party scholar William Crotty describes it as a:

> politically charged and balkanized atmosphere [in which] 'no coalition of interests is strong enough to set priorities for the overall public good . . . and to inspire confidence in political leadership.'

William J. Crotty, *American Parties in Decline*, 2nd ed. (Glenview, Illinois: Scott, Foresman and Company, 1984), 142–43, (quoting John Herbers, "Deep Government Disunity Alarms Many U.S. Leaders," *The New York Times* November 12, 1978, 1).

3. Cynthia Ward describes the separatist propensies of group representation this way:

> [G]roup members begin to see anyone outside the group as the 'other.' The group focus turns inward as it attempts to draw more and more of its members' sense of identity away from general citizenship and toward total immersion in the group. . . . This attitude manifests itself in a siege mentality toward the outside world, increasing alienation, and an emphasis on oppression, in spite of any progress that is made.

"The Limits of 'Liberal Republicanism," *Columbia Law Review* 91: 581, 585 (1991); see also Charles Fried, "*Metro Broadcasting, Inc. v. FCC*: Two Concepts of Equality," *Harvard Law Review* 104: 107 (1990).

4. Cynthia Ward, "The Limits of 'Liberal Republicanism'" *Columbia Law Review* 91: 581, 605–606 (1991).

5. Donald W. Jackson, *Even The Children of Strangers: Equality Under the U.S. Constitution*, (Lawrence, Kans.: University Press of Kansas, 1992), 10–11.

6. Group representation proponent Cass Sunstein admits that this may further marginalize groups rather than help them. The resulting factionalism may "discourage political actors from assuming and understanding the perspectives of others," thereby dampening the deliberative and transformative aspects of politics. Cass Sunstein, "Beyond the Republican Revival," *Yale Law Journal* 97: 1539, 1587 (1988). Iris Marion Young, too, admits to having concerns over the potential to reinstate stigma and exclusion through focusing on group differences. Young, *Justice and the Politics of Difference*, 174.

7. See the expert survey results, Appendix A, p. 197.

8. This typology is a synthesis of a number of works, including Alvin Zander, *Effective Social Action by Community Groups* (San Francisco: Jossey-Bass Publishers, 1990); Norman J. Orenstein and Shirley Elder, *Interest Groups, Lobbying and Policymaking* (Washington, D.C.: Congressional Quarterly, 1978); Carol S. Greenwald, *Group Power: Lobbying and Public Policy* (New York: Praeger Publishers, 1977); and Kay Lehman Schlozman and John T. Tierney, *Organized Interests and American Democracy*, (New York: Harper & Row, 1986).

9. Appendix C provides a more thorough examination of the practical obstacles to implemention of group representation schemes. The author analyzes in detail the empirical and behavioral complexities that accompany attempts to apply neopluralist remedies in any comprehensive or consistent fashion.

10. Herbert Alexander, "Political Finance Regulation in International Perspective," *Parties, Interest Groups, and Campaign Finance Laws*, ed. Michael Malbin (Washington, D.C.: American Enterprise Institute, 1980), 107–151.

11. Zander, *Effective Social Action by Community Groups*, 4, 60–65.

12. See generally the discussion in Appendix C of possible typologies built around these and other possible determinants of group representation, pp. 207–15.

13. See Anne Phillips, "Democracy and Difference: Some Problems for Feminist Theory," *The Political Quarterly* 63 (1992): 79, 81.

14. Fried calls this the worst kind of stereotyping, that "which assumes that members of racial or ethnic groups exhibit distinct ways of thinking, share particular dispositions, or display common patterns of values and behavior." Fried, *"Metro Broadcasting, Inc. v. FCC,"* 123.

15. Larry May, *The Morality of Groups*. May is apparently undaunted. He adopts an expansive definition of harm to members of a group by virtue

solely of their membership in that group. He argues that we ought not
to require that group members suffer actual harm, only that they are
treated indiscriminately as members of a negatively stereotyped group.
Ibid., 120.

16. Fried, 125.

17. See Jackson, *Even The Children of Strangers*, 229.

18. Anne Phillips, "Democracy and Difference: Some Problems for Feminist Theory," *The Political Quarterly* 63: 79, 85.

19. Young concedes that there is no easy way to identify the eligible
groups or to implement group representation. She would require groups
to petition and persuade (the courts or legislature) for their right to
representation. This is marred by an obvious circularity. To qualify for
representation, a group must show itself to be excluded or oppressed.
Yet, real oppression or exclusion of groups may well preclude them from
being effectively heard within the legislative or legal institution responsible for conferring representative status.

20. Anne Phillips concurs that the decisions as to group influence cannot be made apart from politics and political mobilization. She argues
that group classification constitutes a premature freezing of categories
that is inappropriate for issues of representation and political equality.
Phillips, "Democracy and Difference: Some Problems for Feminist Theory,"
The Political Quarterly 63 (1992): 79, 89.

21. John C. Wahlke, "Logic and Politics in Electoral Engineering," *Representation and Redistricting Issues*, eds. Bernard Grofman et al (Toronto:
Lexington Books, 1982), 165–166.

22. For a thorough and thoughtful theoretical exposition of parties and
party systems, see Giovanni Sartori, *Parties and Party Systems: A Framework
for Analysis* (Cambridge: Cambridge University Press, 1976).

23. Giovanni Sartori sums it up this way:

> Parties *must* be aggregating agencies that maintain their com-
> petitive near-evenness by amalgamating as many groups, in-
> terests and demands as possible.

Parties and Party Systems: A Framework for Analysis (Cambridge: Cambridge
University Press, 1976), 192 (Emphasis his).

24. The decline of the political parties is well-documented. For discus-
sions of the reasons for their decreasing relevance, see Gerald M. Pomper,
Passions and Parties (Lawrence, Kansas: University Press of Kansas, 1992);
A. James Reichley, *The Life of the Parties* (New York: The Free Press, 1992).

25. de Grazia, citing E. Pendleton Herring, *Group Representation Before
Congress* (Baltimore: The John Hopkins Press, 1929).

26. See generally Anthony Downs, *An Economic Theory of Democracy* (New York: Harper and Row, 1957).

27. Joseph Schlesinger, *Political Parties and the Winning of Public Office*, 6.

28. This is essentially the rational choice model of political behavior popularized by Anthony Downs. *Ibid.*, 6–15.

29. The Democrats can at least generally be described as the party of labor, pro-choice, gays and lesbians, blacks, and so on. Republicans are similarly comprised of evangelical Christians, pro-business organizations, and other groups. Moreover, the struggle to prevail on election day hinges on the parties' success in attracting other less well-defined or committed groups of voters. Hence the struggle to attract large segments of ethnic groups, various age groups, geographically based blocs (suburban, inner-city, agricultural), and professional and blue collar workers.

30. Mary Ann Glendon, *Rights Talk: The Impoverishment of Political Discourse* (New York: The Free Press, 1991), 75.

31. Note: "The Constitutional Imperative of Proportional Representation," *Yale Law Journal* 94: 163, 183 (1985).

32. Eulau and Prewitt, *Labyrinths of Democracy*, 342.

33. *Ibid.*, 395.

34. *Ibid.*, 395.

35. As a point of clarification, it should be noted that factionalism is used here in the Madisonian sense, as opposed to more contemporary usage of factions existing within party coalitions (i.e., the Christian Right within the Republican Party, the liberal wing of the Democratic Party). Madison defined factions in a broader sense, as a group of citizens (comprising either a majority or minority) united in some common impulse or interest that was adverse to the rights of others or to the permanent or aggregate interests of the community. Alexander Hamilton, James Madison, and John Jay, *The Federalist Papers*, intro. Clinton Rossiter (New York: Mentor Books, 1961), No. 10. p. 78.

36. Hamilton, Madison, and Jay, *The Federalist Papers*, No. 10.

37. Bruce Cain, "Perspectives on *Davis v. Bandemer,*" *Political Gerrymandering and the Courts*, ed. Bernard Grofman (New York: Agathon Press, 1990), 134.

38. Jerome M. Mileur, "Prospects for Party Government," *Challenges to Party Government*, eds. John K. White and Jerome M. Mileur (Carbondale: Southern Illinois University Press, 1992), 214–219.

39. For an early articulation of parties as managers of conflict see E.E. Schattschneider's *Semi-Sovereign People* (New York: Holt, Rinehart and Winston, 1960).

40. Ralph M. Goldman, *Dilemma and Destiny: The Democratic Party in America* (Lanham, Maryland: Madison Books, 1986) (emphasis added).

41. Giovanni Sartori uses the terms "majority principle" and "minority rule." *The Theory of Democracy Revisited*, 131–137.

42. Note: "The Constitutional Imperative of Proportional Representation," *Yale Law Journal* 94: 177 (1985).

43. Daniel H. Lowenstein, *"Bandemer's* Gap: Gerrymandering and Equal Protection," *Political Gerrymandering and the Courts*, ed. Bernard Grofman (New York: Agathon Press, 1990), 84, n. 9.

44. Michael Hess, "Beyond Justiciability: Political Gerrymandering After *Davis v. Bandemer*," *Cambell Law Review* 9: 207, 252 (1987).

45. Leon Epstein, *Political Parties in the American Mold* (Madison: The University of Wisconsin Press, 1986), 27.

46. Richard A. Brisbin, Jr., "Federal Courts and the Changing Role of American Political Parties," *Northern Illinois University Law Review* 5: 68 (1984).

47. This suggests the necessity of party systems alternatives broad enough to acknowledge the role of parties outside the two major parties. The inherent limitations of the two major parties in recognizing all groups and giving them voice indicates that minor or new parties are a legitimate and important presence in the satisfaction of those functions. The analysis must be broad enough for multi-party systems if the party functions are to be adequately performed.

48. For an example of an early criticism of the parties' programmatic makeup, see the 1950 report of the APSA Committee on Parties entitled *Toward a More Responsible Two-Party System* (New York: Rinehart & Co., 1950).

49. At the same time, parties have the ability to incorporate and reconcile a multitude of group claims because they are not the monolithic creatures this discussion has sometimes suggested. Because they are fluid, ever-changing, and adjusting, they are able to build coalitions of groups (and in fact are essentially constituted by those groups), and give them voice in the process.

50. See the results of the canvassing of legal experts and political activists set out in Appendix A, pp. 196–97.

51. *Ibid.*

52. That capability lies in what Van Buren saw as a basic characteristic of the parties, their formation around broad principles rather than narrow ones. Within broad parameters, they serve to create civic identity and cultivate a less self-interested perspective in public affairs.Wilson Carey McWilliams, "Parties as Civic Associations," *Party Reform in America: Theory and Practice*, ed. Gerald M. Pomper (New York: Praeger Publishers, 1980), 60.

53. de Grazia, 210.

54. Sartori, 77.

55. "They aggregate, select, and eventually deviate and distort." *Ibid.*, 28.

56. *Ibid.*, 342.

CHAPTER SEVEN

1. *Gaffney v. Cummings*, 412 U.S. 735 (1973).

2. 412 U.S. 735, 738.

3. 412 U.S. 735, 748 (citing *Reynolds v. Sims*, 377 U.S. 533, 565–566).

4. 412 U.S. 735, 754 (emphasis added).

5. *Ibid.*

6. Nevertheless, political scientists lauded the decision as a step in the right direction toward fairer districting procedures. See Robert G. Dixon, Jr., "Fair Criteria and Procedures for Establishing Legislative Districts," *Representation and Redistricting Issues*, eds. Bernard Grofman et al (Toronto: Lexington Books, 1982), 11; Richard Niemi and John Deegan, Jr., "A Theory of Political Districting," *American Political Science Review* 72 (1978): 1304 (responsive representative bodies are possible only by incorporating "the partisan division of the vote into the criteria for fair districting").

7. For a statement in general agreement with this assessment, see Bruce E. Cain, "Perspectives on *Davis v. Bandemer*: Views of the Practitioner, Theorist and Reformer," *Political Gerrymandering and the Courts*, ed. Bernard Grofman, 117–142. For a contrary view, see Daniel Lowenstein, "*Bandemer*'s Gap: Gerrymandering and Equal Protection," *Political Gerrymandering and the Courts*, ed. Bernard Grofman (New York: Agathon Press, 1990), 70. Lowenstein characterizes *Reynolds* and its progeny as entailing voting rights that were personal and individual in nature, and state action that discriminated against individuals. *Bandemer*, in contrast, confronted the separate right to representation, and state action that impeded the efforts of groups to secure representation by electing representatives of their choice.

8. Davis v. Bandemer, 478 U.S. 109, 124 (emphasis added).

9. *Ibid.*, 132–33.

10. *Ibid.*, 147.

11. If anything, O'Connor's concurrence suggested a preference for treating parties *less* sympathetically than other groups in the districting process. Unlike racial groups which might have been shut out of the political process, parties:

> cannot claim that they are a discrete and insular group vulnerable to exclusion from the political process by some dominant group: these political parties are the dominant groups, and the Court has offered no reason to believe that they are incapable of fending for themselves through the political process. . . . There is no proof before us that political gerrymandering is an evil that cannot be checked or cured by the people or by the parties themselves.

Ibid., 152.

12. *Ibid.*, 131.

13. *Ibid.*, 139–140.

14. In *Badham v. Eu*, 694 F. Supp. 664 (N.D. Cal. 1988), a California district court confronted perhaps the most blatant case of political gerrymandering to come before the courts. In 1981, a Democratically-controlled California legislature passed a Congressional redistricting plan which Republicans challenged. The case followed a torturous procedural path, sputtering along fitfully for years, lying dormant at times and for various reasons, at one point to permit the Supreme Court to decide *Bandemer.* By 1988, when it was finally decided, three election cycles had occurred. Though the Republicans in 1984 received over 50 percent of the statewide vote in congressional races, they won only 40 percent of those races (18 of 45). In 1986, the disparity narrowed, as Republicans garnered 47 percent of the vote and retained the same number of seats. Despite these numbers, the district court was not persuaded that the redistricting unconstitutionally "fragmented and submerged Republican minorities."

The district court read *Bandemer* to require the Republicans to show they "had essentially been shut out of the political process." 694 U.S. 664, 672 (Citing *Bandemer*, 106 S.Ct. at 2814). The court dismissed the complaint, finding that the Republicans had failed to establish that their interests "were 'entirely ignore[d]' by their congressmen." 694 F. Supp. 664, 672. The district court latched onto *Bandemer's* requirement of an absence of political power necessary to establish a statewide discriminatory impact. The Court found it significant that, far from being shut out of the process, California Republicans still held 40 percent of the House, a U.S. senatorial seat and the governorship. These facts belied the Republicans' claim that they could not "exercise potent power in the political process as a whole" due to unfair gerrymandering. *Ibid.*, 672. The Republican presence in California politics statewide was indicative of a degree of political power sufficient to protect them from "political subjugation." *Ibid.*

15. For support for this view, see Bruce E. Cain, "Perspectives on *Davis v. Bandemer*," 126.

16. *Republican Party of Virginia v. Wilder*, 774 F. Supp. 400 (W.D. Va. 1991), involved another Equal Protection challenge to partisan gerrymandering. Republicans challenged a plan for the Virginia House of Delegates, prepared and passed by a Democratically dominated legislature, on grounds that it unfairly coupled incumbent Republicans. The plan paired fourteen Republican incumbents to run against each other, as compared to just two Democrats. The district court conceded that the plan placed a burden on Republicans not similarly visited on their Democratic counterparts. Nevertheless, it held that practices that disproportionately paired minority party incumbents was not necessarily constitutionally infirm. Not every "interference with an opportunity to elect a representative of one's choice" is an Equal Protection violation. 774 F. Supp. 400, 405 (citing *Davis v. Bandemer*, 478 U.S. 109, 133).

17. Only Justice Powell's dissenting opinion demonstrated any degree of enthusiasm for more rigorous restrictions on partisan gerrymandering. Powell proposed a host of "neutral factors relevant to the fairness of redistricting," including the shapes of the proposed districts, adherence to existing political subdivision boundaries, and a review of the legislative procedures, history, and goals underlying the proposed plan. 478 U.S. 109, 162, 165–66. Powell appeared far less concerned about the discriminatory outcome than the intent behind the process. If the intent to discriminate was evident from the neutral fairness factors, discriminatory effect could largely be inferred.

18. 478 U.S. 109, 132.

19. 478 U.S. 109, 140.

20. *Ibid.*, 139 (2814).

21. Two counties consisted of multi-member districts in which, even though Democrats received 46 percent of the vote, they won only three of the twenty-one contested seats.

22. See generally, David E. Price, "The Party Connection," *Challenges to Party Government*, eds. John Kenneth White and Jerome M. Mileur (Carbondale, Illinois: Southern Illinois University Press, 1992), 133–153. It is for this reason that the public's disdain for parties, while a serious concern, is not fatal to legal efforts to lift the parties' standing constitutionally.

23. Leon Epstein, *Political Parties in the American Mold* (Madison: University of Wisconsin Press, 1986), 77.

24. Lowenstein, *"Bandemer's* Gap," 77.

25. For a summary of the classic Burkean conceptualization of the competing delegate versus trustee ideals of representation, see Heinz Eulau and Kenneth Prewitt, *Labyrinths of Democracy: Adaptations, Linkages, Representation, and Policies in Urban Politics* (New York: The Bobbs-Merrill Company, Inc., 1973), 398–443, and other works of Eulau. Eulau contrasts two basic types of representative. Those who act in a purely democratic fashion behave as *delegates*, their function simply to discern and follow the will and wishes of the constituency. Rather than exercise independent judgment, the legislator need only mirror the interests of the people, and act as a conduit through which their desires are channeled.

    The republican ideal of representative as *trustee* is markedly different. In a republic, the ultimate exercise of democratic power is relinquished by the citizenry to elected representatives, people of supposedly superior intellect and judgment and most capable of performing the public service of governing. They are dutybound to exercise their best judgment in pursuit of the greatest good, even when it does not coincide with the immediate wishes of the represented. Rather than relying on the whims of the majority, the representative is trustee of the common good, his informed judgment transcending the people's uninformed, self-interested desires. Thus are the interests of all subjects best assured by the advancement of those "who possess most wisdom to discern, and most virtue to pursue, the common good of society . . ." Alexander Hamilton, James Madison, and John Jay, *The Federalist Papers,* intro Clinton Rossiter (New York: Harcourt Brace Jovanovich, 1955), No. 52.

26. Cain, 152.

27. David R. Mayhew, *Congress: The Electoral Connection* (New Haven: Yale University Press, 1974), 115.

28. Theodore J. Lowi: *The End of Liberalism: The Second Republic of the United States* (New York: W.W. Norton & Co., 1979), xii.

29. 478 U.S. 109, 170 (emphasis added).

30. One group of commentators put it this way:

> Very dubious is the plurality's assertion that minority party voters may not be hurt by a partisan gerrymander because they are not shut out of any considerations by the majority party officeholders. . . . What is an election about if it is not between candidates who offer somewhat different policy alternatives on at least some questions. Parties matter in elections, and parties matter in legislative decisions. It is simply

not true that a legislator gives equal weight to the views and needs of his supporters and opponents.

Charles Backstrom, Leonard Robins, and Scott Eller, "Establishing a State-wide Electoral Effects Baseline," *Political Gerrymandering and the Courts*, ed. Bernard Grofman (New York: Agathon Press, 1990), 157.

31. 478 U.S. 109, 153 (emphasis added).

32. Gordon E. Baker, "The Totality of Circumstances Approach," *Political Gerrymandering and the Courts*, ed. Bernard Grofman (New York: Agathon Press, 1990), 207.

33. Robert G. Dixon, Jr. noted the need to focus on statewide electoral outcomes:

> There is the outcome for the legislature as a whole where an important part of the power equation, and the reality of effective representation, depends on capturing enough district seats to win a legislative majority and be able to control the key committee chairmanships.

"Fair Criteria and Procedures for Establishing Legislative Districts," 8.

34. That preoccupation with formal modes of representation is shared by legal practitioners and political activists, as has been noted. See the expert survey results set forth in Appendix A, p. 195.

35. Once again, it is conceded that this idealizes the parties to make the point. Serious doubts exist as to the electorate's capacity for this advanced level of rationality. The inherent limitations among the electorate to digest a highly substantive campaign temper the assumptions of rational public choice. See generally Angus Campbell et al, *The American Voter* (New York: Wiley, 1960). At the same time, there is ample justification for questioning the ability of parties and their candidates to mount programmatic campaigns, and to inject reason and rationality into the process.

36. Indeed, the injurious impact on choice works a harm against voters belonging to both parties. The complement to safe districts for the majority party's candidates is the packing of as many of the minority party's voters into as few districts as possible. In this way, the number of votes cast for the minority party candidate who will win the seat are maximized. By conceding certain seats to the other party and making the electoral margin as large as possible, the majority wastes as many of the other party's and as few of its own votes as possible. In those districts, those who vote with the statewide majority party are similarly denied meaningful influence or input as to the personal representative of their choice. They are essentially the sacrificial lambs of the majority party, forfeiting their choice so that the party may enhance its majority statewide.

37. David Wells, "Against Affirmative Gerrymandering," *Representation and Redistricting Issues*, eds. Bernard Grofman et al (Toronto: Lexington Books, 1982), 83; Stephen Gottlieb, "Fashioning a Test for Gerrymandering," *Journal of Legislation* 15: 1, 12 (1988).

38. Stephen E. Gottlieb, "Election Reform and Democratic Objectives— Match or Mismatch?" *Yale Law Review* 9: 219 (1991). Bernard Grofman describes:

> political parties and the candidate choices they offer voters [as] the single most important mechanism for incorporating citizen preferences into public policy decisions. To invidiously discriminate against the candidates of a political party is to effectively disenfranchise like voters who support the positions espoused by the party's candidates and thus to dilute the importance of their views in the halls of the legislature.

Bernard Grofman, "Criteria for Districting: A Social Science Perspective," *UCLA Law Review* 33: 112 (1985).

39. Gordon E. Baker, "The Unfinished Reapportionment Revolution," *Political Gerrymandering and the Courts*, ed. Bernard Grofman (New York: Agathon Press, 1990), 25.

40. Baker, "The Unfinished Reapportionment Revolution," 210.

41. Richard Morrill, "A Geographic Perspective," *Political Gerrymandering and the Courts*, ed. Grofman, 212.

42. Grofman, "Criteria for Districting: A Social Science Perspective," *UCLA Law Review* 33: 77, 112.

43. Cain, "Perspectives on *Davis v. Bandemer*: Views of the Practitioner, Theorist, and Reformer," 131.

44. Baker, "The Unfinished Reapportionment Revolution," 49.

45. Richard Morrill succinctly states the case for parties, as opposed to groups, this way:

> The argument that if parties, why not ethnic groups, the elderly or other interest groups, is of course specious, since *it is uniquely parties that are entrusted with governance*—the purpose of voting in the first place.

"A Geographer's Perspective," *Political Gerrymandering and the Courts*, ed. Grofman, 212, 218 (emphasis added).

46. 478 U.S. 109, 136. See Bernard Grofman, "Toward a Coherent Theory of Gerrymandering: *Bandemer* and *Thornburg*," *Political Gerrymandering and the Courts*, 29, 37.

CHAPTER EIGHT

1. Clifton McCleskey, "Parties Before the Bar: Equal Protection, Freedom of Association, and the Rights of Political Organizations," *Journal of Politics* 46 (1984): 347, 348.

2. Mark E. Rush, "Voters' Rights and The Legal Status of American Political Parties," *Journal of Law and Politics* 9 (1993): 487, 500.

3. Anthony Downs provided the reasoning behind the more limited ballot with his articulation of the rational voter choice theory in his classic, *An Economic Theory of Democracy* (New York: Harper and Row, 1957). Downs explained the advantages of a stable two-party system over a multi-party electoral system in promoting voter participation in elections. According to Downs's model, voters' participation was determined in part by the information and decisionmaking costs of making themselves informed to cast a ballot. The two-party system reduced those costs by narrowing the choices on the ballot, making it more "rational" for voters to cast a ballot. *Ibid.*

4. Rush, "Voters' Rights and The Legal Status of American Political Parties," 511–512.

5. *NAACP v. Alabama ex rel. Patterson*, 357 U.S. 449, 459 (1958).

6. Gary Scott and Craig Carr, "Political Parties Before the Bar: The Controversy Over Associational Rights," *University Of Puget Sound Law Review* 5: 267 (1982).

7. Stephen Gottlieb, "Rebuilding the Right of Association: The Right to Hold A Convention as a Test Case," *Hofstra Law Review* 11: 191, 203.

8. *Sweezey v. New Hampshire*, 354 U.S. 234, 250 (1956).

9. 354 U.S. 234, 250–51. In *NAACP v. Alabama*, 357 U.S. 449, 459, Justice Marshall described the association as "but the medium through which its individual members" seek political expression.

10. The right of association was available to members of an array of groups. It encompassed the "right to associate with the political party of one's choice," *Kusper v. Pontikes*, 414 U.S. 51, 56 (1973) but also to political, economic, religious or cultural matters. *NAACP v. Alabama*, 357 U.S. 449, 460. Noting the "virtue of political activity by minority, dissident groups," *Sweezey*, 354 U.S. 234, 251, the Court extended the protections "without regard to the race, creed or political or religious affiliation of the members of the group which invokes its shield, or to the truth, popularity, or social utility of the ideas and beliefs which are offered." *NAACP v. Button*, 371 U.S. 415 (1962).

11. The pervasiveness of state regulation of political parties is well-documented. Many have blamed the decline in party influence on legal

restrictions that relegated parties to secondary status. See David Price, *Bringing Back the Parties* (Washington, D.C.: Congressional Quarterly Press, 1984), 121–25; Gerald M. Pomper, *Passions and Interests: Political Party Concepts of American Democracy* (New York: Praeger Publishers, 1980), 116–131; David Mayhew, *Placing Parties in American Politics: Organization, Electoral Settings, and Government Activity in The Twentieth Century* (Princeton: Princeton University Press, 1986) 308–332 for a thorough description of progressive reforms and regulation of parties; Stephen Gottlieb traces the history of party regulation in "Rebuilding the Right of Association," 196–200.

12. *Williams v. Rhodes*, 393 U.S. 23 (1968).

13. 393 U.S. 23, 30.

14. 393 U.S. 23, 31.

15. For a concurring view, see Clifton McCleskey, "Parties Before the Bar," *Journal of Politics* 46 (1984): 347, 350–351. Mark Rush states that "the state's authority to regulate the parties is thus grounded in a rather broad conceptualization of an individual's right to vote." "Voters' Rights and The Legal Status of American Political Parties," 494.

16. *Whitcomb v. Chavis*, 403 U.S. 431 (1971).

17. 403 U.S. 431, 439.

18. *Ibid.*, 442.

19. *Ibid.*, 441.

20. *Ibid.*

21. *Lubin v. Parrish*, 415 U.S. 709 (1973).

22. 415 U.S. 709, 715.

23. *Ibid.*, 719.

24. *Ibid.*, 716.

25. *Ibid.*, 716.

26. *Storer v. Brown*, 415 U.S. 724 (1973).

27. 415 U.S. 724, 733.

28. *Ibid.*, 736.

29. *Ibid.*, 735.

30. Several commentators have lauded the *Jennes - Storer - American Party* line of cases as exemplifying the Court's recognition of the legitimate functions of parties. Gottlieb, "Rebuilding the Right of Association," 208–209; Rush, 500–501.

31. *Storer*, 746.

32. *Ibid.*, 746.

33. *Ibid.*, 745.

34. For a more generous reading of this line of cases, see Clifton McCleskey's discussion in "Parties Before the Bar," 351. He contends that the cases culminating in *Storer* generally reflect a judicial support for party politics.

35. 460 U.S. 780 (1982).

36. 460 U.S. 780, 787–788.

37. *Ibid.*, 793–794 (emphasis added).

38. *Ibid.*, 806.

39. *Ibid.*, 793.

40. *Ibid.*, 821.

41. McCleskey, 353–354.

42. For a contrary view, see Lee Epstein and Charles Hadley, "On the Treatment of Political Parties in the United States Supreme Court," *Journal of Politics* 52 (May 1990): 414.

43. *Illinois State Board of Elections v. Socialist Workers Party*, 440 U.S. 173 (1979), was similarly illustrative of the subordination of the major parties to minor ones. It involved a discrepancy between two Illinois state laws that had the practical effect of imposing more cumbersome petition requirements upon the Socialist Workers Party than upon other parties. Illinois law required 25,000 signatures from new parties and independent candidacies for statewide elections. A separate law for local races required signatures from at least five percent of those voting in the previous election. When Mayor Daley's death required a special mayoral election in Chicago, the law pertaining to local elections required the Socialist Workers Party to obtain more signatures than would have been required under the law for statewide elections. The Socialist Workers' Party challenged it as a violation of its associational freedoms.

The Court agreed, holding that the rule diminished the "freedom to associate as a political party." 440 U.S. 173, 184. In finding for the Socialist Workers' Party, the Court articulated benefits flowing from third parties that it rarely attributes to the two major parties. It was impressed with the intellectual component of minor parties. It found especially compelling the capacity of third parties to inject substance and fresh ideas into political campaigns. It dwelled on the significant role of third parties in the political development of the Nation, citing the Abolitionists, Progressives, and Populists as examples of how "an election campaign is a means of disseminating ideas as well as attaining political office." *Ibid.*, 185–186.

44. John Moeller, "The Federal Courts' Involvement in the Reform of Political Parties," *Western Political Quarterly* 40 (1987): 717, 720.

45. Ballot access questions especially implicate lesser parties and third parties. Their emerging importance in American politics warrants more careful consideration than has been allotted to them here. For now, suffice it to say that a functionally based theory of representation would at least assist the courts (and others) in placing minor parties on the political spectrum. A party-based theory of representation would provide the Court with a tool for considering multi-party systems, and for dealing with parties outside the two-party system logically and consistently.

46. 414 U.S. 51 (1973).

47. 414 U.S. 51, 57.

48. *Ibid.*, 58. Blackmun minimized the infringement on party association by the statute, which he described in his dissent as a "minor and incidental burden that happens to fall on a few uniquely situated citizens." *Ibid.*, 63–64.

49. 419 U.S. 477 (1975).

50. 419 U.S. 477, 487–488.

51. *Ibid.*, 490.

52. Justice Rehnquist's concurring opinion echoed the basic importance of the party-oriented right of association:

> The right of members of a political party to gather in a national political convention in order to formulate proposed programs and nominate candidates for political office is at the very heart of the freedom of assembly and association . . .

Ibid., 491 (Rehnquist, J., concurring) (citations omitted).

53. Gary L. Scott and Craig L. Carr, "Political Parties Before the Bar," *University of Puget Sound Law Review* 5: 267, 273 (1982).

54. Moeller, "The Federal Courts' Involvement in the Reform of Political Parties," 725.

55. 450 U.S. 107 (1980).

56. 450 U.S. 107, 122.

57. *Ibid.*, 122. The Court relied heavily upon a significant lower court opinion, *Ripon Society v. National Republican Party*, 525 F. 2d 567 (D.C. Cir. 1975). That decision contained a remarkably clear discussion of the na-

ture of parties and their need for political association, perhaps due to the fact that the president of Ripon Society at the time was John Saloma, a political scientist who had authored books related to the importance of political parties. See John S. Saloma, *Parties: The Real Opportunity for Effective Citizen Politics* (New York: Alfred Knopf, 1972).

The Ripon Society had challenged the Republican Party's policy of awarding bonus national convention delegates to states that had voted Republican in certain previous elections, thus violating one person, one vote. Refusing to extend strict one person, one vote principles to procedures for presidential nominating conventions, the appellate court described parties as an "organized attempt to see the most important of [their] views put into practice through control of the levers of government." *Ibid.*, 585. It issued a strong endorsement of the parties' associational rights. Without such a right, the freedoms of speech and assembly were of little value. The D.C. Circuit Court continued:

> What is important for our purposes is that a party's choice, as among various ways of governing itself, of the one which seems best calculated to strengthen the party and advance its interests, deserves the protection of the Constitution as much if not more than its condemnation.... There must be a right not only to form political associations, but to organize and direct them in the ways that will make them most effective.

Ibid. In this context, the First Amendment rights of the Party were superior to voting rights implied by the primary delegate selection scheme. *Ibid*, 588.

58. 450 U.S. 107, 137, n. 13.

59. *Ibid.*, 131.

60. 450 U.S. 107, 137.

61. Political scientists hailed *LaFollette* and *Cousins* as bellwethers for the parties. Brian L. Porto, "The Constitution and Political Parties," *Constitutional Commentary* 8: 433 (1991); Arthur M. Weisburd, "Candidate Making and the Constitution," *California Law Review* 57: 213 (1984). John Moeller proclaimed a newfound judicial preference for party-strengthening reforms over the twentieth century-long progressive reforms aimed at democratizing the electoral system, and speculated about a new pluralism which "includes parties that favor identifiable groups over discrete individuals." He concluded that the decisions might well lead to the effective deregulation of the parties by states. Moeller, 725. David Price interpreted the combined effects of the cases as "legitimat[ing] an increasing autonomous and assertive role for the national parties in the presidential nomination process and other aspects of party life." Price, 141. For a darker view, see Clifton McCleskey, "Parties Before the Bar," 356.

62. Scott and Carr, "Political Parties Before the Bar," 274.

63. 479 U.S. 208 (1986).

64. 479 U.S. 208, 215 (1986).

65. 479 U.S. 208, 215–216.

66. *Ibid.*, 224.

67. *Ibid.*, 224.

68. See *Buckley v. Valeo*, 424 U.S. 1 (1976).

69. 479 U.S. 208, 223–224.

70. Moeller, 720.

71. Moeller asserts that the decision could lead to total deregulation of parties with respect to their internal affairs and their nomination of candidates. *Ibid.* For a more equivocal reading of *Tashjian*, see Leon Epstein, "Will American Political Parties be Privatized?" *Journal of Law and Politics* 5: 239 (1989). Analyzing changes in state law post-*Tashjian*, he concludes that it has generally had no noticeable determinative effect on the constitutional status of parties, or on the success of challenges to state regulation of primaries. Epstein, 253–254.

72. See Mark Rush's commentary in "Voters' Rights and The Legal Status of American Political Parties," *Journal of Law and Politics* 9: 487 (1993). He reads *Tashjian* as ultimately concerned with the state's authority to regulate parties to assure voters a confusion-free electoral process. *Ibid.*, 494. Rush notes the judicial tension between bolstering the parties' collective rights and the Court's ultimate concern with voters' individual rights. *Ibid.*, 488.

73. 479 U.S. 208, 235.

74. *Ibid.*, 237.

75. Scott and Carr, 276.

76. *Ibid.*, 286.

77. The political science profession itself could not agree on the substantive issue of the consequences of open primaries for the parties, as evidenced by the filing of amicus briefs in *Tashjian*. See Epstein, "Will American Political Parties be Privatized?" 256–258. A group of well-known political scientists filed a brief opposing the state law, and asserting the primacy of party autonomy in determining whether the circumstances warranted closed or open primaries. A group of political scientists from the Northeast disagreed, arguing that the goal of responsible parties warranted the state's imposition of a closed primary requirement.

78. Scott and Carr, 276–277.

79. James MacGregor Burns, *Cobblestone Leadership: Majority Rule, Minority Power* (Norman: University of Oklahoma Press, 1990), 97.

80. Burns, *Cobblestone Leadership*, 97–98.

81. Scott and Carr argue that primaries ought to be "the private affair of those groups of individuals who choose to associate with a party to seek political clout." *Ibid.*, 279. Otherwise, the representative and conflict management functions of intraparty politics are lost.

82. Julie E. Guttman, "Primary Elections and the Collective Right of Freedom of Association," *Yale Law Journal* 94: 117, 129 (1984).

83. See the discussion by Scott and Carr at 272–278.

84. *Ibid.*, 277–278.

85. See Anthony Downs's statement of the values and functions of intraparty politics. *An Economic Theory of Democracy*, 109–111.

86. 489 U.S. 214 (1989).

87. 489 U.S. 214, 224.

88. *Ibid.*, 223.

89. *Ibid.*, 217–218.

90. *Ibid.*,223.

91. Brian L. Porto, "The Constitution and Political Parties: Supreme Court Jurisprudence and Its Implications for Partybuilding," *Constitutional Commentary* 8: 433, 445 (1991)cf., Mark Rush, "Voters' Rights and the Legal Status of American Political Parties," 491.

92. Porto, "The Constitution and Political Parties," 448 (citing Kay Lawson, "Challenging Regulation of Political Parties: The California Case," *Journal of Law and Politics* 2: 263, 276 (1985). James Fay argues that party control over nominations is the key to bringing groups into mainstream politics, "offering them incentives to work within the parties." Fay states this relationship in classic group theory terms:

> Such efforts of influence by groups should be welcome for the party ought to function as umbrella organization[s] for a wide variety of constituencies, to aggregate their philosophies and policy alternatives and to encourage those groups to consider their values and goals in relation to those of others.

James S. Fay, "The Legal Regulation of Political Parties," *Journal of Legislation* 9 (1982): 263, 280.

93. Gottlieb, "Rebuilding the Right of Association," 214–216.

94. Gottlieb posits that a return to conventions would allow groups to better pursue their long-term ideological and associational goals through the political parties. He argues that:

> The presence of viable clubs or grass roots groups within the parties working toward generic ideological or practical goals might well help to improve the creativity and reliability of the political process—basic first amendment objectives.

Gottlieb, "Government Allocation of First Amendment Resources," 247. James MacGregor Burns seconds the need to return to a convention system. *Cobblestone Leadership*, 125.

95. Gottlieb, 237. V.O. Key offered a contrary view. He applauded direct primaries as a positive move away from the domination of party machines and toward greater democratization. Direct primaries permitted a more direct expression of electoral choice by party membership on nominations than did caucuses or conventions dominated by party bosses. Under a system of direct primaries, Key maintained that the party machine would continue, but would be forced to be "more solicitous of the sentiment of party membership." V.O. Key, *Politics, Parties and Pressure Groups*, 395.

96. 489 U.S. 214, 228, n. 18.

97. *Ibid.*, 230–231. Unlike *Tashjian*, where Marshall found little significance in the fact of formal party affiliation, he concluded in *Eu* that the threatened associational rights were stronger, since the restrictions impinged on the association between affiliated party members, rather than between party and nonparty voters.

The decision stood in stark contrast to *Marchioro v. Chaney*, 442 U.S. 141 (1979), an early decision in which the Court upheld a Washington statute imposing organizational requirements on the party committees. The Court in *Marchioro* determined the restrictions to be justified by the state's interest in making sure elections were conducted fairly and orderly, and the parties' "critical role . . . in selecting and electing candidates for state and national office." 442 U.S. 141, 195–196.

98. 489 U.S. 214, 232.

99. Moeller, 719.

100. *Ibid.*, 720.

101. 112 S. Ct. 2059 (1992).

102. 112 S. Ct. 2059, 2063.

103. *Ibid.*, 2066.

104. *Ibid.*

105. *Ibid.*

106. *Ibid.*, 2065.

107. *Ibid.*, 2066.

108. *Ibid.*, 2067.

109. Moeller, 732.

110. Clifton McCleskey, "Parties Before the Bar," 367 (1984).

CHAPTER NINE

1. Patronage refers generally to the practice of rewarding the friends of the person or party in power with the benefits of government office. For purposes of this discussion, patronage is used more narrowly to refer to those appointive positions in government that are bestowed either as a reward for past political services or in anticipation of future work. See Frank J. Sorauf, *Political Parties in the American System* (Boston: Little, Brown and Co., 1964), 83. In the context of the legal constraints on patronage, issues arise within the framework of complaints lodged by the "victims" of patronage, those adversely affected by public personnel decisions made on the basis of partisan affiliation. They include decisions of hiring, firing, transfer, and promotion.

2. John Moeller, "The Federal Courts' Involvement in the Reform of Political Parties," *Western Political Quarterly* 40 (December 1987): 717, 730.

3. For general discussions of patronage and its functions see V.O. Key, *Politics, Parties and Pressure Groups*, 335–339; William Goodman, *The Two-Party System in the United States* (New York: D. Van Nostrand Co., Inc., 1964), 107–108; James Jupp, *Political Parties* (London: Routledge & Kegan Paul, 1974), 25–29; Frank Sorauf, "Patronage and Party," *American Political Parties: A Systemic Perspective*, eds. Charles G. Mayo and Beryl L. Crowe (New York: Harper & Row, 1967), 441–449; Comment, "Patronage Dismissals: Constitutional Limits and Political Justifications," *Chicago Law Review* 41: 297, 319–324 (1974); James L. Judson, *American Political Parties in Transition*, 79–80; Louis Cammarosano, "Applications of the First Amendment to Political Patronage Employment Decision," *Fordham Law Review* 58: 101–116 (1989).

4. Goodman, *The Two-Party System in the United States*, 108–109.

5. Comment, "Patronage Dismissals: Constitutional Limits and Political Justifications," *Chicago Law Review* 41: 319–320 (1974).

6. Comment, "Patronage Dismissals," 320.

7. Key, *Politics, Parties and Pressure Groups*, 337.

8. Key, 318.

9. The ability to provide benefits or compensation to its participants, either directly or indirectly, is a primary characteristic of party organization. Joseph A. Schlesinger, *Political Parties and the Winning of Office* (Ann Arbor: The University of Michigan Press, 1991), 19–20. As Martin and Susan Tolchin note, the most basic advantage of the patronage system is its ability to provide "clear-cut rewards in return for good service and unquestioned loyalty." *To the Victor*, 304; James D. Barber, "Leadership Strategies for Legislative Party Cohesion," *Political Parties: Leadership, Organization, Linkage*, eds. David W. Abbott and Edward T. Rogowsky (Chicago: Rand McNally & Company, 1971), 418–423.

For a contrary view, see Frank Sorauf, "Patronage and Party," *American Political Parties: A Systemic Perspective*, 442–449. Sorauf argues that the political usefulness of patronage is overestimated. He doubts the abilities of party leaders to administer or distribute patronage in a responsible or efficient fashion. He also cites examples of states that have flourished without the inducement of patronage appointments. Finally, he contends that the divisions and conflicts over patronage may well do more harm to party unity than good. "Patronage and Party," 442–449. For other skeptical views of the benefits of patronage, see Comment, "First Amendment Limitations on Patronage Employment Practices," *University of Chicago Law Review* 49: 181, 202 (1982).

10. James Jupp, *Political Parties* (London: Routledge & Kegan Paul, 1974), 26.

11. 427 U.S. 347 (1976) (Brennan, J.). For a tracing of the relevant caselaw prior to *Elrod*, see Comment, "Patronage Dismissals: Constitutional Limits and Political Justifications," *Chicago Law Review* 41: 307–317 (1974).

12. *Elrod v. Burns*, 427 U.S. 347, 351. A plurality of the Court held that public employees could not be compelled to sacrifice their political beliefs and associations as the price of maintaining their jobs.

13. *Ibid.*, 383 (citing *Storer v. Brown*, 415 U.S. 724, 735 (1979)).

14. *Ibid.*, 385.

15. *Ibid.*, 379.

16. *Ibid.*, 384 (emphasis added).

17. Powell also considered patronage as important to enhancing the parties' abilities to attract participation among minority and dispossessed groups. *Elrod v. Burns*, 427 U.S. 347, 382 n. 6 (citation omitted). Appointments to government jobs are more than merely the spoils of office, but especially aid disadvantaged groups in their struggle for social acceptance. For an in-depth account and specific illustrations of the use of minority

group and anti-poverty patronage, see Martin Tolchin and Susan Tolchin, *To the Victor: Political Patronage from the Clubhouse to the White House* (New York: Random House, 1971) 73–87.

18. *Ibid.*, 369.

19. The Court's cursory response is attenuated on several grounds. While Jackson is generally given credit for implementing the patronage system, historians and political scientists have observed that it was used to a significant degree as early as the turn of the century. For example, Carl Prince notes the importance of federal patronage to the Democratic-Republican party as early as 1800. "Patronage and a Party Machine: New Jersey Democratic-Republican Activists, 1801–1816," *William and Mary Quarterly*, XXI (1964): 571–578, reprinted in *The Federalists vs. The Jeffersonian Republicans*, ed. Paul Goodman (Huntington, New York: Robert E. Krieger Publishing Co., 1977), 77–81. William Goodman has also concluded that "one of the most famous canards of American political history is the statement that patronage began with the Administration of Andrew Jackson." *The Two-Party System in the United States*, (New York: D. Van Nostrand Co., Inc., 1964), 97. While noting that patronage came into full flower with Jackson, Goodman traces the substantial amount of patronage dispensed within the administrations of Washington, Adams, and Jefferson. See general discussion in *The Two-Party System*, 97–100.

Moreover, the comparison of parties in the early 1800s to those of the present ignores revolutionary changes in the political landscape, changes that render the comparison of highly questionable value. Furthermore, the ascendancy of the dynamic two-party system coincided with the advent of patronage, at least suggesting the possibility that the former was to some extent the result of the latter. Conversely, the Court's statement that parties have survived the movement toward a merit system and away from patronage in personnel decisions is debatable. It ignores what is almost universally accepted as substantial party decline, and political science literature that attributes that decline at least partly to the emasculation of patronage practices. See generally William J. Crotty, *American Parties in Decline*, 2nd ed. (Boston: Little, Brown & Co., 1984); Martin P. Wattenberg, *The Decline of American Political Parties: 1952–1984* (Cambridge, Massachusetts: Harvard University Press, 1990); Gerald Pomper, *Voters, Elections and Parties: The Practice of Democratic Theory* (New Brunswick, New Jersey: Transaction, Inc., 1988).

20. *Elrod*, 427 U.S. 347, 383.

21. *Ibid.*, 369, n. 22.

22. *Ibid.*, 362.

23. This contradicted the Court's explicit acceptance, in other contexts, of the governmental interest in maintaining a stable two-party system.

See generally *Buckley v. Valeo*, 424 U.S. 1 (1976)(campaign finance); *Storer v. Brown*, 415 U.S. 724 (1974)(ballot access).

24. See generally David S. Price, *Bringing Back the Parties* (Washington, D.C.: Congressional Quarterly Press, 1984).

25. The right to associate implies freedom from coerced political affiliation. Forcing an employee to support the in-party to keep his job restrains his freedom to act according to his beliefs and to associate with those who share them. *Elrod*, 427 U.S. 347, 355–356.

26. *Ibid.*, 372.

27. *Ibid.*

28. The decision garnered only a plurality, with three justices joining in the Powell dissent. Justices Stewart and Blackmun concurred in the result, but rejected the plurality's broader indictment of patronage practices in general. They agreed only that it was unconstitutional for a "nonpolicymaking, nonconfidential government employee [to] be discharged or threatened with discharge . . . upon the sole ground of his political beliefs." *Ibid.*, 375.

29. *Branti v. Finkel*, 445 U.S. 507 (1980)(Stewart, J.).

30. *Branti*, 445 U.S. 507, 517.

31. 445 U.S. 507, 518.

32. *Ibid.*, 529, n. 4.

33. *Ibid.*, 527.

34. *Ibid.*, 528.

35. *Ibid.*, 529. In this respect, Powell considered it as important to have people of like mind occupying positions involving implementation of policy as it was in advising or policymaking positions. He was, therefore, unwilling to accept the dichotomy established by the plurality in *Elrod*. *Ibid.*, 530.

36. *Ibid.*, 531.

37. *Ibid.*

38. *Ibid.*

39. *Ibid.*, 532.

40. 497 U.S. 62 (1990)(Brennan, J.).

41. *Rutan*, 497 U.S. 62, 74–75.

42. *Ibid.*, 103–104.

43. *Ibid.*, 104.

44. *Ibid.*, 105. Scalia quoted colorful Tammany Hall legend George Washington Plunkitt:

> I ain't up on sillygisms, but I can give some arguments that nobody can answer. First, this great and glorious country was built up by political parties; second, parties can't hold together if their workers don't get offices when they wish; third, if the parties go to pieces, the government they built up must go to pieces, too; fourth, then there'll be hell to pay.

Ibid., 93 (taken from William L. Riordan, *Plunkitt of Tammany Hall* [New York: Dutton, 1963], 13).

45. *Rutan*, 497 U.S. 62, 106.

46. *Ibid.*, 108.

47. The battle over the propriety of patronage practices may very well not be over just yet. In light of the substantial changes in the Court's make-up, the next patronage case taken up by the Court could be decided much differently. The *Rutan* decision striking down patronage was a narrow one, with only a five justice majority. Three justices in the majority (Brennan, Marshall, and White) have since retired (having been replaced by Souter, Thomas, and Ginsburg), while all four justices joining in the dissent remain (Scalia, Rehnquist, Kennedy, and O'Connor).

48. *Tashjian v. Republican Party of Connecticut*, 479 U.S. 208 (1986); *San Francisco County Democratic Committee v. Eu*, 489 U.S. 214 (1989).

CHAPTER TEN

1. Louis Hartz, *The Liberal Tradition in America* (New York: Harcourt Brace Jovanovich, 1955).

2. Donald Jackson, 218–224. The survey of legal and political experts reveals that those liberal values of individualism that dominate constitutional jurisprudence are held just as strongly by practitioners and participants. Appendix A, p. 196.

3. Harvard law professor Mary Ann Glendon puts it this way:

> Rights talk encourages our all-too-human tendency to place the self at the center of our moral universe. . . . Saturated with rights, political language can no longer perform the important function of facilitating public discussion of the right ordering of our lives together. . . . Our simplistic rights talk simultaneously reflects and distorts American culture. It captures our devotion to individualism and liberty, but omits our traditions of hospitality and care for the community.

Mary Ann Glendon, *Rights Talk: The Impoverishment of Political Discourse* (New York: The Free Press, 1991) xi–iii.

4. Stephen Gottlieb describes these dual functions of democracy as "resolving conflicts and preserving individual rights and creative discussion." "Government Allocation of First Amendment Resources," *University of Pittsburgh Law Review* 41: 205, 225 (1979).

5. The attempt to rearrange judicial attitudes toward parties, however, is only one aspect of what ought to be a larger effort to elevate parties to their proper democratic role. Another aspect would be an educational program aimed at enlightening the public and attacking some of the common misperceptions of parties. Another imperative is for the parties to engage in serious internal assessment and reform, in order to move closer to the functional model and better justify enhanced judicial treatment.

6. While some party functions militate against multi-party systems (such as the translation of electoral support into a guide to governance), others directly implicate the appeal of additional parties. These include the democratizing role of parties, and the need to give expression to additional views which the major parties may overlook. The major parties may not be sufficiently representative of the composition of views in the public. Multiple parties may be necessary to give voice to the existing diversity of groups and interests, something the political market ought to be free to recognize.

7. As this book is in its final stages of publication, the Supreme Court is also awaiting oral arguments in a potentially important campaign finance case. In *FEC v. Colorado Republican Federal Campaign Committee*, 59 F.3d 1015 (10th Cir. 1995), the 10th Circuit remarkably found parties to be a "corrupting" influence on the political process, as it upheld the constitutionality of FECA limits on what political parties can spend on behalf of their candidates. By accepting review of the decision, the high Court may be ready to confront head on the legal status and significance of political parties.

8. Loren E. Lomasky, *Persons, Rights, and The Moral Community* (New York: Oxford University Press, 1987), 7.

9. Pitkin, 232.

APPENDIX C

1. This typology is a synthesis of a number of works, including Alvin Zander, *Effective Social Action by Community Groups* (San Francisco: Jossey-Bass Publishers 1990); Norman J. Orenstein and Shirley Elder, *Interest Groups, Lobbying and Policymaking* (Washington, D.C.: Congressional Quar-

terly 1978); Carol S. Greenwald, *Group Power: Lobbying and Public Policy* (New York: Praeger Publishers, 1977); and Kay Lehman Schlozman and John T. Tierney, *Organized Interests and American Democracy* (New York: Harper & Row, 1986).

2. Norman J. Orenstein and Shirley Elder, *Interest Groups, Lobbying and Policymaking*, (Washington, D.C.: Congressional Quarterly 1978), 35. Arend Lijphart identifies sixteen potential criteria for representation, many of them contradictory to others. Lijphart, "Comparative Perspectives on Fair Representation: The Plurality-Majority Rule, Geographical Districting, and Alternative Electoral Arrangements," *Representation and Redistricting Issues*, eds. Bernard Grofman et al, (Toronto: Lexington Books 1982). 145–147.

3. Herbert Alexander, "Political Finance Regulation in International Perspective," *Parties, Interest Groups, and Campaign Finance Laws*, ed. Michael Malbin (Washington, D.C.: American Enterprise Institute 1980), 107–151.

4. See Alvin Zander's work on organizing and managing action groups in political efforts. Zander, *Effective Social Action by Community Groups*, 213–223. See also Donald Jackson's discussion of "means-regarding equality of opportunity." This vision of equality allows political players to operate within equally applied rules to demonstrate potentially unequal talents. *Even The Children of Strangers: Equality Under the U.S. Constitution*, (Lawrence, Kans.: University Press of Kansas 1992), 24.

5. The varying abilities of groups to effectively participate in political activity inhibits the use of neutral criteria to measure political resources. Knight and Johnson characterize this issue as one of strategic manipulation by groups to advance their self-interest. Strategic behavior involved in group mobilization and the determination of group interests make it difficult to discern any normative status for assigning representation to group voices. "Deliberative Democracy and Cultural Pluralism," Paper presented at the American Political Science Association Annual Meeting, Washington, D.C., 1993.

6. Jane J. Mansbridge, "The Equal Opportunity to Exercise Power," *Equal Opportunity*, ed. Norman E. Bowie (Boulder: Westview Press 1988), 137–138. Mansbridge argues that, while inequality of groups' ability to influence may favor some form of group representation, the same cannot be said for unequal efforts. Political effort produces legitimately unequal political results. Since effort is a measure of the intensity of a desire or need, standards of equal opportunity are satisfied when differences arise out of effort and not ability. This analysis is complicated by the fact that it is not easy to determine whether group differences are due to effort or ability.

7. Norman Ornstein and Shirley Elder, *Interest Groups, Lobbying and Policymaking*, 70–79 ; Carol S. Greenwald, *Group Power: Lobbying and Public*

Policy, 55–56; Kay Lehman Schlozman and John T. Tierney, *Organized Interests and American Democracy*, 121.

8. See David Jessup's catalogue of other means by which associations wield influence besides money. "Can Political Influence be Democratized?", 46. Those resources include grass-roots lobbying, access to the media, knowledge and education, individual commitment of members, and cultural symbols.

9. Greenwald, *Group Power: Lobbying and Public Policy*, 43.

10. Alvin Zander, *Effective Social Action by Community Groups*, 4, 60–65.

11. Ornstein and Elder, *Interest Groups, Lobbying and Policymaking*, 35.

12. Zander, *Effective Social Action by Community Groups*, (San Francisco: Jossey-Bass Publishers 1990), 15–22.

13. *Ibid.*, 29–34.

14. Zander, *Effective Social Action by Community Groups*, 5; Greenwald, *Group Power: Lobbying and Public Policy*, 52–53.

15. Charles Fried, *Metro Broadcasting, Inc. v. FCC*, 125. Iris Young similarly admits the lack of homogeneity within groups in the United States. Social groups:

> mirror in their own differentiations many of the other groups in the wider society. In American society today, for example, blacks are not a single, unified group with a common life. Like other racial and ethnic groups, they are differentiated by age, gender, class, sexuality, region, and nationality, any of which in a given context may become a salient group.

Young, *The Politics of Difference*, 48.

16. See Anne Phillips, "Democracy and Difference: Some Problems for Feminist Theory," *The Political Quarterly* 63 (1992): 79, 81.

17. See Schlozman and Tierney, *Organized Interests and American Democracy*, 64–65.

18. Fried calls this the worst kind of stereotyping, that "which assumes that members of racial or ethnic groups exhibit distinct ways of thinking, share particular dispositions, or display common patterns of values and behavior." Fried, "*Metro Broadcasting, Inc. v. FCC*," 123.

19. Larry May, *The Morality of Groups*. May is apparently undaunted. He adopts an expansive definition of harm to members of a group by virtue solely of their membership in that group. He argues that we ought not to require that group members suffer actual harm, only that they are treated indiscriminately as members of a negatively stereotyped group. *Ibid.*, 120.

20. Fried, 125.

21. Donald Jackson, *Even The Children of Strangers: Equality Under The United States Constitution* (Lawrence, Kans.: University Press of Kansas 1992), 23, 129.

22. See Donald Jackson, *Even The Children of Strangers*, 229.

23. Knight and Johnson, "Deliberative Democracy and Cultural Pluralism", Paper Presented at the American Political Science Association Annual Meeting, Washington, D.C., 1993, 19.

24. Anne Phillips, "Democracy and Difference: Some Problems for Feminist Theory," *The Political Quarterly* 63: 79, 89 (1992).

25. Anne Phillips concurs that the decisions as to group influence cannot be made apart from politics and political mobilization. She argues that group classification constitutes a premature freezing of categories that is inappropriate for issues of representation and political equality. Phillips, "Democracy and Difference: Some Problems for Feminist Theory," *The Political Quarterly* 63: 79, 89.

26. John C. Wahlke, "Logic and Politics in Electoral Engineering," *Representation and Redistricting Issues*, eds. Bernard Grofman et al (Toronto: Lexington Books 1982), 165–166.

BIBLIOGRAPHY

Abram, Morris B. "Civil Rights and Group Preference," *Moral Rights in the Workplace,* ed. Gertrude Ezorsky (New York: State University of New York Press, 1987).

Alexander, Herbert E., *Financing Politics: Money, Elections, & Political Reform,* 4th ed. (Washington, D.C.: Congressional Quarterly, 1992).

——"Political Finance Regulation in International Perspective," *Political Parties, Interest Groups, and Campaign Finance Laws,* ed. Michael Malbin (Washington, D.C.: American Enterprise Institute, 1980), 333–353.

American Political Science Association, Committee on Political Parties, *Toward a More Responsible Two-Party System,* (New York: Rinehart & Co., 1950).

Auerbach, Carl, "Comments on Criteria for Single-Member Districting," *Representation and Redistricting Issues,* eds. Bernard Grofman et al, (Toronto: Lexington Books, 1982).

Backstrom, Charles, Leonard Robins, and Scott Eller, "Establishing a State-wide Electoral Effects Baseline," *Political Gerrymandering and the Courts,* ed. Bernard Grofman (New York: Agathon Press, 1990).

Baker, Gordon E., "The Unfinished Reapportionment Revolution," *Political Gerrymandering and the Courts,* ed. Bernard Grofman (New York: Agathon Press, 1990), 11.

——"The Totality of Circumstances Approach," *Political Gerrymandering and the Courts,* ed. Bernard Grofman (New York: Agathon Press, 1990), 207

——"One Man One Vote and 'Political Fairness'," *Emory Law Journal* 23: 701 (1974).

Banzhaf, John F., III, "Multi-member Districts—Do They Violate the 'One Man One Vote' Principle?" *Yale Law Journal* 75: 1309 (1965).

Baskin, Darryl, "American Pluralism: Theory, Practice and Ideology," *Journal of Politics* 32 (February 1970): 71.

Beer, Samuel H., "The Representation of Interests," *American Political Science Review* LI (September 1957).

Beitz, Charles R., "Equal Opportunity in Political Representation," *Equal Opportunity*, ed. Norman E. Bowie (Boulder: Westview Press, 1988).

Bentley, Arthur, *The Process of Government*, (Cambridge: Belknap Press of Harvard University Press, 1967).

Berry, Jeffrey M., *The Interest Group Society*, (Boston: Little Brown & Co., 1984).

Birch, A.H., *Representation*, (New York: Praeger Publishers, 1971).

Black, Antony, *Guilds and Civil Society in European Political Thought from the Twelfth Century to the Present*, (Ithaca, New York: Cornell University Press, 1984).

Brinkley, Martin H., "Despoiling the Spoils: *Rutan v. Republican Party of Illinois*," *North Carolina Law Review* 69: 719 (1991).

Brisbin, Richard A., Jr., "Federal Courts and the Changing Role of American Political Parties," *Northern Illinois University Law Review* 5: 68 (1984).

Brown, Roger H., *The Republic in Peril: 1812*, (New York: W.W. Norton & Company, Inc., 1971).

Burke, Edmund, "Speech to the Electors," *Burke's Politics*, eds. Ross J.S. Hoffman and Paul Levack (New York: Alfred A. Knopf, Inc., 1949).

———"Speech on the State of the Representation," *Burke's Politics*, eds. Ross J.S. Hoffman and Paul Levack (New York: Alfred A. Knopf, Inc., 1949).

Burns, James MacGregor, *Cobblestone Leadership: Majority Rule, Minority Power*, (Norman: University of Oklahoma Press, 1990).

Cain, Bruce E., "Perspectives on *Davis v. Bandemer*: Views of the Practitioner, Theorist and Reformer," *Political Gerrymandering and the Courts*, ed. Bernard Grofman, (New York: Agathon Press, 1990), 117.

———"Voting Rights and Democratic Theory: Toward a Color-Blind Society?" *Controversies in Minority Voting: The Voting Rights Act in Perspective*, eds. Bernard Grofman and Chandler Davidson (Washington, D.C.: The Brookings Institution, 1992), 261.

Cammarosano, Louis, "Applications of the First Amendment to Political Patronage Employment Decisions," *Fordham Law Review* 58: 101 (1989).

Campbell, Angus, et al, *The American Voter*, (New York: Wiley, 1960).

Center for Party Renewal, *Former Members of Congress View the Role of Political Parties in the Congress: A Report to the Ad Hoc Joint Committee on the Organization of Congress*, (Washington, D.C.: Center for Party Development, 1993).

Cigler, Allan J. and Burdett A. Loomis, eds., *Interest Group Politics*, 2d ed. (Washington, D.C.: Congressional Quarterly Press, 1986).

Claude, Richard, *The Supreme Court and the Electoral Process*, (Baltimore: The Johns Hopkins Press, 1970).

Comment—"First Amendment Limitations on Patronage Employment Practices," *University of Chicago Law Review* 49: 181 (1982).

Comment—"Patronage and the First Amendment After *Elrod v. Burns*," *Columbia Law Review* 78: 468 (1978).

Comment—"Patronage Dismissals: Constitutional Limits and Political Justifications," *University of Chicago Law Review* 41: 297 (1974).

Comment—"*United Jewish Organization v. Carey* and the Need to Recognize Aggregate Voting Rights," *Yale Law Journal* 87: 571 (1978).

Committee on Political Parties, "Toward a More Responsible Two-Party System," *American Political Science Review* 40 (September 1950), Supplement.

Congressional Quarterly, *Congressional Campaign Finances: History, Facts, and Controversy*, (Washington, D.C.: Congressional Quarterly, 1992).

Congressional Quarterly, *State Politics and Redistricting*, (Washington, D.C.: Congressional Quarterly, 1982).

Conlon, Richard, "Commentary," *Political Parties, Interest Groups, and Campaign Finance Laws*, ed. Michael Malbin (Washington, D.C.: American Enterprise Institute, 1980).

Connolly, William E., ed., *The Bias of Pluralism*, (New York: Atherton Press, 1969).

Crotty, William J., *American Parties in Decline*, 2nd ed. (Glenview, Illinois: Scott, Foresman and Company, 1984).

———"The Philosophies of Party Reform," *Party Renewal in America: Theory and Practice*, ed., Gerald M. Pomper (New York: Praeger Publishers, 1980), 31.

Dahl, Robert A., *Dilemmas of Pluralist Democracy: Autonomy vs. Control* (New Haven: Yale University Press, 1982).

———*After the Revolution: Authority in A Good Society* (New Haven: Yale University Press, 1970).

———*Who Governs?: Democracy and Power in the City* (New Haven: Yale University Press, 1961).

——— *A Preface to Democratic Theory* (Chicago: The University of Chicago Press, 1956).

Davidson, Chandler, "The Voting Rights Act: A Brief History," *Controversies in Minority Voting: The Voting Rights Act in Perspective*, eds. Bernard Grofman and Chandler Davidson (Washington, D.C.: The Brookings Institution, 1992), 7.

de Grazia, Alfred, *Public and Republic: Political Representation in America* (New York: Alfred A. Knopf, 1951).

Dewey, John, *The Public and Its Problems* (Chicago: Gateway Books, 1946).

Dixon, Robert G., Jr., "The Courts, The People and One Man One Vote," *Reapportionment in the 1970s*, ed. Nelson Polsby (Berkeley: University of California Press, 1971).

———*Democratic Representation: Reapportionment in Law and Politics* (New York: Oxford University Press, 1968).

———"Fair Criteria and Procedures for Establishing Legislative Districts," *Representation and Redistricting Issues*, eds. Bernard Grofman et al (Toronto: Lexington Books, 1982), 7.

Downs, Anthony, *An Economic Theory of Democracy* (New York: Harper and Row, 1957).

Elliott, Ward E., *The Rise of Guardian Democracy: The Supreme Court's Role in Voting Rights Disputes, 1845–1969* (Cambridge: Harvard University Press, 1974).

Engstrom, Richard L., "The Supreme Court and Equipopulous Gerrymandering: A Remaining Obstacle in the Quest for Fair and Effective Representation," *Arizona State Law Journal* 1976: 277.

Epstein, Edwin M., "Business and Labor under the Federal Election Campaign Act of 1971," *Parties, Interest Groups, and Campaign Finance Laws*, ed. Michael Malbin (Washington, D.C.: American Enterprise Institute, 1980), 107.

Epstein, Lee and Charles Hadley, "On the Treatment of Political Parties in the U.S. Supreme Court," *Journal of Politics* 562: 414 (May 1990).

Epstein, Leon, *Political Parties in the American Mold* (Madison: University of Wisconsin Press, 1986).

———"Will American Political Parties be Privatized?" *Journal of Law and Politics* 239 (1989).

Eulau, Heinz and Kenneth Prewitt, *Labyrinths of Democracy: Adaptations, Linkages, Representation, and Policies in Urban Politics,* (New York: The Bobbs-Merrill Company, Inc., 1973).

Fay, James S. "The Legal Regulation of Political Parties," *Journal of Legislation* 9: 263–281 (1982).

Fiss, Owen M., "Groups and the Equal Protection Clause," *Philosophy and Public Affairs* 5: 107 (1976).

————"Forward: The Forms of Justice, *Harvard Law Review* 93: 1–58 (1982).

Fitts, Michael A., "Look Before You Leap: Some Cautionary Notes on Civic Republicanism," *Yale Law Journal* 97: 1651 (1988).

Fraga, Luis R., "Latino Political Incorporation and the Voting Rights Act," *Controversies in Minority Voting: The Voting Rights Act in Perspective,* eds. Bernard Grofman and Chandler Davidson (Washington, D.C.: The Brookings Institution, 1992), 278.

Fried, Charles, "*Metro Broadcasting, Inc. v. FCC*: Two Concepts of Equality," *Harvard Law Review* 104: 107 (1990).

Friedrich, Carl J., *Constitutional Government and Democracy* (Boston: Ginn & Co., 1950).

————ed., *Responsibility* (Nomos III) (New York: Liberal Arts Press, 1960).

————"Representation and Constitutional Reform in Europe," *Western Politics Quarterly* I (June 1948), 124.

Garet, Ronald R., "Community and Existence: The Rights of Groups," *Southern California Law Review* 56: 1001 (1983).

Garson, G. David, *Group Theories of Politics* (Beverly Hills: Sage, 1978).

Geyh, Charles Gardner, "It's My Party and I'll Cry If I Want To: State Intrusions Upon the Associational Freedoms of Political Parties," *Wisconsin Law Review* 211 (983).

Glendon, Mary Ann, *Rights Talk: The Impoverishment of Political Discourse* (New York: The Free Press, 1991).

Goldman, Ralph M., *The National Party Chairmen and Committees: Factionalism at the Top* (New York: M.E. Sharpe, 1990).

————*Dilemma and Destiny: The Democratic Party in America* (Lanham, Maryland: Madison Books, 1986).

Goodman, William, *The Two-Party System in the United States* (New York: D. Van Nostrand Co., Inc., 1964).

Gosnell, Harold F., *Democracy: The Threshold of Freedom* (New York: The Ronald Press Company, 1948).

Gottlieb, Stephen E., "Election Reform and Democratic objectives—Match or Mismatch?" *Yale Law Review* 9: 219 (1991).

———"Fashioning a Test for Gerrymandering," *Journal of Legislation* 15: 144 (1988).

———"Rebuilding the Right of Association: The Right to Hold a Convention as a Test Case," *Hofstra Law Review* 11: 191–247 (1982).

———"Government Allocation of First Amendment Resources," *University of Pittsburgh Law Review* 41: 205 (1979).

Grady, Robert C., *Restoring Real Representation* (Chicago: University of Illinois Press, 1993).

Greenstone, J. David, "Group Theories," *The Handbook of Political Science*, eds. Fred I. Greenstein and Nelson Polsby (Reading, Massachusetts: Addison-Wesley, 1975).

Greenwald, Carol S., *Group Power: Lobbying and Public Policy* (New York: Praeger Publishers, 1977).

Grofman, Bernard, ed., *Political Gerrymandering and the Courts* (New York: Agathon Press, 1990).

Grofman, Bernard, "Toward a Coherent Theory of Gerrymandering," *Political Gerrymandering and the Courts*, ed. Bernard Grofman (New York: Agathon Press, 1990).

———"Criteria for Districting: A Social Science Perspective," *UCLA Law Review* 33: 77 (1985).

Grofman, Bernard and Chandler Davidson, eds., *Controversies in Minority Voting; The Voting Rights Act in Perspective* (Washington, D.C.: The Brookings Institution, 1992).

Grofman, Bernard, Lisa Handley, and Richard G. Niemi, *Minority Representation and the Quest for Voting Equality* (New York: Cambridge University Press, 1992).

Grofman, Bernard and Arend Lijphart, eds., *Electoral Systems and Their Political Consequences* (New York: Agathon Press, 1986).

Grofman, Bernard, Arend Lijphart, Robert B. McKay, and Howard A. Scarrow, eds., *Representation and Redistricting Issues* (Toronto: Lexington Books, 1982).

Guinier, Lani, "The Triumph of Tokenism: The Voting Rights Act and the Theory of Black Electoral Success," *Michigan Law Review* 89: 1077 (March 1991).

————"No Two Seats: The Elusive Quest for Political Equality," *Virginia Law Review* 77: 1413 (November 1991).

————"Voting Rights and Democratic Theory—Where Do We Go From Here?" *Controversies in Minority Voting: The Voting Rights Act in Perspective*, eds. Bernard Grofman and Chandler Davidson (Washington, D.C.: The Brookings Institution, 1992), 283.

Guttman, Julie E., "Primary Elections and the Collective Right of Freedom of Association," *Yale Law Journal* 94: 117 (1984).

Hamilton, Alexander, James Madison, and John Jay, *The Federalist Papers*, intro. by Clinton Rossiter (New York: Mentor Books, 1961).

Hartz, Louis, *The Liberal Tradition in America* (New York: Harcourt Brace Jovanovich, 1955).

Hayes, Michael T., "The New Group Universe," *Interest Group Politics*, eds. Allan J. Cigler and Burdett A. Loomis, 2nd ed. (Washington, D.C.: Congressional Quarterly Press, 1986), 141.

Henry, Laurin L., *Presidential Transitions* (Washington, D.C.: Brookings Institution, 1960).

Herbers, John, "Deep Government Disunity Alarms Many U.S. Leaders," *The New York Times* (November 12, 1978), 1.

Herring, E. Pendleton, *Group Representation Before Congress* (Baltimore: The John Hopkins Press, 1929).

Hess, Michael, "Beyond Justiciability: Political Gerrymandering After *Davis v. Bandemer*," *Cambell Law Review* 9: 207, 252 (1987).

Holcombe, Arthur N., *Politics in Action: The Problems of Representative Government* (Menasha, Wisconsin: George Banta Publishing Co., 1943).

Jackson, Brooks, *Honest Graft: Big Money and the American Political Process* (New York: Alfred A. Knopf, 1988).

Jackson, Donald W., *Even The Children of Strangers: Equality Under The United States Constitution* (Lawrence, Kansas: University Press of Kansas, 1992).

James, Judson L., *American Political Parties in Transition* (New York: Harper & Row, 1974).

————*American Political Parties: Potential and Performance* (New York: Western Publishing Co., Inc., 1969).

Jessup, David, "Can Political Influence be Democratized? A Labor Perspective," *Parties, Interest Groups, and Campaign Finance Laws*, ed. Michael J. Malbin (Washington, D.C.: American Enterprise Institute, 1980).

Jones, Ruth S., "State Public Financing and the State Parties," *Political Parties, Interest Groups, and Campaign Finance Laws*, ed. Michael Malbin (Washington, D.C.: American Enterprise Institute, 1980), 283.

Jupp, James, *Political Parties* (London: Rautledge & Kegan Paul, 1974).

Kaufman, Arnold S., "Participatory Democracy: Ten Years Later," *The Bias of Pluralism*, ed. William E. Connolly (New York: Atherton Press, 1969).

Kayden, Xandra, "The Nationalizing of the Party System," *Political Parties, Interest Groups, and Campaign Finance Laws*, ed. Michael Malbin (Washington, D.C.: American Enterprise Institute, 1980), 257.

Kester, John G., "Constitutional Restrictions on Political Parties," *Virginia Law Review* 60: 735 (1974).

Key, V.O., *Southern Politics in State and Nation* (Knopf, 1960).

——*Politics, Parties and Pressure Groups*, 5th ed. (New York: Thomas Y. Crowell Company, 1964).

Knight, Jack, and James Johnson, "Deliberative Democracy and Cultural Pluralism," Paper Presented at the American Political Science Association Annual Meeting, Washington, D.C., 1993.

Kornhauser, William, *The Politics of Mass Society* (New York: The Free Press, 1959).

Kousser, J. Morgan, "The Voting Rights Act and the Two Reconstructions," *Controversies in Minority Voting: The Voting Rights Act in Perspective*, eds. Bernard Grofman and Chandler Davidson (Washington, D.C.: The Brookings Institution, 1992), 135.

Kull, Andrew, *The Color-Blind Constitution* (Cambridge: Harvard University Press, 1992).

Latham, Earl, *The Group Basis of Politics: A Study in Basing-Point Legislation* (New York: Octagon Books, Inc., 1965).

Lawson, Kay, "How State Laws Undermine Parties," *Elections American Style*, ed. A. James Reichley (Washington, D.C.: The Brookings Institution, 1987), pp. 240–260.

——"Challenging Regulation of Political Parties: The California Case," *Journal of Law and Politics* 2: 263 (1985).

Lazarsfeld, Paul F., Bernard Berelson, and Hazel Gaudet, *The People's Choice: How the Voter Makes Up His Mind in a Presidential Campaign* 2nd ed. (New York: Columbia University Press, 1948).

Leiserson, Avery, "Problems of Representation," *Journal of Politics* XI (August 1949).

Lijphart, Arend, "Comparative Perspectives on Fair Representation: The Plurality-Majority Rule, Geographical Districting, and Alternative Electoral Arrangements," *Representation and Redistricting Issues*, eds. Bernard Grofman et al (Toronto: Lexington Books, 1982).

Lijphart, Arend and Bernard Grofman, eds., *Choosing an Electoral System: Issues and Alternatives* (New York: Praeger Publishers, 1984).

Lipset, Seymour Martin, *Parties and Governance: The First New Nation* (London: Heinemann Press, 1963).

Lomasky, Loren E., *Persons, Rights, and The Moral Community* (New York: Oxford University Press, 1987).

Lowenstein, Daniel H., "*Bandemer*'s Gap: Gerrymandering and Equal Protection," *Political Gerrymandering and the Courts*, ed. Bernard Grofman (New York: Agathon Press, 1990).

———"Political Bribery and the Intermediate Theory of Politics," *UCLA Law Review* 32: 784 (1985).

Lowi, Theodore J., *The End of Liberalism*, 2nd ed. (New York: W.W. Norton & Company, Inc., 1979).

Main, Jackson Turner, *Political Parties Before the Constitution* (New York: W.W. Norton & Company, Inc., 1973).

Malbin, Michael J., ed., *Parties, Interest Groups, and Campaign Finance Laws* (Washington, D.C.: American Enterprise Institute, 1980).

———"Of Mountains and Molehills: PACs, Campaigns, and Public Policy," *Parties, Interest Groups, and Campaign Finance Laws*, ed. Michael Malbin (Washington, D.C.: American Enterprise Institute, 1980), 152.

Mann, Thomas, foreword, *Controversies in Minority Voting: The Voting Rights Act in Perspective*, eds. Bernard Grofman and Chandler Davidson (Washington, D.C.: The Brookings Institution, 1992).

Mansbridge, Jane J., "A Deliberative Theory of Interest Representation," *The Politics of Interests: Interest Groups Transformed*, ed. Mark P. Petracca (Boulder: Westview Press, 1992).

———"The Equal Opportunity to Exercise Power," *Equal Opportunity*, ed. Norman E. Bowie (Boulder: Westview Press, 1988).

May, Larry, *The Morality of Groups: Collective Responsibility, Group-Based Harm, and Corporate Rights*, (Notre Dame: University of Notre Dame Press, 1987).

Mayhew, David R., *Placing Parties in American Politics: Organization, Electoral Settings, and Government Activity in the Twentieth Century* (Princeton: Princeton University Press, 1986).

McCleskey, Clifton, "Parties Before the Bar: Equal Protection, Freedom of Association, and the Rights of Political Organizations," *Journal of Politics* 46: 347–368 (1984).

McConnell, Grant, *Private Power and American Democracy* (New York: Alfred A. Knopf, 1966).

McDonald, Laughlin, "The 1982 Amendments of Section 2 and Minority Representation," *Controversies in Minority Voting: The Voting Rights Act in Perspective*, eds. Bernard Grofman and Chandler Davidson (Washington, D.C.: The Brookings Institution, 1992).

McWilliams, Wilson Carey, "Parties as Civic Associations," *Party Reform in America: Theory and Practice*, ed. Gerald M. Pomper (New York: Praeger Publishers, 1980), 51.

Merton, Robert K., "The Function of the Political Machine," *American Political Parties: A Systemic Perspective*, eds. Charles G. Mayo and Beryl L. Crowe (New York: Harper & Row, 1967), 423.

Michels, Robert, *Political Parties: A Sociological Study of the Oligarchical Tendencies of Modern Democracy*, trans. Eden and Cedar Paul, intro. by Seymour Martin Lipset (New York: The Free Press, 1962).

Mileur, Jerome M., "Prospects for Party Government," *Challenges to Party Government*, eds. John K. White and Jerome M. Mileur (Carbondale: Southern Illinois University Press, 1992).

Miller, W.E. and D.E. Stokes, "Constituency Influence in Congress," *American Political Science Review* 57: 45 (1963).

Moe, Terry, *The Organization of Interests* (Chicago: University of Chicago Press, 1980).

Moeller, John, "The Federal Courts' Involvement in the Reform of Political Parties," *Western Political Quarterly* 40: 717 (December 1987).

Morrill, Richard, "A Geographer's Perspective," *Political Gerrymandering and the Courts*, ed. Bernard Grofman (New York: Agathon Press, 1990), 212–239.

Neuman, W. Russell, *The Paradox of Mass Politics: Knowledge and Opinion in the American Electorate* (Cambridge: Harvard University Press, 1986).

Niemi, Richard and John Deegan, Jr., "A Theory of Political Districting," *American Political Science Review* 72: 1304 (1978).

Note: "The Constitutional Imperative of Proportional Representation," *Yale Law Journal* 94: 163 (1985).

Note: "Group Representation and Race-Conscious Apportionment: The Roles of States and the Federal Courts," *Harvard Law Review* 91: 1847 (1978).

Olson, Mancur, *The Logic of Collective Action* (Cambridge: Harvard University Press, 1865).

Ornstein, Norman J. and Shirley Elder, *Interest Groups, Lobbying and Policymaking* (Washington, D.C.: Congressional Quarterly, 1978).

O'Rourke, Timothy, "The 1982 Amendments and the Voting Rights Paradox," *Controversies in Minority Voting: The Voting Rights Act in Perspective*, eds. Bernard Grofman and Chandler Davidson (Washington, D.C.: The Brookings Institution, 1992).

Parker, Frank, *Black Votes Count: Political Empowerment in Mississippi After 1965* (Durham: University of North Carolina Press, 1990).

Phillips, Anne, "Democracy and Difference: Some Problems for Feminist Theory," *The Political Quarterly* 63 (1992): 79.

Pitkin, Hannah F., *The Concept of Representation* (Berkeley: University of California Press, 1967).

Pitkin, Hannah, F., ed., *Representation* (New York: Atherton Press, 1969).

Polsby, Nelson W., *Community Power & Political Theory: A Further Look at Problems of Evidence and Inference*, 2nd ed. (New Haven: Yale University Press, 1963).

Pomper, Gerald M., *Passions and Interests: Political Party Concepts of American Democracy* (Lawrence, Kansas: University Press of Kansas, 1992).

——*Voters, Elections and Parties: The Practice of Democratic Theory* (New Brunswick, New Jersey: Transaction, Inc., 1988).

——"The Contribution of Political Parties to American Democracy," *Party Renewal in America: Theory and Practice*, ed. Gerald Pomper (New York: Praeger Publishers, 1980).

Pomper, Gerald M., ed., *Party Renewal in America: Theory and Practice* (New York: Praeger Publishers, 1980).

Porto, Brian L., "The Constitution and Political Parties: Supreme Court Jurisprudence and Its Implications for Partybuilding," *Constitutional Commentary* 8: 433–449 (1991).

Pratt, Larry, "Commentary," *Parties, Interest Groups, and Campaign Finance Laws*, ed. Michael Malbin (Washington, D.C.: American Enterprise Institute, 1980), 86.

Price, David S., "The Party Connection," *Challenges to Party Government*, eds. John Kenneth White and Jerome M. Mileur (Carbondale: Southern Illinois University Press, 1992).

——*Bringing Back the Parties* (Washington, D.C.: Congressional Quarterly Press, 1984).

Rae, Douglas W., *The Political Consequences of Electoral Laws* (New Haven: Yale University Press, 1967).

Reichley, A. James, *The Life of the Parties* (New York: The Free Press, 1992).

Reichley, A. James, ed., *Elections American Style* (Washington, D.C.: The Brookings Institution, 1984).

Riker, William H., "Electoral Systems and Constitutional Restraints," *Choosing an Electoral System: Issues and Alternatives*, eds. Arend Lijphart and Bernard Grofman (New York: Praeger Publishers, 1984).

Riordan, William L., *Plunkitt of Tammany Hall* (New York: Dutton, 1963).

Rogowski, Ronald, "Representation in Political Theory and in Law," *Ethics* 91: 395 (1981).

Rush, Mark E., "Voters' Rights and The Legal Status of American Political Parties," *Journal of Law and Politics* 9: 487 (1993).

Sabato, Larry S., *Paying for Elections: The Campaign Finance Thicket* (New York: Priority Press Publications, 1989).

Saloma. John S., *Parties: The Real Opportunity for Effective Citizen Politics* (New York: Knopf, 1972).

Sartori, Giovanni, *The Theory of Democracy Revisited* (Chatham, New Jersey: Chatham House Publishers, Inc., 1987).

——*Parties and Party Systems: A Framework for Analysis* (Cambridge: Cambridge University Press, 1976).

Schattschneider, E.E., *Party Government,* (Westport, Conn.: Greenwood Press, 1977).

——*The Semi-Sovereign People* (New York: Holt, Rinehart and Winston, 1960).

Schlesinger, Arthur M., Jr., *The Disuniting of America* (New York: W.W. Norton & Co., 1992).

Schlesinger, Joseph A., *Political Parties and the Winning of Office* (Ann Arbor: The University of Michigan, 1991).

Schlozman, Kay Lehman and John T. Tierney, *Organized Interests and American Democracy* (New York: Harper & Row, 1986).

Schuck, Peter, "Partisan Gerrymandering: A Political Problem Without Judicial Solution," *Political Gerrymandering and the Courts*, ed. Bernard Grofman (New York: Agathon Press, 1990), 240.

Scott, Gary L. and Craig L. Carr, "Political Parties Before the Bar: The Controversy Over Associational Rights," *University of Puget Sound Law Review* 5: 267 (1982).

Sorauf, Frank J., "Patronage and Party," *American Political Parties: A Systemic Perspective*, eds. Charles G. Mayo and Beryl L. Crowe (New York: Harper & Row, 1967), 440–452.

————*Political Parties in The American System* (Boston: Little, Brown and Co., 1964).

Stark, Andrew, "Corporate Electoral Activity, Constitutional Discourse, and Conceptions of the Individual," *American Political Science Review* 86 (1992): 626–37.

Stockmeyer, Steven F., "Commentary," *Political Parties, Interest Groups, and Campaign Finance Laws*, ed. Michael Malbin (Washington, D.C.: American Enterprise Institute, 1980).

Sunstein, Cass R., "Preferences and Politics," *Philosophy and Public Affairs* 20 (1991): 3.

————"Beyond the Republican Revival," *Yale Law Journal* 97: 1539 (1988).

Swabey, Marie Collins, *Theory of the Democratic State* (Cambridge: Harvard University Press, 1937).

Thernstrom, Abigail, *Whose Vote Counts? Affirmative Action and Minority Voting Rights* (Cambridge: Harvard University Press, 1987).

Tocqueville, Alexis de, *Democracy in America*, ed. J.P. Mayer (New York: Harper & Row, 1966).

Tolchin, Martin and Susan Tolchin, *To the Victor: Political Patronage from the Clubhouse to the White House* (New York: Random House, 1971).

Truman, David B., *The Governmental Process: Public Interests and Public Opinion* (New York: Alfred A. Knopf, 1951).

United States Senate, Report no. 97–417 (1982).

Verba, Sidney and N.H. Nie, *Participation in America: Political Democracy and Social Equality* (New York: Harper & Row, 1978).

Wahlke, John C., "Logic and Politics in Electoral Engineering," *Representation and Redistricting Issues*, eds. Bernard Grofman et al (Toronto: Lexington Books, 1982).

Ward, Cynthia, "The Limits of 'Liberal Republicanism': Why Group-Based Remedies and Republican Citizenship Don't Mix," *Columbia Law Review* 91: 581 (1991).

Wattenberg, Martin, *The Decline of American Political Parties, 1952–1988* (Cambridge: Harvard University Press, 1990).

Weisburd, Arthur M., "Candidate-Making and the Constitution: Constitutional Restraints on and Protections of Party Nominating Methods," *Southern California Law Review* 57: 213 (1984).

Wells, David, "Against Affirmative Gerrymandering," *Representation and Redistricting Issues*, eds. Bernard Grofman et al (Toronto: Lexington Books, 1982), 77.

Wertheimer, Fred, "Commentary," *Political Parties, Interest Groups, and Campaign Finance Laws*, ed. Michael Malbin (Washington, D.C.: American Enterprise Institute, 1980).

Weyrich, Paul M., "The New Right: PACs and Coalition Politics," *Parties, Interest Groups, and Campaign Finance Laws*, ed. Michael Malbin (Washington, D.C.: American Enterprise Institute, 1980).

White, John Kenneth, *The New Politics of Old Values* (Hanover: University Press of New England, 1988).

White, John Kenneth and Jerome M. Mileur, eds., *Challenges to Party Government* (Carbondale, Ill.: Southern Illinois University Press, 1992).

Wills, Garry, *Explaining America: The Federalist* (New York: Doubleday & Company, Inc., 1981).

Wilson, James Q., *Political Organizations* (New York: Basic Books, 1973).

Winograd, Morley, "Commentary," *Political Parties, Interest Groups, and Campaign Finance Laws*, ed. Michael Malbin (Washington, D.C.: American Enterprise Institute, 1980).

Wolfinger, Raymond, *The Politics of Progress* (New Haven: Yale University Press, 1961).

Wright, "Politics and the Constitution: Is Money Speech?" *Yale Law Journal* 85: 1001 (1976).

Young, Iris Marion, *Justice and the Politics of Difference* (Princeton: Princeton University Press, 1990).

———"Polity and Group Difference: A Critique of the Ideal of Universal Citizenship," *Ethics* 99 (1989): 250.

Zander, Alvin, *Effective Social Action by Community Groups* (San Francisco: Jossey-Bass Publishers, 1990).

Zeigler, Harmon, *Pluralism, Corporatism, and Confucianism: Political Association and Conflict Regulation in the United States, Europe and Taiwan* (Philadelphia: Temple University Press, 1988).

LEGAL DECISIONS—U.S. SUPREME COURT

American Party of Texas v. White, 415 U.S. 767 (1973).

Anderson et al v. Celebrezze, 460 U.S. 780 (1981).

Austin v. Michigan Chamber of Commerce, 494 U.S. 652 (1990).

Avery v. Midland County, 390 U.S. 474 (1967).

Baker v. Carr, 369 U.S. 186 (1962).

Ball v. James, 451 U.S. 355 (1980).

Bates v. City of Little Rock, 361 U.S. 516 (1960).

Beer v. U.S., 374 F. Supp. 363; 419 U.S. 822; vac. 425 U.S. 130 (1973).

Board of Estimates of New York v. Morris, 489 U.S. 688 (1989).

Branti v. Finkel, 445 U.S. 507 (1980).

Brown v. Socialist Workers '74 Campaign Committee, 459 U.S. 87 (1982).

Buckley v. Valeo, 424 U.S. 1 (1976).

Bullock v. Carter, 405 U.S. 134 (1972).

Burdick v. Takushi, 112 S. Ct. 2059 (1992).

Burns v. Richardson, 384 U.S. 73 (1966).

California Medical Association v. Federal Election Commission, 453 U.S. 182 (1981).

Citizens Against Rent Control v. City of Berkeley, 367 U.S. 1 (1961).

City of Mobile v. Bolden, 446 U.S. 55 (1980).

Colgrove v. Green, 66 S. Ct. 1198 (1946).

Cousins v. Wigoda, 419 U.S. 477 (1975).

Davis v. Bandemer, 478 U.S. 109 (1986).

Democratic National Party v. Wisconsin (LaFollette), 450 U.S. 107 (1981).

Dunn v. Blumstein, 405 U.S. 330 (1972).

Elrod v. Burns, 427 U.S. 347 (1975).

FEC v. National Right to Work Committee, 459 U.S. 197 (1982).

First National Bank v. Belotti, 435 U.S. 735 (1978).

Fortson v. Dorsey, 379 U.S. 433 (1965).

Gaffney v. Cummings, 412 U.S. 735 (1973).

Gomillion v. Lightfoot, 364 U.S. 338 (1960).

Gray v. Sanders, 372 U.S. 368 (1963).

Grovey v. Townsend, 295 U.S. 45 (1935).

Hadley v. Junior College District, 397 U.S. 50 (1969).

Illinois State Board of Elections v. Socialist Workers Party, 440 U.S. 173 (1979).

Karcher v. Daggett, 462 U.S. 725 (1983).

Keane v. National Democratic Party, 409 U.A. 816 (1972).

Kirkpatrick v. Preisler, 394 U.S. 526 (1969).

Kramer v. Union Free School District, 395 U.S. 621 (1969).

Kusper v. Pontikes, 414 U.S. 51 (1973).

Lucas v. Colorado General Assembly, 377 U.S. 713 (1964).

Mahan v. Howell, 410 U.S. 182 (1971).

Marchioro v. Chaney, 442 U.S. 191 (1979).

Miller v. Johnson, 132 L. Ed. 2d 762 (1995).

NAACP v. Alabama, 357 U.S. 449 (1958).

NAACP v. Button, 371 U.S. 415 (1962).

Newberry v. United States, 256 U.S. 232 (1921).

Nixon v. Condor, 286 U.S. 73 (1932).

Nixon v. Herndon, 273 U.S. 536 (1927).

O'Brien v. Brown, 409 U.S. 1 (1972).

Pope v. Blue, 121 L. Ed. 2d 3 (1992).

Presley v. Etowah County Commissioner, 112 S. Ct. 820 (1992).

Regents of University of California v. Bakke, 438 U.S. 265 (1978).

Renne v. Geary, 59 U.S. Law Week 4675 (1991).

Reynolds v. Sims, 377 U.S. 533 (1964).

Roberts v. U.S. Jaycees, 104 S.Ct. 507 (1980).

Rogers v. Lodge, 458 U.S. 613 (1982).

Rosario v. Rockefeller, 410 U.S. 752 (1973).

Rutan v. Republican Party of Illinois, 110 S.Ct. 2729 (1990).

Salyer Land Co. v. Tulane Lake Basin Water Storage District, 410 U.S. 719 (1972).

San Francisco County Democratic Committee v. Eu, 489 U.S. 214 (1989).

Shaw v. Reno, 125 L. Ed. 2d 511 (1993).

Smith v. Allwright, 321 U.S. 649 (1944).

Storer v. Brown, 415 U.S. 724 (1974).

Sweezey v. New Hampshire, 354 U.S. 234 (1956).

Tashjian v. Republican Party of Connecticut, 479 U.S. 208 (1986).

Terry v. Adams, 345 U.S. 461 (1953).

Thornburg v. Gingles, 106 S. Ct. 2752 (1986).

United Jewish Organization v. Carey, 430 U.S. 144 (1977).

United States v. Classic, 313 U.S. 299 (1941).

Wells v. Rockefeller, 394 U.S. 542 (1969).

Wesberry v. Sanders, 376 U.S. 1 (1964).

Whitcomb v. Chavis, 403 U.S. 124 (1971).

White v. Regester, 412 U.S. 755 (1973).

Williams v. Rhodes, 393 U.S. 23 (1968).

LEGAL DECISIONS—LOWER FEDERAL COURTS

Badham v. Eu, 694 F. Supp. 664 (N.D. Cal. 1988).

FEC v. Colorado Republican Federal Campaign Committee, 59 F. 3d 1015 (10th Cir. 1995).

LULAC v. Midland Independent School District, 812 F. 2d 1494 (5th Cir. 1987).

Nader v. Schaffer, 417 F. Supp. 837 (D. Conn. 1976).

Republican Party of Virginia v. Wilder, 774 F. Supp. 400 (W.D. Va. 1991).

Ripon Society v. Republican National Committee, 525 F. 2d 567 (D.C. Cir. 1975), cert. denied 424 U.S. 933.

Seergy v. Kings County Republican County Committee, 459 F. 2d 308 (2nd Cir. 1972).

Whitefield v. Democratic Party, 890 F. 2d 1423 (8th Cir. 1989).

INDEX

Alexander, Herbert, 250n
Anderson v. Celebrezze, 150–152
association, right of, 153–160,
    222n, 224n
  and independent voters, 150–151
  and party organization, 155–158
  and political patronage, 167–168,
    172
  in ballot access cases, 145
  in context of campaign finance
    regulation, 101
  in party primaries, 153–160
  organizational basis for, 175–177
  parties' power to limit
    association, 155
  party affiliation, 150, 155–158,
    265n
  See also ballot access; campaign
    finance regulation; political
    parties
Austin v. Michigan Chamber of
  Commerce, 105–106
Avery v. Midland County, 225n

Backstrom, Charles, 263n
Badham v. Eu, 130, 139, 260–261n
  applying the *Bandermer* test,
    260–261n
Baker, Gordon, E., 223n
Baker v. Carr, 5, 35, 57
  See also reapportionment and
    redistricting
ballot access, 143–146, 187
  and associational rights, 145
  legal restrictions on, 143–144

petition requirements for, 267n
regulation of parties in
  elections, 144
rights implicated by, 146
third parties and, 268n
Banzhaf, John F., III, 224n
Barber, James D., 274n
Baskin, Darryl, 239n
Beer, Samuel H., 221n
Beitz, Charles, 221n, 248n
Bentley, Arthur, 68–70, 72
  challenges to, 237n
  on importance of groups within
    institutions of government,
    219n
  See also group politics
Birch, A. H., 217n, 220n, 237n
Branti v. Finkel, 172
Brisbin, Richard A., Jr., 258n
Buckley v. Valeo, 1–2, 97–99, 101,
  187
  See also campaign finance
    regulation
Burdick v. Takushi, 163
Burke, Edmund, 23–25, 220n,
  262n
  and "virtual representation,"
    220n
Burns, James MacGregor, 271n

Cain, Bruce, 226n
California Medical Association v.
  FEC, 99
campaign finance regulation, 1–2,
  96–106

301

factions, 119–121, 257n
"fair and effective representation,"
36, 40, 129, 180
Fay, James S., 271n
Federal Election Campaign Act, 1,
97
1974 amendments, 1, 97
1976 amendments, 251n
FEC v. Colorado Republican Federal
Campaign Committee, 278n
FEC v. Massachusetts Citizens For
Life, 103–104
FEC v. National Right to Work
Committee, 101
Fiss, Owen, 248n
Fortson v. Dorsey, 48
Fried, Charles, 255n, 280n
"functional associations," 94–96

Gaffney v. Cummings, 51–52,
128–129, 132
gerrymandering,
and group right to
representation, 51–58,
138–140
partisan, 44, 51–58, 129–131
racial, 48–50, 62
as depriving voters of choice,
230n, 263n
balkanizing tendencies of, 236n
"totality of the circumstances"
test, 228–229n
See also reapportionment and
redistricting
Glendon, Mary Ann, 222n, 277n
Goldman, Ralph Morris, 258n
Gomillion v. Lightfoot, 48
Goodman, William, 273n, 275n
Gosnell, Harold F., 219n
Gottlieb, Stephen, 222n, 224n
Grady, Robert, 94–96
Grofman, Bernard, 218n, 227n,
228n
group politics, 3, 68–76, 180–181
Arthur Bentley, 68–70

as basis for positive pluralism,
71–76
as key to effective individual
participation, 7
as "raw materials" of politics, 68
Dahl, Robert, 242n
in judicial system, 238n
in theories of representation, 66
Key, V. O., 242n
survey results regarding, 196
Truman, David, 70–71
upper-class bias, 76–77
group right to representation, 42,
180, 186
"democratic cultural pluralism,"
89–91, 248–249n
distinctions between types of
groups, 84, 95–96
divisive tendencies of, 53–54,
62–63, 66, 82, 110–112, 203
equality of policy outcomes,
250n
formal group representation,
181
Grady, Robert, 94–96
group status as basis for,
248–249n
Guinier, Lani, 91–94, 248n
in campaign financing law,
96–106
in constitutional law, 47, 51–58,
63
interest representation, 91–94,
248n
legal standard for constitutional
violation, 58, 61
oppressed groups deserving of,
88–91
partisan gerrymandering and,
51–58, 138–140
problems of definition, 43
problems of implementation,
61, 112–115
racial/ethnic designation, 47
survey opinions regarding, 197

www.ingramcontent.com/pod-product-compliance
Lightning Source LLC
Chambersburg PA
CBHW030641270326
41929CB00007B/160